IN AFGHANISTAN

IN AFGHANISTAN

TWO HUNDRED YEARS OF BRITISH, RUSSIAN AND AMERICAN OCCUPATION

DAVID LOYN

IN AFGHANISTAN
Copyright © David Loyn, 2009.

All rights reserved.

Half-title page: Alexander Burns wearing oriental clothing.
Full-title page: Taliban fighters in 2007 in Musa Qala, a town they
occupied in breach of a controversial deal allowing British forces to
leave. They were forced out in heavy fighting in December of that year.
Photo by Aziz Ahmad Tassal, Institute for War & Peace.
All maps apart from Lieutenant Macartney's (p. vi) by Alex Maxwell.

First published in 2009 by
PALGRAVE MACMILLAN®
in the United States—a division of St. Martin's Press LLC,
175 Fifth Avenue, New York, NY 10010.

Where this book is distributed in the UK, Europe and the rest of
the world, this is by Palgrave Macmillan, a division of Macmillan
Publishers Limited, registered in England, company number 785998, of
Houndmills, Basingstoke, Hampshire RG21 6XS.

Palgrave Macmillan is the global academic imprint of the above
companies and has companies and representatives throughout the world.

Palgrave® and Macmillan® are registered trademarks in the United
States, the United Kingdom, Europe and other countries.

ISBN: 978–0–230–61403–1

Library of Congress Cataloging-in-Publication Data
Loyn, David.
    In Afghanistan : 200 years of British, Russian and American
  occupation / David Loyn.
    p. cm.
    Includes bibliographical references and index.
    ISBN 0–230–61403–5
    1. Afghanistan—History. 2. Afghanistan—History, Military.
  3. Military occupation—History. 4. British—Afghanistan—
  History. 5. Russians—Afghanistan—History. 6. Americans—
  Afghanistan—History. 7. Afghanistan—Strategic aspects.
  8. Afghanistan—Politics and government. I. Title.
DS361.L698 2009
958.1′03—dc22   2008051653

A catalogue record of the book is available from the British Library.

Design by Newgen Imaging Systems (P) Ltd., Chennai, India.

First edition: July 2009

10 9 8 7 6 5 4 3 2 1

Printed in the United States of America.

Dedicated to the memory of H. E. Zahir Shah,
the last king of Afghanistan,
who ruled a united country
with no conflict
for longer than any other leader

A MAP OF THE

KINGDOM OF CAUBUL,

And some of the

NEIGHBOURING COUNTRIES.

Altered from a Map constructed in the Year 1809.

BY LIEUT. JOHN MACARTNEY, 5TH REGT.

Bengal Native Cavalry.

English Miles.

CONTENTS

CONTENTS

CHARACTERS

Note: The "Barakzai" dynasty refers to the family that played a role as "wazir," or chief minister, to the ruling amir, after Ahmed Shah Durrani founded the "Sadozai" dynasty in the middle of the eighteenth century. After his death in 1772 the two families were drawn into a murderous struggle for power lasting for several decades.

AFGHANS (LISTED WITH FIRST NAMES IN ALPHABETICAL ORDER FOR CLARITY)

Abdullah Khan: one of the leaders of the Afghan revolt against British rule in 1841.

Abdul Rashid Dostam: Uzbek militia leader who emerged as head of northern Afghanistan and remained loyal to the communist side until 1992; made and broke many alliances with mujahidin leaders; ousted by Taliban 1997; reemerged after 2001 but never again in undisputed control of the North.

Abdul Rasul Sayyaf: Cairo-educated Wahhabi fundamentalist; commander of mujahidin group in 1980s financed almost exclusively by Saudi Arabia; prominent member of post-2001 parliament.

Abdur Rahman: the "Iron Amir"; grandson of Dost Mohammed; Barakzai dynasty; lost five-year civil war after Dost's death in 1863 and fled north to Russian-controlled territory; returned to Kabul and installed as amir by British in July 1880; united Afghanistan for first time in a century; agreed to Durand Line as border with British India in 1893; stirred up frontier tribes to fight jihad against British control; died in 1901.

Ahmed Shah Durrani: first amir of united Afghanistan, known as the "father of the nation"; founder of Sadozai dynasty; died 1772.

Ahmed Shah Massud: mujahidin commander nicknamed "Lion of Panjshir"; trained as a guerrilla by Pakistan and led the first uprising against reformist government in Afghanistan in 1975 (four years before Soviet invasion); successfully blocked seven Soviet attempts to take the Panjshir Valley; defense minister in post-Soviet government in 1992; lost Kabul to the Taliban 1996; killed by bomb in TV camera two days before attacks of 9/11.

Akbar Khan: son of Dost Mohammed; Barakzai dynasty; killed Sir William Macnaghten in 1841 and presided over slaughter of retreating army; defeated by General Sale, who broke out of the Jalalabad siege in 1842; appointed wazir when Dost returned to power in 1843; died (possibly poisoned) in 1845, age 29.

Amanullah: reformist amir who succeeded his father, Habibullah, in 1919; lost the war against Britain but succeeded in winning full Afghan independence; embarked on a radical program including rights for women; ousted in violent uprising against reforms in 1929.

Ayub Khan: one of several claimants to the Afghan throne in disorder of the late 1870s; led army that destroyed large British force at Maiwand in 1879, before being defeated by General Roberts.

Bacha Saqao: Tajik warlord who seized power in Kabul amid chaos following uprising of 1929; name means "son of a water carrier"; executed when order was restored in the same year.

Babrak Karmal: communist leader of Afghanistan installed by the Soviet invasion in December 1979; ousted when Mikhail Gorbachev took over in Moscow in 1985.

Borjan: *nom de guerre* of veteran of the mujahidin war against Soviet control who was first military commander of the Taliban; died in battle for Kabul, September 1996.

Burhanuddin Rabbani: Cairo-educated professor who led the Islamist underground movement in early 1970s; fled to Pakistan when President Daoud moved against fundamentalists; remained on the Pakistani side of the frontier during the war against Soviet invasion as head of Hezb-i-Islami, one of the main groups fighting against Soviet forces; was briefly president in post-Soviet chaos.

Daoud: Afghanistan's first president; abolished the monarchy in 1973 when he led a bloodless coup against his cousin Zahir Shah; attempted reforms but was killed with many of his family members in the Saur revolution of 1978.

Dost Mohammed: the "Great Amir"; Barakzai dynasty; took power in 1826 after fighting his way to the top of large family of competing brothers; forced out by the British invasion in 1839; returned to power in 1843; ruled until death in 1863.

Ghulam Haider: commander of Abdur Rahman's army in the 1890s; played a key role in fomenting insurrection against Britain on the frontier.

Gulbuddin Hekmatyar: mujahidin commander who began as an Islamist student leader; fled to Pakistan in early 1970s after crackdown by Afghan government; trained as a guerrilla by Pakistan; received the largest share of U.S. funding to defeat the Soviet invasion of Afghanistan; in 2006 announced he was now fighting the United States under the al-Qaeda banner.

Habibullah: amir who succeeded his father, Abdur Rahman, in 1901; assassinated in 1919.

Hafizullah Amin: briefly leader of Afghanistan after murdering Nur Mohammed Taraki in September 1979 to seize power for his faction of the Communist party; his desire for better relations with Western countries and Pakistan provoked Soviet opposition; killed in the Soviet invasion in December 1979.

Hamid Karzai: first president of Afghanistan after Taliban administration ousted in 2001.

Ismail Khan: Afghan army captain involved in the uprising against communist control in Herat ten months before the Soviet invasion in 1979; became leader of mujahidin in the West; governor of Herat from 1992 until forced out by a Taliban attack in 1995; reappointed governor in 2001 but removed by President Karzai after fighting in 2004 and appointed minister of energy.

Jabar Khan: brother of Dost Mohammed; negotiated with British in 1830s; Barakzai dynasty.

Kamran Shah: British-backed ruler of Herat from 1818; Sadozai dynasty; lazy, oppressive and fond of sadistic punishment; killed by his wazir in 1842.

Mahmud Tarzi: intellectual whose magazine inspired Amanullah's radical reforms in the 1920s; became foreign minister.

Mullah Mushk-i-Alam: leader of an uprising against British control of Kabul in 1879; name means "fragrance of all the world."

Mullah of Haddah: known as the "Light of Islam"; Afghan mullah who backed 1897 uprising on the frontier against British control.

Nadir Shah: general who took power after chaos of the 1929 uprising; heir of the Musahiban branch of the Barakzai dynasty.

Najibullah: communist leader of Afghanistan installed by Mikhail Gorbachev in 1985; had been head of the Afghan secret police, the "Khad"; remained in office after Soviet troops withdrew in 1989; forced out by the mujahidin in 1992 and held in safe confinement at a UN compound; tortured and murdered with his brother in 1996 when the Taliban took Kabul.

Mullah Omar: mujahidin commander who became the founding leader of the Taliban in 1994; head of Taliban government, 1996–2001; Taliban fighters still said he was leader in 2008, although in hiding.

Mullah Rabbani: founding member of the Taliban; governor of Kabul after the Taliban seizure of the city in 1996; no relation to the Rabbani who became president.

Mullah Razzaq: founding member of the Taliban; governor of Herat after Taliban seizure of the city in 1995.

Nur Mohammed Taraki: seized power in the communist Saur revolution in 1978; provoked opposition by introducing radical land reforms and rights for women; murdered in palace, September 1979.

Shah Shuja: the "Unlucky Amir"; Sadozai dynasty; ruled in Kabul, 1803–1809; reinstalled with British support in the war of 1839; killed by a mob in 1842.

Shir Ali: son of Dost Mohammed; Barakzai dynasty; became amir in 1868 after civil war that followed the death of Dost Mohammed in 1863; his attempted treaty with Russia led to British invasion, 1878; fled north and died soon afterward.

Shir Ali: no relation of the amir of the same name; Sadozai dynasty; installed as wali of Kandahar in a short-lived British attempt to keep some of the country out of the hands of Abdur Rahman in 1880; fled soon afterward to British pension in Karachi.

Sibghatullah Mujaddidi: Islamic scholar leader of one of the smaller mujahidin groups during the Soviet war; respected as the only survivor of a clan with the role of kingmaker in Afghan history; appointed Speaker of the upper house in first elected parliament after the fall of the Taliban.

Yakub Khan: amir after his father, Shir Ali, fled in November 1878; Barakzai dynasty; negotiated Treaty of Gandamack with the British but did nothing to stop the slaughter of th eBritish mission to Kabul in September 1879; abdicated and went into exile in India.

Zahir Shah: took power in 1933 at age 19 when his father, Nadir Shah, was shot; heir of the Musahiban branch of the Barakzai dynasty; ousted by his cousin Daoud in 1973 while in Rome; returned to Afghanistan after the fall of the Taliban; died in Kabul in 2007.

Zaman Shah: amir who emerged after the bloodbath following death of Timur Shah in 1793; Sadozai dynasty; lost power after rivalry with the Barakzai clan; blinded and sent into exile in India in 1800.

Non-Afghans

James Abbott: British political officer whose mission to release slaves in Khiva in 1840 unnerved Russia; one of Henry Lawrence's "young men"; became administrator of Hazara, a large northern frontier region between Kashmir and the Indus River; the town of Abbottabad was named after him.

Lord Auckland: governor-general responsible for ordering the British invasion in 1839.

Sheikh Abdullah Azzam: wrote *In Defense of Muslim Lands*, the book that inspired Osama bin Laden to take up jihad.

Paolo di Avitabile: Italian who became senior officer in Sikh force in Punjab during 1840s; veteran of European wars including fighting on the French side at the Battle of Waterloo.

Benazir Bhutto: prime minister of Pakistan, 1988–1990, 1993–1996; assassinated December 17, 2007, running for office in the first Pakistani election to be held since 1999.

General Sir Bindon Blood: commanded Malakand field force that put down the 1897 uprising.

Dr. William Brydon: famous as the only survivor of the retreat from Kabul in January 1842; also survived the siege of Lucknow during the 1857 Mutiny; died in bed in Scotland in 1873.

Sir Alexander Burnes: adventurer who became British envoy to Kabul; his first book of travels to Central Asia was a bestseller in the 1830s; failed in his attempt to secure deal with Dost Mohammed in 1837; became deputy head of the British mission to Kabul after Shah Shuja was put on the throne in 1839; killed by a mob in December 1841.

William Casey: director of the U. S. Central Intelligence Agency during the 1980s war against Soviet control of Afghanistan.

Lieutenant Colonel Sir Pierre Louis-Napoleon Cavagnari: frontier political officer who headed the British mission to Kabul in 1879; killed by a mob two months after his arrival.

Brigadier Neville Chamberlain: "most-wounded" soldier in the British army; part of the Army of Retribution in 1842; commanded the force in a tough campaign against Hindustani fanatics in 1863 in Ambeyla; his attempt to move down the Khyber Pass in 1879 would lead to the Second Anglo-Afghan War.

Arthur Connolly: British political officer who first coined the term *Great Game*; made several long trips across the region to gather intelligence; beheaded along with Charles Stoddart in Bokhara in 1842; brother of John.

John Connolly: British political officer who remained in Bala Hissar during negotiations in 1841–42; taken prisoner by Afghans; died of fever in 1842.

Viscount Cranborne: Tory MP who campaigned for the Afghan mujahidin cause in the 1980s; managed huge flow of aid funds; also known as Robert Cecil; became Marquess of Salibury; descendant of the Marquess of Salisbury, who, as prime minister in 1899, detected "an impulse stirring" in the Islamic world to restore a time "when they were victors in every part of the world."

Lord Curzon: viceroy of India, 1899–1905; created the North-West Frontier Province, which put the region under direct central control; also partitioned Bengal; won a gold medal from the Royal Geographical Society for his travel to the source of the Oxus River.

Major Harold Deane: British political officer at Malakand during the uprising of 1897; became the first commissioner of the North-West Frontier Province when it was established in 1901; later knighted.

Colonel (later Brigadier) William Dennie: led "forlorn hope" under withering gunfire to take Ghazni fort in 1839; died in an attempt to break out of the Jalalabad siege in 1842.

Benjamin Disraeli: made his name as a young member of the British parliament questioning the conduct of the first Anglo-Afghan war; as prime minister in the 1870s he launched the disastrous second war.

Sir Henry Mortimer Durand: foreign secretary of India; negotiated the frontier between British India and Afghanistan in 1893 that was named after him; went on to become envoy to Tehran.

Lord Elgin: viceroy of India at the time of the 1897 uprising.

Lord Ellenborough: member of the Secret Committee of the East India Company that drew up the frontier policy in the late 1820s; became governor-general of India after the 1842 Kabul catastrophe; sent in Army of Retribution and took the controversial decision to withdraw forces quickly after sacking Kabul; mocked for removing Somnath gates from Afghanistan that he believed to be ancient Hindu artifacts.

Mountstuart Elphinstone: first British envoy to Afghanistan in 1808; later governor of Bombay and pioneer of education; founded Elphinstone College.

William Elphinstone: British general who took command in Kabul in 1841; cousin of Mountstuart; veteran of Waterloo, but his inability to make decisions was blamed for the Kabul catastrophe; died in Afghan captivity in 1842.

Abdul Rashid Ghazi: mullah in charge of Red Mosque in Islamabad; killed when the Pakistani army stormed the mosque in 2007.

Mikhail Gorbachev: Soviet leader who came to power in 1985; reforms led to the end of communist control of Russia; negotiated withdrawal of Soviet forces from Afghanistan in 1989.

Prince Aleksandr Gorchakov: succeeded Count Nesselrode as Russian foreign minister in 1856; promoted to chancellor of Russia, 1863–1882, keeping control of foreign affairs; architect of Russian expansion into "barbarian" territory to the south.

Sir Lepel Griffin: political officer who negotiated terms for Britain to allow Abdur Rahman take power in 1880; after his retirement in 1893, he led campaign against the division of the frontier that left a large part of ancient Kafir tribe under Afghan control.

General Boris Gromov: commander of Soviet 40th Army; last Soviet soldier to leave Afghanistan on February 15, 1989.

Josiah Harlan: American adventurer who led Sikh army in the 1840s and later became ruler of mountainous Ghor region of Afghanistan; inspiration for Rudyard Kipling's "The Man Who Would Be King."

Colonel Thomas Holdich: geographer who demarcated much of the Afghan border; led the British force that came closest to a clash with Russia during all the years of the Great Game at the Panjdeh oasis in 1885.

Sir Harford Jones: British envoy to Tehran who negotiated the 1808 treaty.

General Konstantin Kaufman: commanded the Russian frontier region from 1867 until his death in 1882; architect of expansion; proposed truce with Britain against what he saw as the common enemy of Islamic fundamentalism.

Sir John (later Baron) Keane: commanded the British force that invaded Afghanistan in 1839; warned of "signal catastrophe."

Colonel James Kelly: British officer who led the raid across high snow-covered mountains to relieve the siege of Chitral in 1894.

Colonel Ali Khanoff: Russian frontier commander who seized the Panjdeh oasis in 1885.

Mohan Lal: author, translator and fixer; described himself as a "gentleman and Kashmirian"; with Sir Alexander Burnes on his adventures in the early 1830s; attached to the British mission in Kabul, 1838–1841, remaining alive and at liberty to negotiate for the lives of British captives.

Lord Lansdowne: viceroy of India at time of negotiations over the Durand Line.

George Lawrence: brother of Henry and John; political officer with Sir William Macnaghten when he was murdered in December 1841; held in Afghan jail; had subsequent long colonial career, told in his *Forty-three Years in India* (outdoing later 41-year literary effort by Field Marshall Roberts).

Henry Lawrence: legendary British frontier political officer in the 1840s; inspired a group known as his "young men" who employed unconventional methods of controlling rebel tribes.

John Lawrence: opposed to any settlement with Afghanistan; as viceroy, was an architect of the policy of "masterly inactivity" outlined in a famous memo of 1867.

General Sir William Lockhart: commanded the largest army assembled under one general during the years of British rule of India to put down the 1897 uprising.

Lord Lytton: viceroy of India appointed by Benjamin Disraeli's new Tory administration in 1876; conducted the most aggressive Forward policy leading to the Second Anglo-Afghan War; lost office when Disraeli replaced by William Gladstone in 1880.

Lieutenant John Macartney: British surveyor; member of Mountstuart Elphinstone's 1808 mission who drew highly influential map of Afghanistan.

Sir William Macnaghten: British Resident in Kabul, (then term for political head of occupying force) heading the mission that installed Shah Shuja on the throne in 1839; murdered by Akbar Khan during negotiations in December 1841.

John Mcneill: British doctor who became a political officer; appointed as British envoy to Tehran, 1835; followed Persian court into Afghanistan for the siege of Herat in 1837; wrote an influential analysis warning of the Russian threat.

Sir John Malcolm: British envoy to Persia; negotiated anti-French treaty in 1800; clashed with Jones mission in 1808.

Charles Masson: real name James Lewis; British army deserter who fled to Kabul to make a new life in the 1820s; gifted archaeologist credited with the discovery of remains of a city built by Alexander the Great north of Kabul; eccentric scholar who traveled widely disguised as a beggar; worked as a British agent in the 1830s but left Afghanistan when not employed by British mission to Kabul in 1839; died in Edmonton in north London in 1853.

William Moorcroft: British adventurer and horse breeder; traveled widely, including a pioneering journey across Himalayas to Mount Kailash and Lake Manasarovar; died of fever near Balkh in 1825.

President Pervez Musharraf: general who led a military coup to become president of Pakistan in 1999; before he took control of the country, he masterminded a Pakistani attack on Indian-controlled Kashmir in the Kargil war; received billions of dollars of U.S. funding in return for support against terrorism after 9/11.

Count Nesselrode: Russian foreign minister from 1816 to 1845; disowned Ivan Vitkevitch after the Briton complained of Russian involvement in Afghanistan in the late 1830s.

General John Nicholson: maverick frontier British political officer; taken prisoner during his first campaign when the garrison at Ghazni surrendered to an Afghan force in December 1841; one of Henry Lawrence's "young men"; famous for no-nonsense tactics in pacifying frontier; object of reverence by a religious cult; died in Delhi in 1857 fighting to suppress the Indian Mutiny.

Lord Palmerston: British foreign secretary at the time of First Anglo-Afghan War.

General David Petraeus: U.S. general who in 2006 conducted the biggest overhaul of counterinsurgency strategy since the Vietnam war; In 2008 after commanding U.S. forces in Iraq, he took over Central Command, which oversees the whole region including Afghanistan.

Lieutenant Eldred Pottinger: British officer who assisted in the defense of Herat against Persian siege in 1836; part of the British force that took Afghanistan in 1839; took over as senior political officer on death of Sir William Macnaghten 1841; taken prisoner by Afghans and subsequently cleared of blame for surrender; died of typhoid in Hong Kong 1842.

Mullah Powindah: fundamentalist leader of insurrection against British control in Waziristan in 1897; continued opposition until his death in 1913.

Robin Raphel: head of the South Asia desk at the U.S. State Department when the Taliban emerged in the mid-1990s; worked in Iraq reconstruction effort after 2003; currently vice president of the National Defense University in Washington, D.C.

Lieutenant Harry Rattray: British commander of a small force at Chakdara fort who held out against assault in 1897 that Winston Churchill compared with the defense of Rorke's Drift, an epic battle in South Africa remembered in the movie *Zulu*.

General Frederick Roberts: British soldier known as "Bobs Bahadur" (Bob the brave); won the Victoria Cross on Delhi Ridge in 1857; saw camp of Hindustani fanatics in 1863; commanded the force that took Kabul after the slaughter of the garrison in 1879; reputation sealed by his forced march to Kandahar to avenge defeat at the battle of Maiwand; later titled Lord Roberts of Kandahar and headed British army as Field Marshall.

Sir George Roos-Keppel: commissioner of the North-West Frontier Province, 1908–1919; wrote an English/Pashtu dictionary that became the standard reference book.

Mullah Sadullah: led the Swat uprising against British rule of the frontier region in 1897; known as the "Mad Mullah" or "Mad Fakir" by British troops.

Lady Florentia Sale: wife of General Sir Robert Sale; survived the retreat from Kabul and wrote a highly critical diary listing military failings; died in Britain in 1853.

General Sir Robert Sale: known as "Fighting Bob"; led the main force into the breach of Ghazni fort in 1839; commanded part of the army detached from Kabul in late 1841 to give a "thrashing" to rebel tribes and to open the pass to the east; besieged in Jalalabad fort for winter, surviving a major earthquake; died in Sikh war in 1845.

Thomas Salter Pyne: British engineer who operated weapons factories for Abdur Rahman in Kabul; left Afghanistan during the cholera epidemic in 1900 and opened a chemical factory in Britain; later knighted.

Sir Robert Sandeman: British agent in Baluchistan in the late 1870s who established a system of control giving power to tribal elders to govern in return for British subsidies; popularized the term "hearts and minds."

Colonel John Shelton: unpopular British officer commanding the 44th Regiment of Foot that was annihilated in the 1842 Kabul retreat; blamed for the debacle; lost his right arm in the Peninsular War in 1813.

Shuja al-Mulk: ruler installed by the British in Chitral in 1895 at age 14; knighted and remained loyal to Raj; died in 1936.

Count Simonich: Russian envoy to Tehran in the 1830s; dismissed after Persia's failure to take Herat.

Ranjit Singh: Sikh ruler from 1799; formed one of the most effective armies in Asia; in 1809 he secured a British treaty marking the Sutlej, the easternmost of five rivers of the Punjab, as his border; died in 1839; the Sikh alliance with Britain broke down in 1845.

Captain Thomas Souter: British officer whose decision to wrap himself in the colors saved his life at Gandamack in 1842.

Colonel Charles Stoddart: British political officer; delivered the message persuading Persia to withdraw from Herat in 1838; taken prisoner on a mission to Bokhara and beheaded in 1842.

Lieutenant John Sturt: engineering officer in British force in Kabul in 1840–1841; played significant role in saving lives during retreat before being shot; gifted artist whose drawings of Kabul in more peaceful times were robbed by Afghans, but later turned up in Britain.

Ivan Vitkevitch: Russian envoy to Kabul, 1837; committed suicide shortly after returning to Russia.

Sir Claude Wade: British political agent in the frontier region in 1830s; blocked Sir Alexander Burnes's attempt to assist Dost Mohammed in negotiations in 1838.

Sir Arthur Wellesley: later the Duke of Wellington; responsible for key victories that took India for Britain at the end of the eighteenth century; defeated Napoleon at Waterloo in 1815 and later became British prime minister; opposed British involvement in first Anglo-Afghan war in 1838.

Congressman Charlie Wilson: masterminded the effort to raise U.S. funding for the mujahidin fight against the Soviet occupation in the 1980s.

Mohammed Yousaf: headed a Pakistani operation to manage the mujahidin during most of the war against the Soviet occupation.

General Zia ul-Haq: took power in a military coup in Pakistan in 1977; hanged the ousted prime minister, Zulfikar Ali Bhutto; backed war against Soviet forces in Afghanistan; killed in a mysterious plane crash in 1988.

GLOSSARY

Akhund: Muslim cleric; term used in Swat region in northwest Pakistan for political leader

Amir: Afghan term for king.

Bala Hissar: means "high fort"; common name in South Asia for fortresses. The Bala Hissars in Kabul and Peshawar are still under military control.

Buzkashi: horseriding game where riders compete ferociously to carry the stuffed carcass of a goat or calf to a marked spot.

Durand Line: name of Afghanistan's eastern border agreed after negotiations between the amir Abdur Rahman and Sir Henry Mortimer in 1893.

Feringhee: means "foreigner" in several South Asian languages; origins lie in the word "Frank."

Ferung: woolen floor-length one-piece Kashmiri garment with a hole through the middle for the head; in the winter wearers carry a small fire-pot in their arms under the ferung to keep warm.

Ghazi: religious warrior.

Ghilzai: subtribe of the Pashtuns living mostly in the eastern border area of Afghanistan.

Governor-General: head of the British imperial administration in India until 1858, replaced by viceroy.

Jezail: long matchlock weapon used by Afghan warriors; used mounted on rest; better range and accuracy than British weapons in First Anglo-Afghan war.

Jihad: mean "struggle"; it is the word used to describe the duty of Muslims to wage war in certain circumstances.

Jowzjani: northern Uzbek militia formed under General Dostam in the 1980s; fought on the Soviet side.

Kilim Jam: common name for General Dostam's Jowjjani militia; literally means "the carpet is gathered up," describing the looting that some experienced when the militia came to call.

Kotwal: chief of police.

Khan: nobleman or lesser king.

Loya Jirga: means "great gathering"; used in Afghanistan for a gathering of elders to discuss issues of national importance.

Madrasa: Islamic school where most of the time is taken up learning holy texts by rote.

Malik: tribal elder.

Mehmandar: courier sent by a king carrying official permission for a visitor to proceed to court.

Munshi: Persian language secretary.

Mujahidin: fighters who have taken up the requirements of jihad.

Pashtu: the majority language in southern Afghanistan and the frontier region.

Pashtun: the largest tribe in Afghanistan, based mainly in the south of the country and across the frontier in what became Pakistan in 1947.

Pashtunwali: honor code of the Pashtun tribe.

Qizalbash: Persian cavalry that had its own fortress in Kabul in the early part of the nineteenth century.

Raja: Indian king

Rissaldar-major: senior-most officers' rank of locally recruited cavalrymen in the British army in India; equivalent to major.

Salwar Kameez: loose cotton pants tied with a draw string worn under long matching shirt; standard wear for men across Afghanistan and Pakistan.

Saur: month approximating April in the Afghan calendar; name given to the 1978 revolution that toppled President Daoud.

Secret Committee: body comprising usually only three members of the board of directors of the East India Company; able to issue secret orders without input from the other directors.

Sepoy: lowest rank of infantry soldier for the British army recruited in India.

Sharia: Islamic legal code.

Shura: Arabic for "consultation"; used in Afghanistan to describe meeting of elders or governing council.

Sirdar: Pashtun nobleman; commander of group of Afghan warriors.

Sowar: lowest rank of cavalry trooper recruited for the British army in India; means "horseman" in Persian.

Stan: common name for the states of Central Asia that emerged in the early twentieth century under the wing of the Soviet Union.

Subedar: officers' rank for locally recruited soldier in the British army in India; equivalent to captain.

Viceroy: term used for British governor of India in 1858 reorganization that followed the mutiny of 1857.

Wali: Afghan term for governor of town or province.

Wazir: chief minister or adviser to the Afghan king (no connection to the frontier province of Waziristan).

Yaboo: small stout horse bred in Afghanistan.

AFGHANISTAN

INTRODUCTION

I first heard the word *Taliban* on a Friday night in September 1994 over a beer in the colonial bungalow that served as the Foreign Correspondents' Club in Delhi. A freelancer had just returned from the south of Afghanistan, where he had come across a new group of fighters using the name. "It might be worth checking them out," he said. "The Taliban seem different to other mujahidin, they are some kind of student militia." The Afghan conflict was then mired in a bloody stalemate 15 years after the Soviet invasion. We did not know that what he had witnessed was the beginning of something that would have implications far beyond Afghanistan.

Two years later, in September 1996, mine was the only TV crew to witness the Taliban takeover of Kabul, driving through the night toward the city past the wreckage of a defeated army. The pace and ruthlessness of the Taliban assault shook Afghanistan, putting more of the country under one administration than at any time since the Soviet invasion. Five years later, in 2001, the Taliban were targeted as the hosts of the 9/11 attackers and forced out after a war that was a technical triumph, victory without tears, at least for the United States, which suffered no combat fatalities. But by 2008 the number of foreign forces in the country rose to 50,000 for the first time, and a call went out for more, to tackle a worsening insurgency.

What had gone wrong? When the Taliban were ousted, few in Afghanistan appeared to lament the fall of these fundamentalist zealots. But that did not take long to change. The Taliban never went away and emerged from underground to win new supporters. The international community had made some fundamental mistakes after 2001, as what the World Bank would call an "aid juggernaut" drove into town, providing funds for itself and living in a parallel world rather than building a new Afghan state. Corruption was allowed to flourish, driven by huge profits from illegal drugs. And a military campaign had focused on arresting terrorists rather than restoring order. But were those failures enough to explain the resurgent Taliban?

Afghanistan had long ago built a reputation of resistance to foreign invaders. In 2009, it is exactly 200 years since Mounstuart Elphinstone, a Scottish political officer working for the Raj, Britain's administration in India, was the first formal envoy sent by any European power to discover who ruled the "Kingdom of Caubul." Another 30 years passed before Britain would attempt its first military expedition. That first war ended in catastrophe, and in the years that followed Afghanistan would inflict other defeats on British forces; Persia and Russia made even less headway. None seemed to learn any lessons from history. As a reporter traveling in Afghanistan, I wondered if there really was something in the nature of the people and the country itself that made it so hard to conquer.

Afghanistan was the farthest outpost of the region I covered as the BBC's South Asia correspondent in the mid-1990s, and the common complaint at the club bar was that it was then a forgotten war. Editors were not easily persuaded to invest in travel to a country locked in the confusing and bitter conflict that followed the pullout of Soviet troops in 1989. Besides, it was very dangerous, as I was reminded when a local journalist working for the BBC, Mirwais Jalil, was targeted and killed in cold blood in July 1994. Fighting in those years between rival *mujahidin* did far more damage to Kabul than the preceding decade of guerrilla warfare against the Soviet invasion, but received hardly any coverage worldwide.

Journalists who ventured there told of narrow escapes in a city that crackled with the constant sound of gunfire, their days spent risking movement through hostile checkpoints and their nights sleeping in basements with a shovel nearby to dig themselves out if the house above was struck by a rocket. They told tales too of the resilience and hospitality of Afghans despite everything, with an honor code—the *pashtunwali*—that meant that although Afghans were ruthless to their enemies, they would risk their own lives to guarantee the safety of their guests.

I saw this in action 20 years later in October 2006 when I interviewed a senior Taliban commander in Helmand Province, who was leading the renewed campaign against British troops. The invitation came from the Taliban, and my safety depended on his word, a system tested when a group of battle-weary fighters arrived after a gun battle with British soldiers and said they wanted to shoot me. In the subsequent argument for my life, he resisted their demands to hand me over, saying they would have to kill him first.

By then I had amassed a collection of classic books about Afghanistan, many of them copies reprinted in dusty back alleys in Peshawar on the North-West Frontier and sold in small ramshackle shops squeezed in among the carpet and curio dealers, who were still hoping that one day it would be safe for tourists to return.

Elphinstone's account of his mission was the best, but on the shelf alongside him in Saaed's Book Bank sat Connolly, Vigne, Moorcroft, and others—tales told by horse dealers, spies, thieves and scholars. There was an extraordinary account of survival through the thick of battle by a redoubtable general's wife, Lady Florentia Sale, and Sir George Robertson's story of the relief of Chitral, after Colonel Kelly led troops that fought their way across high mountain passes, forcing mules that ferried field guns through the snow. Robertson described a world on the frontier where "even fairy tales had a crimson atmosphere. Sensuality of the grossest kind and murder, abominable cruelty, treachery or violent death, are never long absent from the thoughts of a people than whom none in the world are more delightful companions, or of simpler, gentler appearance."

The books described an Afghanistan with characteristics that were still recognizable, peopled by men of enormous charm and grace, with elaborate codes of dress and hospitality alongside unspeakable cruelty. One hardly met any women. The pashtunwali, the honor code that had saved my life, demanded respect for mullahs and loyalty to commanders, restricted contact between the sexes, turned women into virtual commodities, and ensured that revenge would be carried down through generations. This harsh moral code—guaranteeing life to friends and death to strangers—was carved out of unforgiving mountains and deserts. The Kabul plateau is almost 600 feet above sea level, surrounded by mountain ranges that go even higher—a wild lunar landscape of breathtaking beauty. My screen saver shows a picture of a man on a horse, alone in a wilderness where little grows, behind him the sheer bare face of a blue mountain. Elsewhere the mountains are gray green or red, or broken into dust-colored folds that seem to stride over the horizon; and behind it all, like the icing on a cake, the white peaks of the Hindu Kush cut across the center of the country, with the Suleiman Mountains to the east.

Apart from the Pashtuns, I had now traveled among the Mongol-looking Hazaras, Turkic-featured Uzbeks and their neighbors the Tajiks, and high in the mountain fastness of the East, Nuristanis, tall paler-faced people, often with fair hair, blue eyes, and freckles. This tribal diversity told of a complex history lived in a landscape that had been fought over and traded through since the dawn of time.

In the north of Afghanistan lie the ruins of the world's first city, Balkh. In the same region, Avicenna, the founder of modern European medicine, was educated in an Islamic school, a *madrasa*. What had happened in the thousand years since he went to school, that these madrasas had become internationally notorious, known only for the most restrictive fundamentalist education? In the Bamiyan Valley, carved into the wall of the Hindu Kush, had stood two giant Buddhas, until they were blown up by the Taliban. I had lain on the head of the bigger Buddha only a few months before its destruction, gazing at the fragile frescoes on the ceiling—visions of the pleasures of the flesh, painted longingly 1,500 years ago by monks who had abandoned that life for austerity in a cave.

The Buddhas have gone, and the monks' caves have filled with refugees, the smoke from their fires blackening the red rock.

There was another question raised by foreign engagement in Afghanistan during the 200 years since Elphinstone's trip in 1808: Why was holding the country far more difficult than taking it? Seeking an answer would set me on a trail that would involve deeper reading than the reprints available on the frontier. The extraordinary collection of letters and memoirs in the British Library is a treasure trove. Lady Sale turned out to be a gifted artist, whose exquisite watercolors were as much a revelation as her highly critical account of the military failings that led to British defeat in Kabul. She was 50 years old when she moved to Kabul, and cast from an empire-building mold, having already witnessed an uprising in Gwalior in India. She found things to say in the darkest of moments, retaining her leather-bound notebooks in a bag around her waist when she had lost everything else. The morning after her soldier son-in-law died in her arms, and she and other women were taken away from the ranks of the retreating British army to an uncertain fate by Afghan tribesmen, she still noted, "I could not but admire the romantic tortuous defile we passed through, being the bed of a mountain torrent, which we exchanged for the terrific pass I have mentioned." Before the defeat and catastrophic retreat, the letters sent by Sir William Macnaghten, the British envoy to Kabul, show with unbearable poignancy his nagging fear of how things might turn out. He wrote, "we shall be high and dry ere long."

But the most telling account of Britain's failure in its first attempt to take Afghanistan was left by an Indian, Mohan Lal. He was an unassuming man, virtually ignored by some historians of the period, who dismissed his books as the writings of an embittered *munshi* getting above his station as a translator. But Lal showed that he had the better understanding of how hostility grew to British rule. His unthreatening character allowed him to remain at liberty in Kabul, even after his colonial masters were besieged in their garrison. His worth was shown early, when he was a member of a British mission to Kabul facing competing claims from Russia. In 1838 Lal found his way to report on an Afghan royal new year's party at which the Russian envoy was the guest of honor, but the flamboyant British envoy Sir Alexander Burnes had been snubbed.

I recognized Lal because he was the sort of companion I would have chosen if he had been available to work as a fixer for a journalistic assignment. Good locals who can speak the right languages and find their way around obstructions are the key to foreign reporting: people like Rahimullah Yusufzai, whom I traveled with frequently during the early days of the Taliban, including the seizure of Kabul, or Najibullah Razaq, gentle, multilingual, and cunning. Finding out what is happening under the surface in a complex society, where manners and hospitality remain even in wartime, is the key to success. From men like

Rahimullah and Najibullah I learned to wait and drink the green tea and eat the sugared almonds that lubricate business in Afghanistan, squatting on dusty carpets while lunch was prepared and permissions considered.

Again and again in the past, the local dynamics of Afghanistan were not considered important enough to warrant attention by empire builders. In 1893, half a century after the defeat of the Kabul garrison, Henry Mortimer Durand traveled to Kabul. This was the man who would leave his name on the Afghan frontier—still known as the Durand Line. Every night of his visit he, or sometimes a secretary, would copy his correspondence into a letter-book, using a pencil. His plans, read alongside the account left by the Afghan amir Abdur Rahman, reveal just how far Durand underestimated his opposite number, whom he regarded "a brutal savage."

By the late nineteenth century Russia too was threatening Afghanistan, but made even less progress than Britain. A map from the period shows railway tracks from the west, north, and east stopping at the Afghan border. Both Britain and Russia had by then taken vast tracts of Asia, but neither could penetrate Afghanistan. British anxiety over Russia led to the translation of many key Russian documents, just as the United States translated Soviet and Afghan documents after the 1970s, and for the same reason: to understand a potential foe. Britain's translations were published in Calcutta, while the U.S. translations have been available online since Freedom of Information laws kicked in. But were these lessons of former conflicts being learned in the twenty-first century by those nations that had once again gone to war in Afghanistan?

I thought I detected a constant theme running from Britain's first intervention in the early nineteenth century up to the imposition of democracy after 2001: Policy was to be shaped from outside whatever the local Afghan circumstances. The most shortsighted example of this was the indiscriminate foreign funding for the mujahidin fighting against Soviet forces in the 1980s, much of the money coming from the United States. The fundamentalist Islamic creed professed by rebel leaders such as Gulbuddin Hekmatyar and Ahmed Shah Massud was overlooked—they were accorded celebrity status as guerrillas who were on the "right side."

But when forces loyal to the two men turned on each other after the defeat of Soviet forces, the Western diplomats who had funded and praised them fell silent. And few appeared to want to understand the Taliban phenomenon when the movement first emerged in the late 1990s, or in its resurgence in 2006. The belief was that since democracy had come to Afghanistan, "it was not thought necessary for us to understand the tribal system," in the frank admission in 2007 by the European Union representative in Kabul, Francesc Vendrell.

But British forces had seen warriors like these before in their history. In 2006 the British faced their first intense firefights in Helmand Province in

Sangin, the same town where a British invasion force faced its first major battle in the South in 1878. And then, as now, Afghan defenders were inspired by the demands of *jihad*, waging holy war against invaders. In the nineteenth century these fighters were known as *ghazis*, religious warriors. The Taliban had clear antecedents in the ghazis and Hindustani fanatics of the past, as well as the mujahidin struggle against the Soviet invader—different terms in different times for holy warriors for whom martyrdom is their highest calling.

Jihad was even motivated with exactly the same messages across the centuries. The amir who negotiated the border with Durand in 1893, Abdur Rahman, always protested that he was completely loyal to Britain when uprisings erupted along the frontier, but I had heard that he had written a book about jihad, which had been widely distributed in mosques at the time, although I had never seen a translation. I found a very rare original copy in a Kabul market, and my fixer Najibullah translated it, turning to his father, a retired judge, for some of the more obscure Koranic references. The book was a revelation, and a long way from the consoling messages Britain had heard from Abdur Rahman at the time: It was a ringing call to arms against the British, extolling the virtues of overnight horseback ambushes and the beauty of paradise for martyrs. Most interestingly, the Koranic extracts used were the same as those used both by the Taliban and Osama bin Laden in their appeals for *jihad*—identical calls to holy war across the same frontier a century apart.

Reporters who spent a lot of time in Afghanistan gathered knowledge about the particular nature of how conflicts work there and power changes hands. I learned a lot from the veteran cameraman Peter Jouvenal, who has been filming news in Afghanistan since the time of the Soviet invasion. Whether a group of fighters was communist, mujahidin or Taliban is never important to Peter. It is their constant character as Afghans that he believes determines their behavior. He could strip conflict down to a few rules. This was a land with strong centrifugal forces, where loyalty was always to individual local commanders and not to the state, although all tended to unite against outsiders. Commanders would change sides often, seemingly without principle, to follow power. He knew too the ferocity that was expected when towns did change hands and were looted as if by locusts. But full combat was to be avoided at all costs. Commanders would do deals rather than fight wars, in a country where, as one observer put it, "the mere appearance of force is half the battle of ordinary business." The ties that bound warriors to warlords were stronger than the demands of the state. Elphinstone himself had noticed 200 years ago: "They are assembled in tribes under powerful chiefs...which circumstances have prevented any encroachment by their own sovereign on the rights of the local chiefs."

Building a central government and national institutions was never going to be easy. The forces pulling the country apart were as strong against the major nineteenth-century amirs—Dost Mohammed and Abdur Rahman—as against President Hamid Karzai since 2002. The only period of stability was the long reign of Zahir Shah, from 1933 to 1973, helped for all of the later period of his rule by the frozen balance of the cold war. Afghanistan became a far richer and more developed country by the end of this period, a fact often forgotten by aid workers who came in after 2001 and believed they were starting from scratch, but in the end it was pent-up demands for social and political progress that pushed Zahir Shah out of power, leading to the spiral downward toward the Soviet invasion in 1979 and the country's long nightmare.

The porous border across the frontier with Pakistan remained an open back door, useful to the United States when it sent arms and aid along the mule tracks in the mountains to aid the mujahidin struggle against the Soviet invasion in the 1980s, but 20 years later the boot was on the other foot. Pakistan did nothing effective to combat the safe haven for the Taliban on its side of the frontier, and in April 2008 the outgoing U.S. commander of the North Atlantic Treaty Organization (NATO) forces in Afghanistan, General Dan McNeill, said the upsurge in cross-border attacks on his forces inside Afghanistan was "directly attributable to the lack of pressure on the other side of the border." Relations worsened as Pakistani troops were killed by U.S. missiles.

This unstable frontier was the one drawn up by Durand in 1893. Its treacherous mountain ranges could not be crossed by an army except in three places, the best-known being the Khyber Pass. The mountains and valleys of the frontier were natural guerrilla territory that define Afghanistan's strategic relationships. Britain never secured full stability and control during the century when this was the western border of British India, despite a policy known at the time as "butcher and bolt": constant raids to hunt elusive enemies—burning villages in punishment attacks, killing without controlling—directed at men who, in 1897, Winston Churchill called "northern savages, impelled by fanaticism or allured by plunder."

The failure of Pakistan to do any better to combat insecurity on the North-West Frontier after 2001 meant that NATO armies in Afghanistan were fighting as if with one hand tied behind their back, while in front of them corruption, illegal drugs, the failure to build institutions of state and lack of development steadily eroded support for their presence among Afghan people. The initial U.S. plan after the fall of the Taliban did not include widespread military operations across the country. Beyond the hunt for Osama bin Laden and others deemed terrorists, always under a separate command structure, very few forces were sent out beyond Kabul, and their role was very limited. Democracy was seen as a virtue that would spread peace on its own. Comments at the time echoed those made in 1839 by Lieutenant Colonel Dennie, after British forces had installed their choice of amir: "The war may now be considered at an end, the King being once again on his throne." That first war would go on for another three years, and Dennie was killed in its closing stages. In June 1879 General Sam Browne signaled "the Kabul campaign may now be regarded as terminated." After the slaughter of the British mission sent to Kabul, that war would go on for another two years.

Again in 1980, two months after the Soviet invasion, there were plans to withdraw troops, since, in the words of an official report, "having solidified the new Afghan government...they have fulfilled their main task." A month later these troops were replaced by a larger force sent to combat a growing mujahidin insurgency in a war that went on for another nine years.

Similar misunderstanding surrounded Afghanistan in 2001, when the Taliban were believed to be so unpopular that they could never rise again. It took several years and the arguments of commanders like the British general David Richards to scale up the counterinsurgency effort. But when the call went out for more international forces, many countries imposed such rigid conditions around the use of their troops that they were contemptuously known as pot plants by NATO planners, of ornamental use only. With only a small number—mainly Canada, the Netherlands and France—willing to put forces in harm's way, the United States and Britain shouldered an increasing burden, and increasing casualties. In 2008 memories of the bloodless victory of 2001 were long gone as monthly U.S. casualties in Afghanistan were higher than in Iraq for the first time.

A U.S. intelligence estimate toward the end of 2008 was the most pessimistic since the invasion, concluding that Afghanistan was in a "downward spiral" and casting doubt on the ability of the Afghan government and armed forces to contain the insurgency or combat the corrupting effects of the narcotics trade, now bigger than the country's conventional economy. In 2008 U.S. marines were sent for the first time in force to Helmand Province, the main area where opium poppies are grown, to assist British and Canadian forces fighting the most intense warfare against a renewed Taliban insurgency. The fighting had not been anticipated by the British government, whose defense secretary said that troops would be happy to leave "without firing one shot."

Unlike U.S. forces, this army had been to Afghanistan before. In garrisons across Britain hung regimental banners with battle honors from Kandahar, Ghazni, and Khyber stitched into them, and stirring Victorian paintings depicting defeats of the past: the last stand of the 44th at Gandamack, a horse carrying the sole survivor of the Kabul garrison limping into Jalalabad, and the battle of Maiwand.

Afghanistan has a history of confounding the optimism of invaders.

PART ONE

FIRST ENCOUNTERS AND THE FIRST ANGLO-AFGHAN WAR, 1808–1842

KABUL in the NINETEENTH CENTURY

BEMARU HEIGHTS

BRITISH CANTONMENT 1879

CANTONMENT 1840-1841

Canal

Kabul River

THE OLD FALL

to Charaiab

BALA HISSAR

PALACE

BAZAAR

DURRANEE HOUSES

QUIZIL BASH QUARTER'S

BABUR'S TOMB

1

WILD AND STRANGE

In Afghanistan "a small army would be annihilated and a large one starved."
—Arthur Wellesley, Duke of Wellington

Elphinstone was dazzled by the jewels. Beneath a crown from which nine-inch-long spikes encrusted with diamonds shone out in all directions, the Afghan amir wore what looked to him like a suit of green armor. On closer inspection, Elphinstone saw that the armor was studded with emeralds. It was the first meeting between an envoy from a European power and an Afghan king, and amid all the finery the Briton at first hardly noticed that Shah Shuja wore a shining rock of a startling size hanging from a bracelet around his wrist: the Koh-i-noor diamond.

When he had left Delhi on October 13, 1808, Mountstuart Elphinstone, a 29-year-old British political officer, had prepared a mission of "great magnificence," since he had heard that the court at Kabul was "haughty, and supposed to entertain a mean opinion of the European nations." His retinue included 600 camels and 12 elephants laden with presents. It was the beginning of a relationship that would lead directly to Britain's worst defeats in two centuries of imperial power in Asia.

The background to Elphinstone's mission lay in Britain's realization of Afghanistan's strategic importance to India. It was only four years since British forces under Arthur Wellesley, later Duke of Wellington, had secured military dominance of India. But this control was threatened when Napoleon set his eyes on Britain's new empire in the East; and the balance of power in Europe had just shifted decisively in his favor. Napoleon's embrace with Tsar Alexander on a raft in the center of the river that divided their armies at Tilsit, in the north of Europe, ended a war that had cost the lives of about 50,000 troops, sealing a new alliance that sent shockwaves not only across Europe but the world.

British spies brought news of a secret clause in the Tilsit treaty creating a joint Russo-French force of 70,000 troops to invade India. Russian territory was far from India, and on the wrong side of the high plateau of the steppes and vast mountain ranges. But what if the invasion came directly from the west, across Persia? Russia had been threatening Persia for years. Now Napoleon sent a mission there, with money, guns and military skills, to train the Persians in the arts of European warfare. If Persia was brought in on the side of the Russo-French alliance, then only Afghanistan would stand in the way of a full-scale assault on India.

John Crokatt, an analyst with the East India Company, which at this time ran India, wrote: "events seem rapidly approaching which threaten with immediate danger, if not with total subversion, the British government in India."

Even if France and Russia stayed out, Britain was already fearful of Afghan aggression toward India, and kept forces in the west as a deterrent. Crokatt remembered recent history, when "Zaman Shah, the brother and immediate predecessor of the reigning monarch, was led by predatory and ambitious motives to meditate acts of hostility against the [East India] company. At this momentous crisis it is of considerable importance to ascertain whether the present King is guided by similar views." This was the reason for Elphinstone's mission.

Britain knew little about Afghanistan. There had been travelers' tales from a few individual adventurers but, until Elphinstone set out, no determined attempt to discover the reality of the land beyond the five rivers of the Punjab, at that time the effective western border of British India. Britain did know of Afghanistan's warrior history. It was within living memory that an Afghan amir had ruled in Delhi itself after conquering half the continent. That was Ahmed Shah, founder of a dynasty, and still revered as the father of the Afghan nation, whose dynasty was known as *Durrani*, meaning "pearl of pearls." Shah Shuja, the amir who met Elphinstone, was his grandson.

The Afghans were known for their banditry and lawlessness. An early British traveler to Afghanistan, George Forster, like so many after him, was attacked in 1783, as he went through the Khyber Pass, the long winding pathway through the Suleiman range, the soaring mountain fastness that conceals Afghanistan from the rest of South Asia. Although he had paid a toll to the keepers of the pass, protection money in effect, he was knocked off his mule and kept his money only because it was wrapped in gaiters around his legs. He saw that the "freebooting life" was aided by "a chain of rocky mountains, whose scanty slips of valley afford but the coarsest provision for human wants. This rude race of men have made so slow a progress in civilization, that the greatest part of them, like the storied Troglodites of old, dwell in caves, or rather in the fissures of rocks."

Forster grew a beard to blend in. He did not want to admit to being British, and decided against pretending to be French; he thought it too likely that he would encounter a real Frenchman, because of the "the wandering temper of that people, who stray into every corner of the earth." After 15 months traveling west from India, as he was having his beard shaved on a Russian frigate in the Caspian, he regretted its passing. He reflected on "the general importance of an Asiatic beard, the essential services which mine had rendered, and our long and intimate association."

But neither Forster nor any other of the handful of Europeans who had been into Afghan lands before 1800 had left maps or detailed guides. Incredible as it may seem, Elphinstone was using accounts left by Alexander the Great, written more than 2,000 years before, as he probed the land beyond Britain's known Indian world. He had only Alexander's names for the rivers that crossed the flat country of the Punjab, until he came to the wide barrier of the Indus itself, the defining geographical feature of the region.

Not yet 30 years old, Elphinstone was a brilliant classical scholar, and spoke fluent modern Persian as well as Hindi. Personally charismatic, as a teenager he had startled visitors to Edinburgh Castle, where his father was governor, by marching around with his long blond hair swept back in the French manner, singing revolutionary songs he had learned from French prisoners. An uncle in the East India Company in Calcutta obtained a post for him in India, where he quickly caught the attention of Arthur Wellesley. He was sent as a political officer to secure a peace deal with the Mahrattas, the last major threat to British control of the subcontinent, and when peace talks broke down, he played a crucial role on Wellesley's staff at the battle of Assaye in 1804, when the Mahratta army was defeated once and for all. Wellesley told him he should have become a soldier.

Guided only by accounts of ancient battles but fueled by apprehension of a French invasion, Elphinstone's mission left Delhi in 1808 and headed southwest across modern Rajasthan toward, although they did not know it, one of the largest deserts in the world. The journey took on an epic quality. Soon the camels could go in single file only on shifting tracks through sand hills "rising one after another like the waves of the sea, and marked on the surface by the wind like drifted snow." Marching at night, sleeping fitfully through the heat of the day, the two-mile-long caravan made slow progress. The heavy sand became too much for the *sepoys*, the Indian soldiers fighting for the British, so they were allowed to ride in turns, two to a camel. Securing water was a constant problem, and even when they found it, the wells were sometimes as deep as 300 feet, emptied in a single night by bullocks turning a winch.

Securing food and water was not made any easier by the decadence of the rulers they encountered, who were constantly drugged by alcohol or opium. Elphinstone found he could conduct business with them only in a brief window of time in the afternoon—"the interval between sobriety and absolute stupefaction"—after the first fix had eased the pain of the hangover and craving, and before they were too drugged again.

But the difficulties he encountered with minor tribal leaders, who all swore allegiance to Britain—when sober enough—were as nothing compared to the civil war that Elphinstone was nearly drawn into when he reached the region carved up by the five main Rajput rulers. He found the kings of Jodhpur and Jaipur fighting over the hand of the princess of Udaipur, who must have been a beauty, for this South Asian Helen of Troy had little land.

As the desert became more threatening and the war closer, the trickle of desertions from among Elphinstone's camp followers turned into a flood. Any expedition then relied on a village of people moving with it, to keep it on the road. Each horse required its own "grass-cutter," to gather fodder and water, and a groom to tend it. There were farriers, carpenters and leather workers for the animals, and cooks, water gatherers, and laundrymen for the officers. Elphinstone now put the whole expedition onto a military footing, separating out the wives and children and sending them back, and hiring 150 local horsemen to help guard their progress. But the desertions stopped only when they were so far from safety that returning was more dangerous than going on.

Three weeks after leaving Delhi, the British arrived in the city of Bikaner, capital of the richest and largest of the five Rajput kingdoms. It was under attack. The British saw the evidence of the war for the princess's hand in bodies on the ground and "disorderly bands of ragged soldiers in all directions." Elphinstone had to fend off attempts by the warring kings to draw him in. His well-trained and battle-hardened sepoy force, with its British officers, might have been decisive. The raja of Bikaner exerted pressure by denying his wells to the British force, and sickness and the harsh conditions began to take their toll. From what had not been a large force, 40 men died in the first week after they arrived at Bikaner. But the raja knew about the threat of the French, and once he had demonstrated his power, he relented, gave the British water and promised them his full support, even trying to press the keys of the city onto Elphinstone, who declined since his mission was not to take territory.

When the force moved on from Bikaner they marched by day, since they feared bandits at night, although it meant using more water. The desert sand was firmer now, and they made faster progress, with the camels moving a dozen abreast. Still only just across into modern Pakistan, east of the five rivers, and a long way short of the modern Afghan border on November 21, the British encountered Afghan troops for the first time.

Elphinstone was impressed. The Afghan force, 150 soldiers on camels, which they managed as if they were light horses, had an appearance that "was altogether novel and striking." Two men sat on each camel, each with a long matchlock rifle, highly decorated in black and white checkered wood and mother-of-pearl. This was the weapon the British would later learn to call a *jezail* and come to respect, since it was surprisingly accurate at a distance. The Afghans brought 100 camels carrying skins of fresh water, with four separate jars of water for the British officers, sealed by their leader, the chief of the most southerly of the regions owing allegiance to Kabul.

Elphinstone's trip now took on the appearance of a medieval adventure overlaid by the courtly manners of the rulers he moved among, a long winter where his days were spent hunting and his nights feasting and watching dancing girls. Two hundred years ago, Afghans had quite different customs from today.

After the ordeal of the desert and the drunken indolence of the Rajput rulers, Elphinstone now found himself handed from khan to khan, on his way to meet their overall amir, the ruler of Kabul, whom most of them had never met. They may have been suspicious of Elphinstone's intentions and feared he wanted to take their land, but they hunted with him and mostly treated him well. Expecting to face incessant demands for gifts, "as is usual on such occasions in most parts of India," instead he often found it hard to give things away without elaborate negotiation. And in return he found himself the owner of horses, hawks, greyhounds, guns and fine cloths. The khans saw him not as an imperial emissary but the representative of a power like their own. In those early days of Britain's settlement of the subcontinent, there was far more equality between the two sides than later, at the height of the Victorian empire.

Some of the khans were more graceful than others. Elphinstone was stuck in the ancient capital of lower Punjab, Multan, for three weeks until the arrival of a *mehmandar,* an official courier sent to escort an important visitor to the Afghan court. The khan of Multan was suspicious, speaking quickly and saying often "You are welcome, you are very welcome" but meaning the opposite. When he finally agreed to visit the British camp, his large armed party marched in at speed, almost sweeping aside Elphinstone's tent and his secretary: "Mr Strachey's horse was nearly borne to the ground, and only recovered himself by a violent exertion." But even this khan settled down after this first farcical encounter, and the caravan moved on.

While still east of the Indus, the British caught their first sight of the Suleiman Mountains, the mesmerizing and complex wall running from north to south, with only a few navigable passes, the most important being the Khyber, through to the high plains of Afghanistan beyond. These mountains, 400 miles long and 200 miles wide in places, would come to dominate Afghanistan's relationship with the outside world over the next two centuries. "Their appearance was beautiful; we clearly saw three ranges, the last of which was very high, and we often doubted whether we were deceived by the clouds, or really saw still higher ranges beyond." The Afghanistan on the other side of the mountains took a powerful hold on Elphinstone's imagination; he knew only that "beyond the hills was something wild and strange."

Three months after leaving Delhi, the British crossed the Indus at a point where it was 1,000 yards broad, but the flow of the river was weakened as it was broken by islands. The elephants swam across, as those in Alexander the Great's force must have done, while the horses crossed in large flat-bottomed boats, and the camels had their feet tied and "were thrown into the boats like any other baggage." By now the British had been in the region long enough for rumors to have spread about them. They were said to carry "great guns packed up in trunks; and…certain small boxes, so contrived as to explode and kill half a dozen men each" without hurting themselves. Another story was a version of an old Asian folk tale that said the British had made a magic sheep which looked real, but when it was sold was found to be made of wood. Elphinstone's men were among a superstitious and rumor-fueled people.

There was suspicion everywhere. In a nomad camp Elphinstone was asked why they were there, rather than being "contented with our own possessions, Cawnpore, Lucknow, and all those fine places?" Two of Elphinstone's officers took a day to try to climb to "King Solomon's throne," the snow-covered peak that had given the Suleiman Mountain range its name. But they found the top of the mountain inaccessible and were robbed on the way back, while in another village a man cocked his matchlock at the two climbers. As the caravan continued north, word arrived with a convoy carrying mule-loads of fruit from Kabul that they would not need to go all the way to the capital; the amir would greet them in Peshawar.

It was the Mogul emperor Akbar who gave Peshawar its name, meaning "advanced post," in the sixteenth century, designating it as the gateway for the defense of India against Afghanistan. It was a substantial town of mud-walled houses with flat roofs around a teeming bazaar, with a fort, the Bala Hissar, that was "of no strength" to Elphinstone's eye. From there it was only a morning's ride to the eastern entrance of the Khyber Pass, the narrow pathway through the mountains into Afghanistan. The British party arrived in Peshawar on February 25, 1809, "after some confusion about the mode of our reception." Armed horsemen had to beat back the huge crowds who came to see them.

More than two weeks later, amid a huge noise "like a charge of cavalry, which was occasioned by the iron-heeled boots of the guards," Elphinstone was welcomed in to the Afghan court, a complex series of ornate buildings with ponds and fountains, and fine silk carpets hanging from the walls. To the sound of drums and trumpets he was led from person to person through inner courtyards and gardens, and announced with some ceremony outside, before the curiously downbeat moment as he made his way into the presence of the king. As was the custom, in order not to be seen to be making a recommendation, the courtier did not announce him with any formality but in an offhand aside, as if saying "Well, here he is, but I don't vouch for him."

Elphinstone was greeted by the sight of the amir perched on a gold-colored throne, elevated above the heads of his eunuchs. "His appearance was magnificent and royal: his crown and all his dress were one blaze of jewels." But despite the dazzling finery, Shah Shuja was in a weak position. Elphinstone correctly assessed that this "all bore less the appearance of a state in prosperity than of a splendid monarchy in decay." He discovered in conversation with one of the amir's key advisers that the man thought Calcutta was in England.

The curse of the Koh-i-noor, which is said to bring bad luck to any male ruler who owns it, may have contributed to Shah Shuja's problems. (This belief continues to the present day. The diamond has been worn by only two rulers since being seized by Britain: Victoria and Elizabeth II. British kings have ordered it to be put into their female consort's crown.) But it would have taken a statesman of extraordinary quality to have stabilized Afghanistan in the early nineteenth century, a period of intrigue and royal bloodletting uniquely awful even in a country with such a murderous history.

While the ceremony to welcome Elphinstone was going on, his soldiers and servants were having a hard time trying to hand over the gifts they had brought for the amir. Not only were the camels bearing the gifts taken by force by the amir's men, so were other riding camels that had come in by mistake. British livery was taken off the backs of the elephant drivers, and there was an attempt to kidnap two servants. It was symbolic of what was taking place across the land. Royal power did not even extend as far as the royal stables. On his way to Peshawar Elphinstone had noticed how even people who worked closely with the amir would speak openly against him, "I was a good deal surprised at the freedom with which all my visitors spoke of the government, and of the civil wars."

What was happening was a fight to the death between two rival clans. Both were old Pashtun noble families from the South. When Ahmed Shah Durrani, who came from the Sadozai clan, founded his dynasty in the middle of the eighteenth century, the chief of the other big southern clan, the Barakzais, had stood aside for him, crowning him symbolically with a sheaf of corn (remembered still in a symbol on the national flag). After Ahmed Shah's son Timur died in 1793 the succession was disputed. Initially one of Timur's 23 sons, Zaman Shah, ruled successfully with the assistance of Payendah Khan, the clan leader of the Barakzais, as his *wazir* (chief minister). This was the king Britain had feared enough to keep troops garrisoned in the West. But voices at court conspired against Payendah Khan, and Zaman Shah had him killed. The power struggle between the two clans would take a further 40 years to resolve, drawing both Persia and Britain into wars in Afghanistan.

Zaman Shah had made too many enemies and lost his throne in 1800; caught trying to escape, he was blinded in a savagely symbolic act and thrown into jail. In the chaos of the following years, he was released and fled to exile as a pensioner of the British in India, beginning the nineteenth-century trail of discontented and dispossessed members of Afghan ruling families who would take rupees from the British while plotting their return to power. Guest houses in Ludhiana and Rawalpindi became royal waiting rooms.

When Shah Shuja, brother of the blinded Zaman, met Elphinstone in Peshawar in 1809, he had just taken Kandahar and Herat, the two principal cities in the South, and the ones Britain had been most concerned about, for they lay on what was believed to be Napoleon's likely invasion route. But Shah Shuja's hold on power was precarious. In the months that Elphinstone was with him, he lost Kashmir to local rivals and was not sure it was even safe to return to Kabul. In their discussions, Elphinstone did secure a treaty against Napoleon, but he did not demand much, certainly much less than he had sought at first, because the expectation of a French invasion had receded. While Elphinstone had been hunting and hawking on his way to the Indus through the winter of 1808–9, his mentor Arthur Wellesley had proven that he was not just a "sepoy general." He was pinning down French forces in the Peninsular war in southern Europe, blocking Napoleon's wider ambitions. This had a profound impact on events in the Indian subcontinent.

Elphinstone's instructions when he first set out from Delhi had been to secure an aggressive pact, binding the Afghans to attack Persia if French forces appeared over the horizon, with promises of troops and substantial military aid. French reverses in the Peninsular war led to a change of plan. Elphinstone returned to Delhi after agreeing to a treaty with Afghanistan that offered far less than had been originally considered—a defensive alliance, with terms that provided for British aid for "arms, ordnance, and military stores, rather than of troops." Shah Shuja was the first in a long line of Afghan kings to find himself on the receiving end of a British policy that was determined only by British interests, not helping his hold on power or considering wider regional security.

The risk of the French winning the support of the Persian government had receded despite one of the most ludicrous episodes in the history of British diplomacy. Unlike Afghanistan, which would not be safe enough for permanent embassies from abroad for another century, Persia did admit foreign embassies. Britain had responded to the threat of French influence in the region by sending not one but two missions to Persia, from London and from India, with contradictory orders.

Persia was bemused by the desire of the great powers to court support. When the Persian ambassador in Bombay was killed by chance in a brawl outside his home, the British paid lavish recompense, fearing offense. A Persian minister said, "the English might kill ten ambassadors, if they would pay for them at the same rate." Britain had already concluded a rabidly anti-French treaty with Persia in 1800, amid general European hysteria about the threat of republicanism spreading after the French Revolution. Despite vigorous protests from France, the treaty effectively bound the Persian government to kill French civilians on sight.

With Russia and France now threatening again in 1808, the government in India sent Brigadier John Malcolm, the same man who had secured the original bloody anti-French treaty. But before he set out for Tehran, Malcolm heard that the East India Company was planning to send another emissary, under the direct command of London, headed by Sir Harford Jones, newly knighted for the occasion.

Malcolm had fallen out with Jones before, and the row that ensued between London and Calcutta had a personal edge. Malcolm wrote to the governor-general of India, complaining of Sir Harford's "character and former petty animosities...Sir Harford is not in possession of that high local respect and consideration in the countries to which he is deputed that should attach to a national representative."

But Malcolm's powers of persuasion failed him this time. He arrived in Persia, bearing gold and threats, and was received very coldly. He watched French artillery officers giving the Persians advice and French surveyors helping them to map their territory, while he had to leave with nothing. His rival Jones was now ready in Bombay, and by the time Malcolm had returned and persuaded the government in India to take a tougher line, and threaten military action against Persia, Jones had already set sail. A black comedy followed, with Malcolm securing agreement from the government in India to put together a military force of 2,000 men to attack Persian islands in the gulf while Jones found his missives ignored by a government that was refusing even to settle his bills, as he continued trying to negotiate peace.

Things became dangerous for Jones when the governor-general, Lord Minto, threatened to damage his reputation in Persia: "In the event of you not complying, without further reference or delay, with the instruction conveyed in this letter, by closing your mission and retiring from Persia, it has been determined, and measures have been taken accordingly, to disavow your public character in that country."

Jones was nevertheless able to ignore Calcutta because his orders came directly from London, and he carried on laying the diplomatic groundwork for a treaty that was beginning to look possible. He was lucky as well. He had already proved he was an unconventional diplomat in the way he continued to go forward despite specific orders. As the treaty came closer to being agreed, the senior Persian negotiator complained about a clause that was unclear and called the British diplomat a very undiplomatic name meaning "cheat." Jones pushed him against the wall, told him he was an idiot, kicked over the candles and stormed out. Whatever he did, it worked, although Malcolm fumed away, advocating force and complaining that Jones could never achieve success, which "every child with him sees is unattainable through the means he uses."

Jones finally secured his treaty, with a specific clause barring British military assault on Persian islands in the gulf, inserted by Persia to deal with Malcolm's threat. The turf war meant a loss of face for the government in India. British relations with Persia were conducted directly from London for most of the rest of the nineteenth century.

Other long-term consequences emerged from this episode of diplomacy. Persia had its own ambitions for Afghanistan at the time—as in the conflict two centuries later, when Persia is called Iran. In the early decades of the nineteenth century, the divisions inside Afghanistan made a Persian advance seem possible. The power struggle between the southern Afghan clan leaders was settling into a pattern that would affect regional balances for generations to come. Kabul became the natural capital of the country, replacing Kandahar, which would now be routinely fought over between Kabul and the semi-independent city of Herat, close to the Persian border in the west.

All of this felt remote and distant to the British in India. Even after Elphinstone's first mission, they knew little of what was really going on. Elphinstone had not even crossed the Suleiman Mountains, instead meeting the amir east of the Khyber Pass. Afghanistan remained a closed book. A surveyor traveling with Elphinstone, Lieutenant Macartney, drew a map from accounts he was given by travelers, in an effort to understand the country. He had not seen Afghanistan either, but his perspective would define military thinking about the land across the Indus for a century. The "wild and strange" land beyond the mountains was an imaginary country—an Afghanistan of the mind. Macartney's drawing defines the routes in and out of Afghanistan much more clearly than a modern map, where the sheer complexity of the mountain ranges can conceal understanding.

Macartney's map peers over the mountains, making an educated guess about how Afghanistan looked. The most significant feature beyond the Indus was the Suleiman Mountain wall, virtually impassable and, according to Elphinstone, reaching "up to the sky." (Modern surveys show the range to have peaks that reach 11,500 feet.) Beyond these mountains on Macartney's map lay uninhabitable wasteland and then another solid wall crossing the center of the country—the Hindu Kush, a fabled snow-topped mountain range with few known passes through it; its name translates as "killer of Hindus."

These two ranges—the Suleiman Mountains running north-south and the Hindu Kush in an east-west gash across the middle of the country—were the defining features for British strategists. In their mind's eye, Afghanistan was huge and treacherous, dominated by these walls set at right angles, and this image informed all of their thinking. They knew very little about the precise topography, but they did know that Alexander the Great had found his way through from the other side and had crossed the Indus. For the defense of India, Britain needed to have a relationship with the people beyond the mountains. Macartney shows too the vital importance of the Helmand River in the southwest, and the impenetrable mountains to the north and west of Helmand. The map demonstrates clearly why the battles of the next 200 years were always fought in the same places. Nowhere does geography more define war than in Afghanistan.

It took until the end of the nineteenth century for Britain to decide which of the two key barriers, the Indus River or the Suleiman Mountains, was the better Afghan border. How far "forward" did it need to go to project military power and diplomatic influence in order to defend India? The solution the British came to in 1893 was to draw a line down the *middle* of the mountains, a line that became the border between Afghanistan and Pakistan and has remained a permanent source of instability into the twenty-first century.

The Afghanistan of the mind that developed from Lieutenant Macartney's map was part of a defensive wall on a chessboard. The amir may have dressed as a king, but he was just a pawn, expendable in a bigger game. At the start of the century of British dominance of world events, the Afghan amir was offered neither protection nor support, but instead a demand that he should support British imperial interests. Later in the century Afghan amirs would ask for more protection in return for Britain controlling their foreign policy, but they would not receive it, and this weakened them in their battles for succession.

Britain offered Afghanistan no permanent guarantees of its own security but sought temporary defensive deals that lasted only for the reign of the amir who negotiated them. And when the British tried to influence who should be in power in Kabul during two catastrophic wars in Afghanistan in the nineteenth century, they did so in pursuit of narrow British defensive interests.

— — —

So what did the Europeans think of the Afghans they first encountered? Elphinstone, a highly sensitive and articulate man, was the first of a long line of British writers who developed a genuine regard for them. To him, the straightforwardness, courtesy, and looks of Afghans, were appealing compared to the Indians he lived among. They had neat houses "so unlike those of Hindoostan," and they were more pleasing to his eye: "their appearance and complexion continued to improve as we got northward." Afghans tended to be tall, with paler skin than Indians, and a Grecian nose. Many had blue eyes, and some from the North had fair hair.

Elphinstone went into admiring detail about the exercise routine of the Afghans, especially their use of Indian clubs, swung around their heads. He was very struck by one exercise in particular: "the performer places himself on his hands and toes, with his arms stiff, and his body horizontal, at a distance from the ground. He then throws his body forward, and at the same time bends his arms, so that his chest and belly almost sweep the ground. When his body is as far thrown forward as possible, he draws it back to the utmost, straightens his arms, and is prepared to repeat the motion."

He described approvingly how beneficial this was, saying that one of his officers could soon do 600 of the exercises at a time. The British army had discovered push-ups.

The British force adopted an Afghan giant of a man called Rasool, calling him "Rasool the Mad" and equipping him with a full British uniform and helmet. He had come to their notice when they first arrived, as he enthusiastically beat back the crowds. Praise for the looks and manly virtue of the Afghans, compared to Hindu plains Indians, was a constant thread in the writing of male British writers from that first traveler George Forster onward. It was as if the British recognized something they admired once they came close to the mountains that was easier to deal with than the dark complexities of India with its many gods.

The Afghans' faith, Islam, was also seen in a more favorable light than Hinduism. One of the early travelers, Alexander Burnes, admired a Hindu on his staff who converted to Islam in the frontier region. Islam would not "satisfy a Christian" but was still a move in the right direction. "It is no small step to advance from Hindooism, its superstitions and abominations, to Mohammedanism, even with all its imperfections and absurdities."

The British had no illusions: Afghans were always to be characterized as predatory, murderous and barbarous, with, as Forster put it, a "fixed contempt for the occupations of civil life." But they were believed to be honorable, robust and hardy. Victorian British travelers also shared a preoccupation with local sexual practices, culminating in a magisterial collection of stereotypes, laid down by an adventurer who went on to govern India as viceroy at the end of the century, Lord Curzon. "At Chitral I fraternized with fratricides, parricides, murderers, adulterers and sodomites...I start tomorrow for Kabul where a female donkey is the object of favourite solicitude." he wrote in 1895. The often soft and familiar way that men would walk together, for example holding hands in public, was easily construed as meaning that homosexuality was widespread, although Forster admired what he believed to be a hard line against "that unnatural passion to which many of the Mohametan sects are addicted; and the perpetrators are punished with severity."

Elphinstone was told that Afghan men and women could marry for love rather than by arrangement, a situation "unique for the east" from his Indian-trained perspective. Certainly from the way he describes village life, it appears that Pashtun women had far more liberty then than they do today: "as the women there go unveiled, and there is less restraint...between the sexes, the match generally originates in the attachment of the parties, and all the previous negotiations are saved." If a man were to cut a lock of a girl's hair or take her veil, then that would be enough to win her as a fiancée. With the complicity of the bride's mother, a groom might be allowed to slip in to spend nights with her before the wedding.

If young couples were forced to elope, then he was told that Pashtun hospitality rules would give them sanctuary with another clan or tribe. Elphinstone was an acute observer of both extremes of the *pashtunwali*, their code of honor, that gave protection to guests while guaranteeing death to strangers.

Elphinstone understood aggression toward strangers and travelers as an inevitable and proper part of a system that demanded loyalty. Lone travelers had no relations or tribe so there was no provision for their security, and it was reasonable to rob them. The system was a closed one, depending on a balance of strength. "To sum up the character of the Afghans in a few words; their vices are revenge, envy, avarice, rapacity and obstinacy; on the other hand, they are fond of liberty, faithful to their friends, kind to their dependants, hospitable, brave, hardy, frugal, laborious and prudent."

The strength of their clan and tribal ties gave Afghans the ability to survive without effective central government and at the same time made it harder for central government to impose its will. The violence and bloodshed caused by continual weakness and war at the center must have given the country beyond the Suleiman Mountains something of the same feel in 1808 as it had 200 years later, when the U.S.-led invasion had not provided stable government.

But it was better than neighboring Persia, which did not have the Pashtun honor code. "We find Persia in a state of decay, after twenty years of entire tranquillity; while Afghanistan continues the progressive improvement which it has kept up during twelve years of civil warfare." Education was valued, although even then it was too often in the hands of "half-taught Mullahs, who rather impede than promote the progress of real learning."

After Elphinstone returned home to Bombay, a young Anglo-Indian called Durie came to his door having traveled across Afghanistan. He had pretended to be a Muslim and had politely declined an offer of circumcision on the spot when his real identity was discovered. Elphinstone quoted Durie's conclusion that military success in Afghanistan was possible: "It is evident that a regular courageous army, having provisions, can make them all submit completely." Military men of more experience than Durie would make the same mistaken prophecy often during the next two centuries.

— — —

While Elphinstone had been probing west of the Indus to secure Afghan support in case of a French attack, another of Wellesley's young stars, Charles Metcalfe, was behind him, ensuring that the Sikh army between India and

Afghanistan did not stray beyond the land of the five rivers. One of the most influential rulers in South Asia in the nineteenth century, Ranjit Singh, was just coming into his prime—uniting the Sikhs and pushing his elbows into Afghan territory to his north and west, as well as toward British India to the east. After British forces pushed Sikh cavalry back west of the Sutlej River without a fight, Metcalfe forced a defensive alliance on Ranjit Singh in Lahore in March 1809. Once again the long shadow of Wellesley's success in Spain would help negotiations in India. Ranjit Singh could not count on France, and agreed that British forces could cross his territory if they needed to move west into Afghanistan.

Sikh forces made easy work though of defeating the Afghan amir Shah Shuja, aided by their European artillery and European, mainly French, soldiers of fortune. Within six months of his meeting with Elphinstone, Shuja had lost his throne, fleeing to regroup the remnants of his army just inside British India. He returned to retake Peshawar in 1812 but could offer nothing to the chiefs there, who took a bribe to hand over the ex-amir to the Sikhs. He was held in jail for a year while complex negotiations went on for control of the Koh-i-noor diamond, the symbol of power across the region since the days of the Mogul Empire.

In the end it fell into the hands of the new strongman in the region, Ranjit Singh, who signed elaborate promises in return, none of which he fulfilled. Shah Shuja's run of bad luck did not stop once he had lost the cursed stone. After escaping from his Sikh jail dressed as a beggar, he bribed a Hindu army with his last money to retake Kashmir, but they were defeated by the snows. He fled in 1816 to join his sightless brother Zaman Shah amid the growing colony of ex-Afghan rulers living on British pensions.

The struggle for control of Afghanistan did not stop with Shuja's flight. When the British horse breeder William Moorcroft visited Peshawar in the early 1820s, he found the Bala Hissar, the fort overlooking the city, reduced to a pile of rubble. Sikhs had demolished the remaining signs of Mogul and Afghan rule and even damaged some mosques. The elaborate courtyards where Shah Shuja had ruled from his golden throne were no more.

Moorcroft rejected an offer by four princes from the next generation of the Barakzai dynasty to "become the channel for negotiation for placing the whole country under British rule." Afghanistan was for sale to Britain for 300,000 rupees (about $3 million in today's money). As he moved toward the mountains, even the Waziris, the most ferocious, independent and warlike of the Afghan tribes, asked for British protection from the cruelty of their own rulers and the threat of the Sikhs. They were "torn to pieces by intestine feuds, village being armed against village, and man against man." But Moorcroft was driven only by the imperative to improve Indian bloodstock. Among the Waziris he noted two horse breeds: one was called *Dagla-gala*, meaning "thieves' brood."

The reputation of those who lived hidden in the folds of the remote mountain ranges of Waziristan imprinted itself on generations of travelers. Elphinstone had been told to fear the Waziris, who were said to be savages who ate human flesh. The region contained no routes into Afghanistan that were useful in military terms but dozens of mountain tracks that were perfect for thieves, smugglers and, in the wars that broke out after the Soviet invasion in 1979, Islamist insurgents. By then Waziristan was on the Pakistani side of the Afghan border and provided the staunchest support for the U.S.-backed war against the Soviet Union in Afghanistan, and later the best refuge for Osama bin Laden's foreign fighters. By 2006, when the insurgency in Afghanistan against the post-Taliban government intensified, it was the remote mountain regions of Waziristan that again hid Taliban and al-Qaeda fighters. The region an early British colonial officer called "the plague spot" of the frontier again added to its reputation.

Moorcroft faced the usual threats when negotiating his way through the Khyber Pass into Afghanistan, paying protection money while fearing throughout for his security. He found the Khyberees "tall for mountaineers, and of a singularly Jewish cast of features." This referred to an old belief of the Pashtuns that they were the lost tribe of Israel. "Some of the young women had an arch, lively look, but we saw none that could be described as pretty." His companion George Trebeck was robbed while they were camping within sight of Kabul.

Moorcroft was the most adventurous of the European travelers who penetrated the farther reaches of Asia in the early years of the nineteenth century, even crossing the Himalayas to Lake Manasarovar, at the foot of Mount Kailash, the holiest mountain for both Hindus and Buddhists. He and Trebeck both died of fever in northern Afghanistan in 1825 and were buried outside the walls of the oldest city in the world, Balkh, near the Oxus River.

But deaths on distant mountainsides did not deter exploration by other British adventurers. Alexander Burnes, a brilliant linguist with a rakish reputation and a flair for self-publicity, first came to Punjab in 1831, bearing the fantastic gift to Ranjit Singh of five British dray horses, four mares and a stallion, the biggest horses in Asia—and a specially built carriage fit for a maharajah. He brought them up the Indus on a flat-bottomed barge. The trip was a boast with a hard-headed commercial objective: If Britain could take a carriage and five cart-horses up the river, then why not normal trade?

A few months later Burnes set out west from India again, pretending to be poor, with pots and pans tied to his saddle. This time he led a very small party, including an Indian, Mohan Lal, who was surprised to see his companions sitting on the ground "which I never saw an Englishman do before." And they were willing to sleep out without a tent, even when there was frost.

The choice of Mohan Lal was a curious link with the 1808 mission; his father had been Elphinstone's secretary on that journey. Lal was part of the

Indian elite that received a first-class education and skillfully navigated the cultural minefields between British India and Afghanistan. He was an acute observer of the Afghan temperament: "The Afghans are bold and careless, with a mixture of rudeness. They are accustomed to shoot on horseback, and a good marksman is always respected, although he may be of low family. They quarrel for an insignificant thing, and kill each other for a trifling offence. They boast of their heroism, and think themselves the most incomparable warriors of the age…They cut off a man's head with as much indifference as we cut a radish."

The most powerful and successful military leader in the region, the Sikh king Ranjit Singh put on a show for them before they left. Mohan Lal was unimpressed. The short lecherous Sikh ruler was already showing signs of the skin cancer that would kill him: "His one eye is ever inflamed, either by the use of opium or wine," Lal was shocked to find Ranjit Singh talking familiarly to dancing girls—"improper in the opinion of the wise." Worse, he was accompanied by a beautiful boy, whose family he had enriched.

Burnes enjoyed the debauchery of the Sikh court before disappearing into his not-very-plausible disguise as a pauper; his confidence in his own abilities reflected in the name he used: Sikander, Alexander in the local language. The only Sikander remembered on the frontier is Alexander the Great. And he chose as his second name Khan, meaning king.

— — —

By the 1830s, Russia had replaced France as the country Britain thought most likely to threaten their control of India. A Russian mission was massacred in Tehran, as Lord Ellenborough, a member of the Board of Control that supervised Indian affairs in London, noted in his diary with some satisfaction. "These accounts only confirm what we had already heard of the arrogance and violence of the Russians. They deserve their fate." But he was concerned enough to put out a secret order to arrest Russian spies, and recommended that Britain should occupy Kabul if there were any hint of a Russian move south.

Ellenborough, a pompous manipulative man, would be the person called on to clean up after the disaster of the war in Afghanistan that was to come in 1838. Back in 1829, he laid out a policy that would not change much in its essentials until Britain pulled out of India in 1947. First he wanted information. "We know nothing of these passes, nothing of the country beyond them, nothing of the course of the Indus." Preparations were made for 70,000 troops, with as many mounted as possible, and his tactics had an icy cynicism. "We should have full information so as to be able to crush an advancing enemy, by making the whole country hostile, which money would do."

The region was to be controlled with cash and cavalry. Britain's long obsession with India's northwest frontier had begun.

2

A WAR OF ROBBERY

A war of robbery…a new crime in the annals of nations—a secret war. It has been made by a people without their knowledge, against another people who had committed no offence.

—East India Company Select Committee report

The appearance of two dogs, exhausted and thirsty, one evening at the besieged British garrison in Kabul in December 1841, was the first sign of a missing British force. Lady Florentia Sale recognized the dogs immediately. They belonged to officers serving in the occupying force commanded by her husband, General Sir Robert Sale, "Fighting Bob," who had set out from Kabul to give rebel tribes a "thrashing." But there had been no firm news from the missing army for several weeks.

As the sun dropped below the hill behind Kabul city to the southwest, soft remnants of evening light picked out the dark shapes of Afghan warriors, moving into position among the scrubby larch and oak trees for another night of firing down from the Bemaru Hills above the British garrison into the poorly defended area below. Lady Sale took in the dogs and ordered servants to feed them, although she knew that the remaining dogs in the garrison were already eating the corpses of horses and camels that had died of starvation.

Were the officers' dogs harbingers of doom, or messengers, coming ahead of the army, on its way back to relieve Kabul, where the British occupation force was now in desperate straits?

For weeks General Sale's letters to her had somehow got through the chaos. They talked of far fiercer fighting than expected in the passes to the east, with dozens of British dead, until Sale moved into to defend the fort at Jalalabad, and then nothing. Appeals from Kabul for help went unanswered. Colonel John Shelton, who had lost his arm in a previous Indian war, did not endear himself to

Lady Sale, saying her husband would not be back, since "being out of a scrape, keep so." Shelton promptly moved into the Sales' house in the Kabul cantonment, complaining that it was too cold to sleep outside as winter approached.

Lady Sale was not to see her husband again for another nine months. And by the time she did, he had withstood a siege in Jalalabad, during which he saw his defenses collapse in an earthquake, and she had emerged from Kabul as one of a handful of survivors of Britain's greatest Asian defeat—a heroine who had taken command of troops when the men around her failed to rise to the challenge. It was her new houseguest Shelton—a stiff and unimaginative man, "a tyrant to his regiment"—who was to be responsible for the catastrophe that engulfed the garrison, alongside an old and sick veteran of Waterloo who had not seen action for years, General William Elphinstone (first cousin of Mountstuart Elphinstone). But the military mistakes of Shelton and Elphinstone were just the closing chapter in a story of political miscalculation, hard reality against vain hope, humiliation after hubris—dealt out to another invader by Afghanistan.

It had begun with a note sent to the foreign secretary, Lord Palmerston, by his ambassador in Tehran in 1836, warning that Russia was urging a Persian advance on Herat in the west of Afghanistan—then not governed from Kandahar or Kabul but an independent city-state. Full of mosques, minarets and gardens that told of old wealth gathered from centuries of trade on the crossroads of Asia, Herat was the legacy of one extraordinary woman, the fifteenth-century Gohar Shad Begum, who married the son of the great warlord Tamerlane and used the wealth of conquest to bring the best artists from around the known world to adorn the city.

The ambassador who had sent the note John McNeill, was the author of a highly influential analysis of Russia's threat to British control of India, which pointed out how fast the Russians were moving south. "Russia alone threatens to overturn thrones, to subvert empires, and subdue nations hitherto independent." He warned of the knock-on effect if Herat went, weakening Britain's "moral influence" across Asia.

Britain was backing the ruler of Herat, Kamran Shah, to balance power within Afghanistan, a country that was still divided into several kingdoms. Herat was the only part still in the hands of the Sadozai dynasty, descendants of Ahmed Shah Durrani. An opium addict and wine drinker, Kamran Shah would steal from merchants and the public to pay his troops. "In lieu of distributing justice, he spends the whole of his life in ornamenting himself with handsome robes, and his abominable conduct…has rendered him most obnoxious throughout the whole of Afghanistan."

Kamran Shah was fond of devising new methods of torture, such as ripping open the bellies of prisoners and tying them upside-down to camels that were driven through the bazaar, coloring the sand red. He wanted better backing against the threat of Persia, telling a British visitor "any boy of four years of age in this country knew well that the Persians were the intimate friends, and even the slaves, of Russia."

What any boy of four knew was certainly believed by Lord Palmerston at the Foreign Office in London: Russia was now the puppet master pulling the strings in Persia, ending decades of British influence. Britain's aim was to avoid military confrontation with Russia while neutralizing its power. It was the same foreign policy thinking used by the United States in the days of the cold war in the second half of the twentieth century. And on both occasions it ended up with Afghanistan becoming a battlefield.

Palmerston's main concern was much farther west than Afghanistan: Avoiding war with Russia over Turkey while retaining access through the Dardanelles and influence over Constantinople was the main objective. Afghanistan was a remote and distant piece on the board, to be shaped and moved into place by the master strategist according to his grand vision, not for its own good but as a defensive wall against Russia, "the best rampart India could have."

The player chosen to fit Afghanistan into Palmerston's design was Alexander Burnes, now the most famous British adventurer of the age. After presenting Ranjit Singh with his carriage and cart horses, he had written an account of his epic trip through Afghanistan and across the Oxus north to the mysterious kingdom of Bokhara in 1831 that became an instant best seller. Now he was going back to Kabul to try to prevent a war.

The Afghan capital in the 1830s was a teeming cosmopolitan trading post, with one of Asia's most important bazaars, built in the crook of the Kabul River as it turned a right angle between three high hills that reared up around the center. On the southern side, set away from the river, lay a fort complex, a military town within a town, known in Peshawar as the Bala Hissar. Overlooked by the ruins of an earlier castle above a large walled area that housed the royal palace and a garrison of troops, it jutted out like an apron into Kabul—its walls and towers grand vestiges of two centuries of Mogul supremacy in Kabul before the eighteenth century.

Kabul seethed with armed men, including thousands of *qizalbashes*, Persian cavalry for hire, who lived in a separate walled compound not far from the Bala Hissar. While nearly all Afghans were Muslim, there was a large Hindu quarter, and also Sikhs, Jews and Christians—a kaleidoscope of Asian humanity as it was before the monochrome of the modern Muslim world. Armenian Christians, valued for their prowess in making guns, had their own church in the Bala Hissar itself. Alcohol was freely available, and "females, both of high and low family, desert the path of virtue and pursue bad principles." This was so well known that there was an old Pashtun proverb: "As the flour of Peshawar is always tainted by a little barley, so the women of Kabul are not without lovers."

Burnes had an appetite for all Kabul had to offer, although he was initially made "melancholy" by the sight of women in their standard dress, shrouded from head to toe in a burqa with just a lattice window to see and breathe through. He went to the races and recorded that while the first prize was a girl, the second rider took home 50 sheep and the third won a boy; the prizes then went down through a cow, horse and camel, until the seventh man won a watermelon, and was the object of "ridicule and banter for the rest of the meeting."

Burnes's initial cover story, as he traveled across Punjab and up the Indus toward the Khyber Pass, was that he was surveying the river looking for trading opportunities. But no one believed it. And by the time he arrived in Kabul in September 1837, his secret orders had become more urgent. He wrote to a friend that he had been sent "to see into affairs and judge what was to be done hereafter; but the hereafter has already arrived."

Persia had carried out its threat to besiege Herat, the shah himself coming from Tehran and setting up camp on Afghan territory. And on the eastern side of Afghanistan, while waiting to go through the Khyber Pass, Burnes had seen the bodies of men and horses still littering the battlefield at Jamrud, where sizable Sikh and Afghan armies had fought each other to a standstill some months before—a battle that had taken the life of the Sikh commander in chief. Britain wanted to stop another Afghan army roaring through the pass to confront the Sikhs, now in control of Peshawar and other former Afghan land west of the Indus. Britain's promotion of the interests of the Sikh leader Ranjit Singh was their first mistake.

On his arrival in Kabul in September 1837, Burnes was greeted warmly as an old friend by the amir's son Akbar Khan and carried in some ceremony on the back of an elephant through narrow streets where people shouted up at him, "Do not destroy Kabul." He was honored with lodgings in a spacious royal guest house next to the palace itself inside the Bala Hissar complex. The buildings were on a colossal scale. In front of Burnes's window was a formally laid-out square garden 500 feet across, with the clear waters of a stream flowing through elaborately constructed halls of audience at each end.

The day after his arrival, Burnes walked out through the entrance of his grand lodging and across a square lined with petitioners waiting to see their amir, Dost Mohammed, who could be seen sitting on a raised dais, in a large audience chamber one floor up. Burnes thought he seemed "more alert and full of intelligence than when I last saw him." Later in the day he had the curious honor of being taken to see the brother of the amir, Jabar Khan, in his bath.

Dost Mohammed, who became known as the "great amir," was one of the two dominating Afghan characters of the nineteenth century. And like the "iron amir," Abdur Rahman, at the end of the century, the longest and most successful part of his reign was to follow a failed British military intervention. These two men stood like giants at each end of a period of intense British involvement in the affairs of the country, and a crucial part of the mix that brought success for both was the way they exploited political Islam for their own ends.

Dost's aim was to knit together the frontier tribes in a jihad, a holy war, against the Sikh invader. The willingness to sacrifice everything for the promise of paradise beyond this life was a powerful imperative for Islamic holy warriors in Afghanistan, then as later. They responded to kings who would define jihad not as many thought—a personal inward struggle—but a call to war.

Dost Mohammed was the first Afghan leader to realize what power this had. He was preoccupied with retaking Peshawar and the other former Afghan territory east of the Khyber Pass. He even went as far as to declare himself Amir al-Mu'minin—the spiritual leader not just of Afghanistan but of all Muslims, after a very rare public display of Afghanistan's most precious object, a cloak believed to have belonged to the Prophet Mohammed himself. The next person to take out the cloak and declare himself Amir al-Mu'minin was Mullah Omar, the leader of the Taliban, in 1996.

Dost Mohammed, a man of "tall stature and haughty countenance," had fought his way to the top. He was one of the youngest of 20 half-brothers of Fateh Khan, the main Barakzai claimant to power, but Dost had no status, as his mother was the daughter of a qizalbash, a Persian mercenary. He remedied that when, just 14, he killed an enemy of Fateh Khan's with a knife. Dost emerged as amir from a vicious civil war as the most powerful of the Barakzai brothers, after Fateh Khan overreached himself and was literally cut to pieces—first his ears, then his nose, then his hands and feet, before his throat was cut.

Dost had enjoyed wine as a youth, but like Shakespeare's Prince Hal, he turned away from his former self when he assumed power. Some British travelers mocked his conversion. "Of later years, by all accounts, he has been ambitious of the character of a saint, pretending to have celestial visions." But Burnes did not mock him; he liked the amir, who had offered him command of the Afghan army when they had last met, believing that much of the strength of the Sikh force lay in its European officers. Burnes wanted Dost Mohammed as a British ally, but he had been given impossible orders.

Britain's alliance with Ranjit Singh's Sikh kingdom dominated the discussions in Kabul, with Burnes being ordered to persuade Dost to make peace at any price. If Dost would apologize for Sikh losses in the battle of Jamrud in 1836 and pay tribute to Ranjit Singh, then there might again be an Afghan prince in Peshawar—but under Sikh domination, and not Dost himself. Instead, Britain would install another Barakzai brother in Peshawar—an enemy of Dost, who was discovering how bitter was Britain's game of divide and rule.

But Burnes's ability to negotiate was being undermined. Beneath Palmerston's empire-building map of the world lay layers of British-Indian public officials.

The Afghan negotiations were not directly run by the governor-general in India but by a political officer, Sir Claude Wade, who had far more influence in the system than the maverick young adventurer Burnes and put his own spin on the reports as they passed both ways.

Burnes soon realized that Wade had his own agent in Kabul, a man calling himself Charles Masson and claiming to be an American adventurer from Kentucky. He was in reality a deserter from the East India Company's army called James Lewis, pardoned for desertion at the insistence of Burnes himself, who had pressed his case in London after meeting "Masson" on his first trip to Kabul in 1831.

Masson did not repay the favor. He was the sort of character often washed up on the shores of Afghanistan—independent, resourceful, hugely talented and duplicitous. He had traveled widely across the country in the guise of a beggar and had an encyclopedic knowledge of its history and a fine coin collection. Burnes was a threat to his small income as a company spy, and from his mud house, carved out of the hill in the narrow winding streets of the Armenian quarter below the palace in the Bala Hissar, Masson conspired against the flamboyant adventurer who had come onto his patch.

Worse than the presence of Masson, who was at least supposed to be on the same side, was the news soon after Burnes arrived that a Russian envoy was also on his way. Dost Mohammed asked Burnes what he should do, and what Britain would offer if he were to turn away the Russian envoy. Burnes was ready for the question. He had his own spy at court and knew that Dost was planning to see both of them no matter what he offered, so he bowed and gracefully gave the amir his "permission" to see the Russian. Messengers were now galloping daily through the Khyber Pass, carrying the assessments of Burnes and Masson in one direction and orders the other way. The letters often crossed, and Burnes made two offers for which he had no authority, to keep ahead of Persia and Russia. He offered financial help to Dost's brothers in Kandahar to head off a Persian attempt to dominate the town, and then he offered Dost direct help to take Kandahar for himself.

But Britain did not back its own envoy. The British strategy was to keep Kandahar, Herat and Kabul divided and do nothing to threaten the Sikh leader Ranjit Singh to the east of Afghanistan, a strategy that ignored the crisis brewing to the west, where the hawkish envoy McNeill was still writing virulent messages about the Russian threat: "The evidence of concert between Persia and Russia, for purposes injurious to British interests·is unequivocal, and the magnitude of the evil with which we are threatened is, in my estimation, immense."

McNeill was seeing the threat at firsthand. As ambassador he had had to move with the Persian court onto Afghan soil when the shah began his siege of Herat, and had seen him take money and artillery advice from the Russian ambassador and shamelessly greet the Russian envoy, who was on his way to meet Dost Mohammed in Kabul.

In desperation, on December 23, Burnes wrote a personal note to the governor-general of India, Lord Auckland, going over Wade's head. The high-handed move was a risk, especially as Wade was already recommending that Burnes should be reprimanded for offering far more than Britain wanted to deliver. In his personal note Burnes put Dost's case against the Sikhs, and said the Afghans had wanted connection with British but had received "cold and distant replies to their solicitations." He said it was impossible to negotiate through Wade and was a "matter of great moment that this question should be speedily adjusted."

While waiting for an answer to his plea, Burnes, with characteristic flair, sent an invitation to the newly arrived Russian agent Ivan Vitkevitch to join him for Christmas dinner. Vitkevitch came to his sumptuous quarters, deep in the Bala Hissar, in the full uniform of a Cossack officer: two of the most gifted mavericks ever drawn to Afghanistan face to face at dinner in the city at the heart of the Great Game—the imperial struggle for influence across Asia.

Vitkevitch had a colorful past. Stripped of his noble title for organizing a secret far-right revolutionary society, the Black Brothers, he had escaped execution and was banished instead in what was seen as an almost equivalent punishment—serving as a ordinary soldier on the wildest fringes of Russia in Orenburg, the garrison town facing south to the untamed vastness of Central Asia.

He was a natural spy, resourceful and with a gift for languages and deception that quickly drew him to the attention of Russian intelligence. In Kabul, he had far more money to offer and more scope to make promises to Dost Mohammed than Burnes had. The Afghan amir had already been in touch with Russia to try to secure that nation's support. The arrival of Vitkevitch meant he was being offered something other than Britain's arid, repetitive humiliating demand that he should pay tribute to the Sikh maharajah Ranjit Singh—an infidel who had taken *Afghan* land.

Dost Mohammed continued to tell Burnes that he would prefer to do a deal with the British: "I wish no countenance but that of the English, and you refuse all pledges and promises, and mean...to do nothing for me." But Vitkevitch was offering so much more, and it was clear that Burnes's mission was hopeless by the time of the spring equinox in March, when Afghans celebrate the new year. Vitkevitch was Dost's guest of honor, while Burnes was not invited. Mohan Lal, the discreet Indian master fixer, succeeded in getting an invitation, but only at the last minute, scrabbling together the symbolic gifts of salt, sprouting rice and a purse of money to take with him.

At the party, Vitkevitch took Lal aside and boasted that he would rouse "all the discontented chiefs of India to rebel"; 50,000 Russian soldiers were ready at the border. He claimed he had offered Dost enough money to move through the Khyber, retaking Peshawar *and* Kashmir. Vitkevitch sneered, "The English, who are not soldiers, but merely mercantile adventurers of Europe, would not dare to assist Ranjit Singh, knowing that the Afghans are succored by the warlike nation of Russia."

Burnes's position became impossible. His advice to the government in India continued to be distorted by Wade, whose notes condemned Dost's "extravagant expectations." Burnes had to threaten to leave, knowing it would mean war, but still had no response. He had trouble hiring mules to carry his baggage home: Kabul's bankers had lowered Britain's credit rating. When he went to say good-bye to Dost, the amir carried on coldly playing a chess game, neither rising nor turning his face to the British envoy. But as Burnes rode away, two fine horses followed him to the Khyber as a personal gift from the amir.

Burnes was ambitious, but he was also loyal. Although he could not directly oppose policy, he could perhaps express incredulity at the direction it was heading. In one of his last and most poignant notes before abandoning his mission in Afghanistan, he subtly hinted at what he thought was really behind Britain's increasingly tough line. He wrote that he did not understand apparent noninterference in Afghanistan, unless it was intended to put back in power the "ex-king at Loodiana, secure through him a footing in these countries, and sweep the present rulers from their authority, which has happily never been contemplated."

Burnes's worst fear was exactly what was now being contemplated. The ex-king was Shah Shuja, the "unlucky amir" Elphinstone had met in such finery in Peshawar on the first British mission a generation before. Shuja had never stopped trying to reclaim his throne, taking an army into the field as recently as 1835, with some British financial support, but failing to defeat Dost Mohammed and the other Barakzai "pretenders" in running battles near Kandahar. Now old and in exile in British India, Shuja pressed his ancestral claim on Wade, the political officer running the negotiations, persuading him he had substantial Afghan support against the usurper Dost.

The Wade/Shuja relationship was a combination that Burnes could never match. The complex reality experienced by the agent on the ground did not count as much as the bureaucratic analysis of the desk officer; it never has.

As Burnes led his small mission out of Kabul, there were celebrations in the large Persian community in the city, who thought Persia would beat the British-backed ruler in Herat too. The loudest roars of delight came from the qizalbash cavalry, but the Afghan majority was quieter and more concerned. The British misread this, believing it meant that Dost Mohammed was unpopular and that Shuja would be welcomed back. The analysis would have fatal consequences.

Burnes never saw Vitkevitch again. After the new year celebrations, signaling the spring and the start of another fighting season in Afghanistan, the Russian envoy went on to Kandahar, with a treaty from Dost in his pocket and Russian money to support Dost's brothers and the other *sirdars*—the tribal chiefs whose support was and is always uncertain, always expensive and always essential for waging war successfully in Afghanistan. With Russian backing, 250 Kandahari horsemen set off to help the Persian army surrounding Herat.

It was the best chance to break a siege that had gone on in a desultory way for more than six months. When the Kandahar sirdars came in on the Persian side, the remaining support in the countryside for those besieged began to ebb away. But in Herat the opium-soaked tyrant Kamran Shah was lucky in having a young British artillery officer on hand. Eldred Pottinger had been traveling in disguise across Afghanistan, first as horse dealer and then a holy man, with a loose commission from the Intelligence Department in India to report what he found. Pottinger, in Herat when the siege began, promptly dropped his disguise, organized the defenses of the city and trained its troops.

The arrival of Russian support on the Persian side in June led to the fiercest fighting. The city nearly fell as Pottinger's defenses were breached by a determined assault. The defenders fought for their lives, encouraged by the bounty that Kamran Shah offered for the head of an enemy. In one epic day of fighting 400 enemy heads, including that of a Russian officer, were stuck onto pikes above the city gate.

Enough was enough. Palmerston had wanted to avoid military entanglements with Russia, concerned as he was about the possibility of war over Turkey, but he dispatched a fleet to threaten Persia and called in the Russian ambassador in London to demand that Russia stop its military adventure in Afghanistan. As Herat held out through the relentless heat of a long desert summer, British marines took an island in the gulf, planted the Union Jack on Persian soil and threatened to advance onto the mainland.

Britain's ultimatum to the shah of Persia was couched in diplomatic language, but as it was being read to him by Colonel Charles Stoddart at his camp near Herat, the shah interrupted and said, "The fact is that if I don't leave Herat there will be war—is that not it?" Stoddart put down the paper and nodded. A month later, on September 9, 1838, he sent a message that the Persian army had lifted the siege and was heading home.

Palmerston did not stop there: He wanted the Russian ambassador to Tehran, Count Simonich, recalled, and when Simonich returned to St. Petersburg, he was disowned by those who had sent him to Persia. Russian frontier policy rewarded the success of those willing to take risks, but failure was a chilly place. The Russian government was able to tell London that Simonich had exceeded his instructions. The freeze extended to Vitkevitch too. British intelligence reports from the Russian capital reported that when the envoy returned from Afghanistan, he could not get a meeting with the foreign minister Count Nesselrode, who said he knew no one of that name, "except for an adventurer…lately engaged in some unauthorised intrigues in Kabul and Kandahar."

This was absurd given the lavish funding that the Russian agent had at his disposal in Afghanistan and the fact that following him on his way home were gifts from Dost Mohammed, including an elephant for the tsar. But neither side wanted to question the foreign minister's account. Even if Vitkevitch had in fact been warmly greeted and congratulated on his return, if Russia could say the opposite then so much the better, since it would divert awkward questions from London; and Britain did not want to be triumphalist so it preferred to believe that the envoy had gone well beyond any orders he might have had. The British game of portraying Russia as "a riddle, wrapped in a mystery, inside an enigma" has deep origins that on this occasion suited diplomats on both sides.

Vitkevitch would never tell his side of the story. A week or so after arriving in St. Petersburg he was seen in high spirits, "chatting gaily" with friends at the theater. He then went to his lodgings, and after giving orders that he should be called in the morning, he closed his door, burned all his Afghan papers and shot himself in the head.

Shuja agreed to everything that Dost would not; he would do anything to get back into power in Kabul. He even acceded to British demands that he give up all the former Afghan lands east of the Khyber Pass and pay what Dost would have considered a humiliating annual tribute to the Sikh leader Ranjit Singh, listed in exhaustive detail, beginning with "fifty-five high-bred horses, of approved colour and pleasant paces, eleven Persian scimitars," going through melons, grapes and pomegranates, and down to "an abundant supply" of almonds, raisins, pistachios and chestnuts. In return the Sikhs agreed only to send various cloths to Kabul. Britain noticed encouraging signs from inside Afghanistan that Shuja would be welcomed, including the arrival of a note from a chief who supported him against Dost, which said: "the faggots are all laid, it requires but the torch of the British government to light them."

Ranjit Singh was delighted with the way things were going. When told of British plans to reinstate Shuja, he said, "That would be adding sugar to milk." Twenty years before he had humiliated Shuja and held him in prison for a year, wresting the Koh-i-noor diamond from his grasp; he knew how to deal with him. And he was beginning to realize that he could deal with the British by promising them much more than he was ever prepared to deliver. Britain expected significant Sikh military forces to back Shuja in his attempt to retake the country. Ranjit Singh was never going to commit his forces, but he nevertheless signed the treaty.

The summer of 1838 was one of the high peaks of British imperial grandeur. The young Queen Victoria was crowned, and a military parade in Hyde Park displayed the pomp and ceremony of a country that believed its military forces could not be bettered. Before she was queen, when only just a teenager, Victoria had met the glamorous adventurer Burnes after his previous trip across Afghanistan to Bokhara. Now he was knighted and promoted two ranks in the army; the British mission that was to support Shuja in Kabul would include Lieutenant-Colonel Sir Alexander Burnes under the leadership of Sir William Macnaghten. In the afterglow of the coronation, Palmerston approved a "great operation in Affghanistan; to push on Runjeet Singh, send an English Corps to act with his army."

To Palmerston, the case for war was obvious. Dost Mohammed was troublesome, and a constant threat to Britain's alliance with Ranjit Singh's Sikh kingdom. The solution was on hand: reinstate a king, Shah Shuja, who had a better ancestral claim than Dost Mohammed, and would be loyal to Britain. When the war plans had been first considered, Persia's siege of Britain's other Afghan ally in Herat was another reason for military action. But Persia's withdrawal did not alter the main reason for the war.

Not taking military action risked leaving Afghanistan in the hands of others. "If the Governor-General were to leave the chiefs of Kandahar and the Amir of Kabul to pursue their own plans," wrote Mohan Lal, "the result would be that Persian agents, superintended and directed by Russian officers, would be placed in the court of the above chieftains; and intrigues would have been conducted and extended by them, even to the very heart of India." The effective declaration of war in the "Simla Manifesto" on October 1 accused Dost Mohammed of unprovoked attacks on the Sikhs and a "hostile policy" toward the English.

Old South Asia hands—retired generals of the sort who would in a later century appear on the Sunday morning talk shows to talk gravely about military affairs—warned of the dangers of the war and worried about Britain's preoccupation with that "superannuated puppet" Shuja. Both the victor at Waterloo, the Duke of Wellington, and that first Afghan envoy Mountstuart Elphinstone urged caution. Thirty years after his first mission, Elphinstone's analysis of Afghanistan was prescient, both for the war that was to come and the war that followed the defeat of the Taliban in 2001. Holding Afghanistan was harder than taking it. "I have no doubt you will take Candahar and Caubul and set up Shuja; but for maintaining him in a poor, cold, strong and remote country, among a turbulent people like the Afghans, I own it seems to me to be hopeless...I never knew a close alliance between a civilised and an uncivilised state that did not end in mutual hatred in three years."

But as would happen often when Britain threatened Afghanistan, the press swung in on the side of the most hawkish policy. "The Russian fiend has been haunting and troubling the human race" thundered *The Times* in 1838, building popular support for the war. Politicians faced competing pressures, with military men and officials in India urging caution, while the press thought war easy.

Even when one of the main causes of the war went away, as the Persian army withdrew from Herat, the British "Army of the Indus" did not break step for an instant in its march toward Afghanistan. The initial mobilization included around 15,000 troops, including one detachment under the "ex-king at Loodiana," the unlucky Shah Shuja, and some 40,000 camp followers. One regiment brought its pack of foxhounds, and others took fine linen, furniture and large tents. A brigadier had 60 camels for his personal use.

Few were to survive. Of the 5,000 camels in the advance column to Kabul, only 500 made it all the way. Captain Thomas Seaton wrote, "The whole system of loading is bad: the saddles are very rude, clumsy, and difficult to pack, and are perfect instruments of torture to the poor ill-treated animals." Seaton discovered that a measure of whisky would revive his animals when they fell, so they would not be abandoned with the rest.

But such problems were in the future as the Army of the Indus marched west to glory. The governor-general, Lord Auckland, reflected on the sheer scale of what he was undertaking as he was borne in his carriage toward a ceremonial meeting with his ally Ranjit Singh: "The magnitude of the measures in which I am embarking is alarming even to myself, and it will be for others to pronounce whether I am attempting at too great a hazard and at too great expense to establish and to maintain a British influence throughout the nations of Central Asia...I have looked upon my course to be strictly one of self-defence. I embarked on it most painfully and unwillingly."

Auckland was an unlikely war leader, a competent administrator who had been a stopgap appointment at a time when Britain needed consolidation in India, not foreign conquest. He had come a long way since the first letter he wrote to Dost Mohammed on his appointment two years before the war: "My friend, you are aware that it is not the practice of the British government to interfere with the affairs of other independent states'."

Ranjit Singh greeted the force in a ceremony on the banks of the Sutlej, the effective eastern border of Sikh territory—the frontier of British India. The "distant clangor of a band of indescribable musicians" announced his approach, which was signaled by salutes fired from small guns mounted on the backs of squatting camels and witnessed by around 300 British officers, in dress uniform and full regalia, "a picture of military splendor rarely exhibited in India." The empire felt unstoppable.

Ranjit Singh arrived on an elephant, and put on a performance of the kind that Burnes had enjoyed on his previous trips but which another officer thought "an unseemly display of dancing girls," with evening entertainment that was "still less decorous," washed down with fierce locally distilled alcohol that the Sikh king pressed on his guests.

The following day the Sikh force put on an impressive military display for the British. They were unnervingly good: better dressed and as well drilled as British troops; a "sad blow to our vanities," said Auckland's sister, Emily Eden. Led by foreign experts, notably the U.S. adventurer Josiah Harlan, an Italian Paolo di Avitabile and several experienced French officers, with a number of British deserters as sergeants, and the Sikh warrior tradition behind it, Ranjit Singh's army was a formidable force. But he would not commit it beyond the Khyber Pass. By then that did not matter. The Army of the Indus was so big, and its confidence so high, that the Afghan campaign was as good as over. The invasion went ahead even when Ranjit Singh reneged on another agreement, refusing to let such a large British force cross his territory and forcing it to go south and take Kandahar first rather than follow the more direct route up the Khyber.

The Indus was overcome with a bridge of planks on top of 74 boats lashed together to make a road that would carry wheeled traffic including artillery. "Hurrah for the Bolan Pass and Affghanistan," shouted the commander of the leading column General Sir William Nott, "for poverty, a fine climate, and a gallant race of people."

The hurrahs were short-lived. The engineers took time to build a military road to allow them passage through the Bolan Pass, the gateway through the southern range; winter and lack of food took their toll of the camels. One of the two columns trying to find a way through ran out of beef cattle to eat as they took so long to move. The second column passed the somber sight of the bodies of animals and men left to rot in the pass.

They arrived in Quetta, at the western end of the Bolan, on half rations, having suffered murder and plunder along the way. Thieves even managed to take two elephants belonging to Macnaghten, and a local ruler, the khan of Khelat, asked: "You have brought an army into the country, but how do you propose to take it out again?" He went on to betray the British, who were forced into a battle that cost them 100 lives.

Once the British force had fought its way clear of the frontier, Kandahar itself fell without a fight. Authority shifted in the Afghan way, as the Barakzai sirdars fled across the Helmand River to the west and local chiefs came across to the new power in the land. But before the British moved forward, they had to wait for Shah Shuja to catch up. "Can this be done in the vain hope of giving plausibility to the fiction, of the 'Shah entering his dominions surrounded by his own troops,'" said Colonel William Dennie impatiently, "when the fact is too notorious to escape detection and exposure, that he has not a single subject of Affghan among them?" Shuja's high-handed manner with British officers had not made him any friends. He would shout and keep them waiting, standing for hours.

The day after Kandahar fell, Shuja appeared under a canopy in front of 7,500 British troops to display his pomp, but hardly any Afghans saw the parade. The British force was sowing the seeds of its later destruction by not playing the local power game with the tact or subtlety required. Mohan Lal understood this well, complaining later that Afghan local leaders "were forgotten through our vain pride of power." At the time, he kept this analysis to himself, loyal to the Raj to the end, but bitter at how bad his masters on this expedition appeared to be at anything beyond the exercise of raw military power.

Lal himself seemed too gentle to be a threat to anyone; hiding a calculating mind beneath a veneer of subservience and courtly manners, he went under the surface to discover the cultural and political levers that mattered. When a local chief, at some personal risk, came over to the British with stolen secret documents, the promised reward was not paid. Lal saw the effect on other powerful tribal elders: "instead of joining us, and facilitating our march towards Ghazni, they moved their families with their valuables into the interior, and continued annoying and plundering us all the way on our flanks."

Ghazni is the southern point of the triangle of relatively level land in the center of the country, with Kabul its northern point and Jalalabad its eastern, that any conqueror of Afghanistan needs to take. Beyond this triangle to the east lies the Suleiman range and the frontier; to the north the Hindu Kush; to the west the sprawling, deceptive mountain ranges that stretch out like the fingers of a hand clutching the ground, at the end of an arm that rises across Afghanistan to the uninhabitable wastes of the Himalayas; and to the south the flat desert that rolls out to Herat and beyond to Persia.

The Army of the Indus set out north from Kandahar toward Ghazni at the end of June 1839, leaving a detachment behind to control the South. Burnes was offered the senior political role in Kandahar by Auckland but turned it down. He was only 34, and he had his eye on the bigger prize of deputizing for Macnaghten in Kabul and then succeeding him.

As they marched in the sapping heat of high summer, news came that Ranjit Singh had died. War had been planned when there was a Persian threat to the west and a powerful Sikh force to the east of Afghanistan; now there was neither.

Even Wade, the administrator whose analysis had made Burnes's negotiations with Dost Mohammed in Kabul so difficult, was now having second thoughts. He changed his advice with the shameless silken ease of a born public servant who could argue that black was white. He proposed that Dost should be left in power, since the defensive priority was to ensure a Sikh succession in Britain's favor. But in the Punjab, there was a black farce as Karrack Singh,

Ranjit's Singh's successor, died soon after taking power, then the next in line was crushed to death by an arch falling on him at Karrack Singh's funeral.

Despite this chaos in Punjab, Auckland was planning to leave a large occupation force in Afghanistan after dislodging Dost Mohammed. "The only objection is that of expense," he wrote. "But it would be an act of extravagance to leave our work incomplete, and our strength should not be recalled to this distance until Afghanistan is settled, and the integrity of Herat well assured."

When the main army arrived outside Ghazni, the city's defenders were well dug in behind sheer walls of a tall solidly built fortress, standing foursquare above the river. The British had left their heavy siege guns behind in Kandahar but took the fortress in a daring operation. The assault was made possible by good intelligence from a spy who told of one gate on the northern side that was not barricaded and bricked up like the rest. In the dead of night a small group of volunteers made their way to the gate carrying simple mines made from leather bags packed with gunpowder. It was an act of extraordinary bravery: the way to the gate was up a steep narrow track winding through the outer defenses of the castle.

After the charges successfully blew open the gate, 200 men, the "forlorn hope," dashed through the breach in the dark, and fought their way along an L-shaped entranceway while missiles and bullets poured down on them from above. They were followed by the main assault force led by "Fighting Bob" Sale, wounded in the face during the fighting. Seventeen British soldiers died for 600 of the defenders. Ghazni woke to see the flag of Sale's 13th Light Infantry flying from the fort. The assault was one of the British military landmarks in Asia in the nineteenth century. It sent a signal across the country about British military ability and shook Dost Mohammed out of power in Kabul.

Dost Mohammed's son, Afzul Khan, rode fast to Kabul with the news, abandoning elephants, baggage and guns in his camp near Ghazni. Dost immediately sent his brother Jabar Khan, who was well known to Burnes, to the British camp as a mediator. He brought a proposal that Dost should stand aside and act as wazir to Shah Shuja, resuming the ancient relationship of the Barakzais to the ruling Sadozai amirs. Britain turned him down, not wanting Dost to retain any power, but no one could give a good response to Jabar Khan when he said: "If Shah Shuja is really a king...leave him now with us Afghans, and let him rule if he can." Afghans would make similar challenges often in the wars that followed, up to and including the appointment of President Hamid Karzai by the United States.

There was another curious incident in the battle for Ghazni with twenty-first century resonance. Among the prisoners were 50 black-shirted warriors fighting under a green banner, most of them not Afghans but Indians. During an assault the day before the fort fell, they had fought with an almost suicidal intensity that British forces would come to know well in Afghanistan and on the frontier. They were ghazis, Islamist fundamentalists, who had answered Dost Mohammed's call to fight a jihad against the alien invader. Later in the century they would become known as Hindustani fanatics, men prepared to die for a cause bigger than Afghan nationalism, and the forerunners of al-Qaeda. Taken into Shuja's presence, they were all immediately executed on his orders—a policy of zero tolerance for fundamentalism. The butchery took place behind his tent, and was chanced on by a British officer, who was appalled as much by the casual approach of the executioners as the killing itself: "They were laughing and joking, and seemed to look upon the work as good fun."

Dost's son Akbar Khan continued to sound the bell for jihad, especially where he had the most eager listeners, on the frontier itself. But by April 1839, six months after British forces first entered Afghan territory, a new force of 11,000 men, half British and half Sikh, was now heading down the Khyber Pass. Ranjit Singh's death had made it possible for Britain to insist on Sikh support. As the Army of the Indus moved north from Ghazni, Dost Mohammed knew his time had come. In the first week of August he fled northwest to the Bamiyan Valley, at the western end of the Hindu Kush.

A chief who had come across to the British side in Kandahar, Haji Khan Kakur, was put in charge of 2,000 of Shah Shuja's Afghan troops to go in pursuit. But in Afghanistan, issuing orders did not mean they were carried out—there were other loyalties beneath the surface not recognized by Britain. At the time appointed to set out by Major James Outram, the British officer commanding the operation to capture Dost, "not more than three hundred effective men could be mustered, the residue of those present consisting of from four to five hundred Affghan rabble, mounted upon yaboos, and starved ponies."

They were only a day behind the fleeing Amir, Dost Mohammed, whose progress was slow as his son was ill and needed to be carried, but they never caught up. Kakur had fierce daily arguments with Outram, insisting that they wait for reinforcements, at one point actually grabbing the British officer's reins and trying to pull him from his horse. When they tried to set out at night, Kakur took away his guides so the British were marching blind. Outram heard rumors of significant support for Dost among his supposed allies: "many of our own Afghans were traitors upon whom in the hour of need no dependence could be placed."

In the end Outram planned a virtual suicide mission: to ride fast into Dost's escort force with the aim of killing him, deploying only his 13 British officers, and not relying on their Indian sepoys or Afghans. As he slept in the snow, on the high pass heading into Bamiyan, Outram was "no more happy than on this night, under the exciting expectation of so glorious a struggle in the morning. All prospect of danger on such occasions as these is met by the soldier with the gratifying conviction that should he fall, he will have earned an enviable place in the recollection of those loved."

But Outram's sacrifice would have to be postponed. He arrived in Bamiyan to find that Dost Mohammed had fled north of the Hindu Kush the day before—out of reach. The British force had failed to catch him because of betrayal by a tribal leader who had pledged allegiance to them and disloyalty by troops in the pay of the king they had installed. It was not an auspicious start to the occupation. But the warning signs were ignored.

With Dost Mohammed out of the way, there was to be no battle for Kabul itself. Shah Shuja moved into the city in August 1839, crossing the bridge over the moat into the Bala Hissar fort complex, through the narrow dog-leg entrance onto the main street, with low mud shops of its bazaar on either side, to a "respectful, decorous, even cold reception." Some 5,000 people lived inside the fort, but there was little sign of emotion at the return of a king who had last ruled 30 years before. He dismounted from his elephant in the palace courtyard, to occupy the palace that had been built by his father, Timur, giving Macnaghten the large guesthouse overlooking a garden on the other side, the same one that Dost had given to Burnes on his failed peace mission two years earlier.

The buildings were in a "ruinous state"; the splendor of the Afghan court that Shah Shuja remembered was no more. The ancient Mogul fort above would remain in ruins. A British proposal to restore it and station troops there was rejected by Shah Shuja, because it looked over his quarters. He felt it would draw attention to his alliance with the British and "the feelings of the inhabitants would be hurt."

Lieutenant Colonel William Dennie, who had led the forlorn hope through the breach at Ghazni, wrote to his family, "The war may now be considered at an end, the King being once again on his throne."

In October 1839, most of the invasion force was withdrawn, with its commander, General Sir John Keane, giving advice to a young officer as they went: "I cannot but congratulate you on quitting this country; for, mark my words, it will not be long before there is here some signal catastrophe." The young officer was Lieutenant Henry Durand, who had lit the fuse on the mine at Ghazni, an act of unusual bravery, and whose family would play a central role in the affairs of Afghanistan and the frontier.

By the spring of 1840, Kabul had become a fashionable destination for the more adventurous sort of British travelers from India, and for the next two summers there was horseracing, boating on the Wazirabad Lake and hunting in the hills. Amid relative peace, at least in the capital, Sir William Macnaghten set up home in some style. His wife arrived with a group of other garrison wives, and a line of elephants and baggage animals behind them carrying rugs, chandeliers, fine china and cases of wine. The high dry mountain air of Kabul was a relief from the sapping heat of the Indian plains.

Lady Sale, a woman whose nature was quarried from empire-building granite, planted a fine kitchen garden, growing peas, potatoes, artichokes, turnip and radishes, all from seeds brought from India, and melons from local seed—topped with color from sweet peas and geraniums, as if she were in England. She found the "Cabul lettuces hairy and inferior to ours, but the cabbages superior and milder." Her daughter, married to a lieutenant in the engineers posted to Kabul, came to live with her.

Sir Alexander Burnes created a job for his brother Charley, who came out to live with him in a fine house in town, outside the garrison walls. Burnes bought Russian mirrors in the market and scraped the quicksilver off the back to fit Kabul's first windows into his house. He and his brother entertained lavishly, and with other officers enthusiastically tested what he had heard about the morals of Kabul women—a pursuit that would contribute directly to Burnes's death.

But while foreigners lived in complacent splendor, the Afghanistan beyond the racetrack and boating lake was in ferment. From exile north of the Oxus, Dost Mohammed was writing inflammatory letters all over the country: "Religion is his watchword, and he hopes to raise the whole country against us...I hope we are to be really well prepared for the worst that may happen," wrote Macnaghten, who too saw the threat of instability spilling over from the frontier region.

The appearance of two Islamist spies in August 1840, "carrying money and a Koran in an amulet," who were handed over to Burnes by a tribal elder friendly to Britain, was a rare piece of hard evidence amid rumors of fundamentalist plots being stirred up against the British presence in Afghanistan. The older one, whose name was Khodameer, was identified from the style of his cap as coming from the Khyber. The other, Khodadad, "had a ruddy complexion with a few marks of small-pox." They said they were on their way to see Dost Mohammed in the mountains and to try to recruit men to join Dost's allies, who were now conspiring with the Sikhs in Peshawar against British control.

Against British wishes and despite Macnaghten's warnings, Sikh armies were pushing farther north and west into the mountains adjoining Afghanistan. "The cession by the Sikhs of all the countries west of the Indus is what I should think the chief object; next a subsidiary force in the Punjab." But when Macnaghten wrote with this intelligence in November 1840, it was ignored along with his other warnings, although he thought he had enough against Dost Mohammed's brother in Peshawar to "hang him ten times over." The Sikhs were supposed to be British allies but were acting against British interests everywhere Macnaghten looked. He wrote warning letters constantly, until "the stumps of my fingers are nearly worn out," but he found himself sidelined, the government preferring instead to think the Sikhs honest, "most firm friends and most steadfast allies," believing the assurances of Wade.

Events in 1840–41 unfolded in a way that was replayed after the invasion and occupation by international forces after 2001: a growing Islamist insurgency, supported by a power on the eastern side of the Khyber Pass that claimed to be backing the occupation force at the same time as conspiring against it; overstretched foreign troops unable to quell a widening and worsening conflict; a cultural clash in Kabul as the occupiers behaved in a way that offended local sensibilities; an amir who could not rule without foreign support; increasing tension between the occupying power and the amir; and growing anger among tribal elders about foreign promises of financial support that they believed were not honored. In the First Anglo-Afghan War, this set of circumstances would lead to the worst disaster suffered by the British during the whole period of the Empire in Asia.

Britain's biggest concern was always regional security: the possibility of a Russian move south toward Afghan territory. The British knew very little of the land north of the Hindu Kush mountains, or the power of the rulers of Samarkand, Bokhara and Khiva. One of the most adventurous British Afghan travelers, Arthur Connolly, had been up to the remote slave-owning kingdom of Khiva and won a treaty of friendship with its khan, but Russia now sent a deputation there, "the most unhappy step taken during the campaign" for Burnes, who said the Russian moves "torture all my thoughts and opinions."

These warning signs were ignored in India, where the governor-general, Lord Auckland, saw the situation in Afghanistan as settled and considered pushing farther north. "I am far from able to decide where occupation should end, and the exercise of peaceful influence begin."

In the summer of 1840 Dost reappeared in Afghanistan, after escaping from virtual house arrest. "Silver handcuffs" had held him for almost a year as a guest at the court in Bokhara, north of the Oxus. He rode his first horse so hard during his getaway that it died under him, and he continued his escape in a basket on a camel, his beard dyed black. But he failed to make any serious military headway against British forces, despite some advances, including at one point encircling Burnes and a number of other senior British officers in Charikar. Colonel Dennie, the hero of Ghazni, defeated Dost's forces at the beginning of October, leaving 600 Afghan dead and almost capturing Dost and his son Akbar Khan.

A month later there was a fierce exchange at Parwan, where Britain's locally hired cavalry hung back, with the excuse that "they did not like the English swords they had been given," and Dost's force nearly won the day. Dost himself was seen on the field, dressed all in white under a blue banner, urging his men to "drive these Ferengee Kafirs out of the country or I am a gone man." He took off his white turban and waved it in the breeze. The Afghan cavalry rode into British troops that were "cut like a flock of sheep." Among the officers lost on the British side was Dr. Percival Lord, who had traveled with Burnes on a former trip and was a leading expert on Afghanistan.

The day after this battle, Macnaghten was out riding in Kabul when a single horseman came up to check who he was, before Dost Mohammed himself appeared and dismounted, surrendering personally to the British envoy. Macnaghten courteously told him to mount his horse again, and they rode on. When they arrived in the Bala Hissar, Dost handed over his sword, but Macnaghten said he should keep it: "he seemed gratified for this mark of confidence." His manner and bearing impressed Macnaghten. "We ejected the Dost, who never offended us, in support of our policy, of which he was the victim."

Dost Mohammed went into exile in India in November 1840 on a British pension. And the British government took the opportunity to carry out a reshuffle of its own commanders and forces: "Major General Elphinstone succeeded Sir Willoughby Cotton in the Affghanistan command, and HM 44th Regiment under Colonel Shelton, replaced the Bengal Europeans."

The 44th marched into Afghanistan, but only a handful would make it out alive. On Christmas Day 1840, Macnaghten wrote to the government in India, "I am greatly apprehensive that we shall be high and dry ere long." He would not live to see another Christmas.

Dost Mohammed's departure did not make security any easier; Macnaghten wrote "this country is one mass of loose gunpowder." As the insurgency spread, the hardest fights faced by the British were in Helmand in the southwest, where there was almost continual campaigning, including during the winter months of 1840–41. With Britain distracted, Persia saw the opportunity to move again on Herat, where Shah Shuja's cousin Kamran Shah was still in power. Britain's influence in Herat was, if anything, weaker now that it held Kabul than before. Attempts to introduce tougher laws, turning it into a "Utopia of justice" by Pottinger and Stoddart, the two political officers in charge, had led to their expulsion. "Why is it that Englishmen everywhere are rough, overbearing, without tact, and address, and more disliked by foreigners than any other people?" asked John Colvin, Auckland's private secretary.

Kamran Shah now changed sides and conspired with Persia against Britain. Palmerston saw this as cause for war on Herat: "The Iron is hot; let us strike it; if we let it grow cold it will be too hard for our blows." But the day the order to attack was agreed in London, June 4, 1841, was the day the government lost a no-confidence motion to Robert Peel's Tories by one vote. Amid the political confusion, a letter from Auckland arrived warning of the huge cost of an assault on Herat, requiring 12,000 men. Diplomacy in Tehran was tried instead, and although British influence there was much reduced as Russia became more dominant, Persia would not move on Herat again.

Shah Shuja was now openly conspiring against Britain. He sent letters to a number of chiefs complaining about his lack of authority, maintaining that the British were governing Afghanistan as they pleased. When a tribal elder friendly to Britain went to Charikar, north of Kabul, to resolve an issue, Shuja's agents went ahead to spread the word that he was "an infidel, and acting for the ruin of the Shah, and of the faithful of the country." Shuja become even more difficult to manage when the probability emerged of Burnes taking over when Macnaghten left. He knew that Burnes had tried to keep him out of power.

But it was financial issues that led to the biggest crisis. Grain was going up in price because of the requirements of the large garrison, and when Shuja ordered prices to be fixed, the British vetoed this in the interests of free trade. (The amir's thugs imposed their will in their way, nailing the ear of a trader to a block in his shop for a day when he raised his prices.) At the same time the British cut the wages of the builders employed in the new cantonment area set apart from Kabul, because they needed to keep them in line with what Shuja was paying. High food prices and low wages were a recipe for disaster, and both could be blamed on British policy.

Just as the financial consequences of all this began to bite, the government in India cut the amount it had been paying loyal tribal elders to maintain forces. It seemed prudent housekeeping now the war was over, and the amount went down from 80,000 to 40,000 rupees.

This last measure was the prime cause of the rebellion that General Sale was sent to quell in the provinces to the east in the autumn of 1841. The campaign was not expected to be extensive—just a skirmish to open the passes to the east. Macnaghten sighed at the amount of thrashing that was needed: "I fear these fellows will require many a hiding yet before they settle down into peaceable citizens." Securing the route east was important as Britain wanted to reduce its forces in Afghanistan, and Macnaghten was preparing to leave with the departing troops, on his way to a new job in India, leaving the senior post to Burnes. hen Sale set out to quell the uprising, his wife was confident that she would be joining him in three days.

As Sale's men set up camp on their first night in the passes to the east, they heard the unearthly clang of the loading of jezails echoing through the darkness around the bare crags, "a loud ringing noise, that can be heard at a considerable distance, so unmistakable in its character that it can never be forgotten by those whose ears have once been startled by the unfamiliar sound."

The sound was of balls, each about one ounce in weight, being rammed down barrels with an iron ramrod. Hundreds would be fired at the British before the night was out.

3

Retreat

*When Burnes came into this country, was not your father entreated by us to kill him;
or he would at some future day bring an army and take our country from us?*

—Afghan tribal chief talking to Akbar Khan, son of Dost Mohammed

The event that sparked the uprising that drove the British out of Kabul was an argument over a woman.

November 2, 1841, was the third Tuesday of Ramadan, the period when good Muslims are expected to fast for the hours of daylight. The aging and ineffectual British commanding officer, General Elphinstone, was recovering in bed after a heavy fall from his horse the day before. Apart from Burnes and some other officers who still lived in the city itself, since the departure of Sale's army the British force had based itself in a poorly defended cantonment area about a mile north of Kabul. Its "serious defects" were obvious even to Colonel Shelton, who said it had "a rampart and ditch an Afghan could run over with the facility of a cat."

At first light dawn watchers in this poorly located and ill-defended cantonment saw smoke rising from the city, and shortly before 8 A.M., a report arrived that Sir Alexander Burnes had been injured, followed soon afterward by news that he was dead.

The storm clouds had been gathering for weeks. Shah Shuja's failings had become apparent to some British officers: "as great a scoundrel as ever lived" said one general, observing shrewdly, "We are becoming hated by the people." But Macnaghten, who was coming to the end of his term of office, had not seen the final storm coming, and talked of "a season of such profound tranquillity" when he had gone to say good-bye to Burnes, the afternoon before the uprising. He did not appear to be concerned about the continued lack of firm news from the troops led by General Sale, which had set off to secure the passes to the east, nor the general unrest provoked by the economic situation.

But there were other signs of an impending emergency if only he had known where to look. Mohan Lal reported perhaps the most important—although its significance was not recognized at the time by the British: Mosques in Kabul stopped praying for Shah Shuja. Forged letters had also appeared in the bazaar claiming strong support from the Sikh government across the frontier for Dost Mohammed—to encourage the idea that he was on his way back. There were rumors too that Macnaghten was planning to round up all the troublesome tribal elders and cart them off to prison in India.

Burnes had made himself unpopular over high-handed demands to tribal elders allied to Britain. At the same time as cutting the subsidies given to them to raise troops, they were expected to provide actual troops for the money for the first time. He attempted to regularize their forces with professional ranks that took no account of tribal structures. One astute officer, Captain Seaton, complained of inconsistency in the British approach, "a mixture of iron and clay...utterly unsuited to the fierce tribes of the country, who soon detected the weakness of their rulers." The result was similar to that which followed the swift introduction of democracy and a Western system of government after 2001—a violent reaction to the threat to traditional power.

The drama that played out on the night of November 1–2 started when the favorite mistress of a powerful Afghan leader, Abdullah Khan, was taken into the house of a British officer. Abdullah sent his nephew to investigate, who was kept at the front door, from where he heard the rustling of skirts and caught a glimpse of the girl he sought being pushed into a back room. The British officer had attempted to hold the door shut, denying she was there. Abdullah complained to Burnes, who did nothing.

Burnes had already made an enemy by firing the *kotwal* of Kabul, the police chief, to block an investigation into a claim by another Afghan that his mistress had been spirited away across the roof of his house by a British officer. And Burnes and his brother had tested Afghan moral patience by having Kashmiri women living with them.

On November 1 Mohan Lal warned Burnes of a plot to get rid of him, seeing him just after Macnaghten had visited with his talk of "profound tranquillity." When Burnes saw the specific death threat contained in an anonymous letter, he told Lal, "the time is arrived that we must leave the country." But he did not act, wanting not to show fear. "The Affghans never received any injury from him...he was quite sure they would never injure him."

At 3 A.M. on November 2, one of Burnes's servants, Bow Singh, received word that merchants all around were removing valuables from their shelves and sealing up their shops. He was afraid that Burnes would reprimand him if he woke him but found the wazir, Nuzamat Dowlah, who went to rouse Burnes. When a message arrived from the Bala Hissar calling the wazir to Shah Shuja's side, Burnes refused to go with him.

The deposed police chief began the insurrection, setting fire to the gates of Burnes's house, the cue for a mob attack. A detachment of Shah Shuja's troops led by a British officer set out from the Bala Hissar nearby to try to restore order but was quickly cut to pieces, losing two field guns. One British officer was killed as the fire took hold of Burnes's house. Burnes ran upstairs and shouted down from a balcony, offering a reward to any who would save his life. But the city he had tried to make his own deceived him in the end. In the melee, a Kashmiri came and offered to take Burnes and his brother out by a safe route, in disguise, then betrayed them, calling out, "Here he is. Here is Sikander Burnes."

Burnes's brother, Charley, ran into the garden with his sword, killing six before he was cut down. But when Sir Alexander knew his own end was unavoidable, he walked out with a black scarf tied round his eyes so he would not see who killed him. Three men were at the front of the crowd and struck the first blows—the police chief fired by Burnes, the man whose complaint against the British he had not investigated and Abdullah Khan himself. All were connected with the disputes over women.

The next few hours were a critical test for British resolve, and General Elphinstone failed to respond effectively. Lady Sale's son-in-law, Lieutenant John Sturt, was horribly injured with a wound in the throat, and staggered, covered in blood, through the entrance of Shah Shuja's audience chamber. Shuja made threats to put down the insurgency but did not act. His soldiers were considered almost useless: "the worst set up and most disorderly body of troops calling themselves a regiment that can be imagined," said Lady Sale. "We seem to sit quietly with our hands folded and look on."

Within days, the British force had lost nearly all of its supplies, stored in a fort inexcusably located outside the main cantonment, and a general uprising involving tens of thousands of Afghans threatened every British soldier in the country. British officers were killed by their men in Kandahar and Ghazni. A British Gurkha regiment in Charikar was encircled and defeated—its survivors taken into slavery, although one of its two British officers made it to Kabul, riding in agony after having his hand cut off. There was widespread desertion by Indian and Afghan soldiers in the British forces, some of whom joined the enemy. The British fired artillery shells into the city of Kabul without much effect, and worst of all, the indecision of officers led to a catastrophic collapse in morale. Lady Sale complained that any story was believed by the "panic-stricken garrison. It is more than shocking, it is shameful, to hear the way that officers go on croaking before their men."

Elphinstone and Shelton could not decide whether to prepare for retreat, move into the Bala Hissar, or try to defend the position they were in. When Macnaghten proposed a raid on the nearby Bemaru Hills, because of constant firing down from them, the orders did not go out until the afternoon after fierce arguments by Shelton, who would fight only if Macnaghten signed a form taking responsibility.

Lady Sale stood on the roof of her house watching the fighting, ducking behind the chimney as rounds flew by. A cannonball embedded itself in the wall of the room where her pregnant daughter was sleeping. She developed respect for the military ability of the enemy: "my very heart felt as if it leapt to my teeth when I saw the Affghans ride clean through...The onset was dreadful. They looked like a great cluster of bees." She noticed how their cavalry could fire while riding and carry an infantryman with them to the scene of the action, "where he is dropped without the fatigue of walking to his post." Two Kabul snipers, said to be a blacksmith and a barber, were able to pick off people in the cantonment from 300 yards.

The fighting went on without a pause for several weeks, as autumn turned to winter, and British stocks of food, ammunition and willpower fell daily. The death of the main rebel leader Abdullah Khan at the end of November was one piece of good news, but it was a rare glimmer of light. It emerged that the conspiracy had been months in the planning, backed by a secret pact against the British by tribal leaders signed on the Koran. Dost Mohammed's son Akbar Khan, powerful among the eastern Ghilzai chiefs, arrived in Kabul with 6,000 men, raising Afghan morale. In the middle of December, Shah Shuja abandoned the British, setting his seal on a proclamation urging all good Muslims to kill the *feringhees* (foreigners). It was only "two days since the king was to have come into the cantonments, in rather light marching order, to accompany us to the provinces," Lady Sale remarked dryly, as Shuja issued his anti-British proclamation and gave the insurgent force access to firing positions in the ruins of the upper fortress of the Bala Hissar.

Macnaghten, whose departure from Afghanistan had been delayed by the uprising, was still hoping for an honorable way out, but had less and less to negotiate with. Through Mohan Lal, still living discreetly in Kabul, he sent messages to Akbar Khan and other chieftains while separately trying to secure support from the qizalbash mercenaries and Afghans loyal to the British, including a chief who offered sanctuary in the hills. Macnaghten had turned down an offer to surrender British weapons and hand over women and children as hostages, saying he preferred "death to dishonour." But he was forced into a series of deals, handing over outlying forts in exchange for food. His room for maneuver diminished daily, as he fell into the maw of a disparate and complex rebellion.

Afghan spies could penetrate inside the British cantonment easily, a British soldier spying for Russia was found and arrested while removing barricades, and when Sturt was standing at the front gate, an Afghan came up to ask if he was an officer. When asked why he wanted to know, the Afghan drew his sword and said "to fight." Horses in the cantonment were reduced to chewing on tent pegs; there was nothing else to eat.

On December 23 Macnaghten rode out of the fort for his last fateful meeting with Akbar Khan. The young Afghan commander had laid out a large rug in a cleared patch in the snow, on a rise just 300 yards from the cantonment. Macnaghten had requested that two British regiments should be made ready to arrest Aminullah Khan, a key rebel leader, since he believed that he could secure Akbar Khan's support, and divide the enemy. Akbar Khan wanted to become wazir, while offering to let Shah Shuja remain on the throne, but Macnaghten did not really know what shifting alliances he faced in the snow.

Shelton failed to have the force Macnaghten had requested ready in time, and made an excuse not to join him for the meeting at the last minute. Just before he left, Macnaghten went white as he read a message from Mohan Lal warning of a plot to kill him. He tried to seem scornful: "A plot! Let me alone for that—trust me for that!" He was carrying as presents a pair of fine pistols and an Arab mare admired by Akbar Khan in the past. In his last recorded words he said, "Dangerous it is, but if it succeeds, it is worth all risks; the rebels have not fulfilled one article of the treaty, and I have no confidence in them, and if by it we can only save our honor, all will be well; at any rate, I would rather suffer a hundred deaths than live the last six weeks over again."

The manner of his killing must have felt like a hundred deaths. With three British officers he sat cross-legged on the rug opposite the Afghan leaders they knew so well. One of the officers, George Lawrence, crouched warily, believing they were not safe, as a large number of Afghans mounted on horses, identified as religious warriors, ghazis, moved in closer to the group. Akbar Khan told Lawrence to relax, but in almost the same breath he cried out, "Seize them!" Lawrence found his hands pinioned behind him so he could not reach his weapons, and he and the other two officers were thrown roughly behind riders on the backs of horses and taken into captivity. The last they saw of Macnaghten was him being dragged headfirst, screaming, down the bank away from them. A shot rang out from one of the pistols he had just given to Akbar Khan, but only wounded him. Macnaghten was cut to pieces, and his hands, feet and torso paraded through the streets of Kabul, the head displayed in a horse nosebag in the bazaar.

The humiliation for Britain continued as Macnaghten's carcass was displayed contemptuously in front of the cantonment, his fine uniform cut from it. Lady Sale fumed, "strange to say no endeavour was made to recover it, which might easily have been done by sending out the cavalry." One of the three officers who had been with Macnaghten was also killed, but the other two were held for several days, taunted by one of Macnaghten's bloody hands waved on a stick outside the bars of their jail. Akbar Khan paraded through Kabul with a bloodstained sword boasting that it was he who had killed the envoy, but to the British he claimed it was the ghazis who had done it and showed his good faith by returning the two captives safely.

The options available to the garrison were now "a disgraceful treaty or a disastrous retreat," according to Lady Sale. The decision was made to negotiate; the terms agreed involved the British force giving up almost all its artillery pieces, handing over hostages to the Afghan side and paying a large sum. Major Pottinger, the hero of Herat, had taken over from Macnaghten, and signed the treaty quickly along with the senior military commanders.

Lady Sale now heard a rumor that was to be a ghastly prophecy. "We are informed that the chiefs do not mean to keep faith; and that is their intention to get all our women into their possession; and to kill every man except one, who is to have his hands and legs cut off, and is to be placed with a letter *in terrorem* at the entrance of the Khyber Passes, to deter all *feringhees* from entering the country again."

The British retreat from Kabul began on January 6, 1842. "All was confusion from before daylight. The day was clear and frosty; the snow nearly a foot deep on the ground; the thermometer considerably below freezing point." Sturt had been out all night building a bridge of gun carriages across the Kabul River at Shelton's insistence, although Sturt said it was easily forded, and the soldiers' feet would be wet anyway in the snow. The camp followers lined up to cross it, and progress was slow. Shelton had ordered that they bring dozens of planks, dragged by bullocks, in case they needed to cross other rivers en route, which also hampered the retreat. By evening they had gone only six miles, despite the urging of friendly Afghans that they should push onto the gorge at Khurd Kabul—a name that would etch itself into the collective memory of Victorian Britain. They made camp in the open.

The remnants of the rearguard did not arrive until 2 A.M., with stories of terrible slaughter that had begun before they had even left the cantonment. The Afghans began by firing jezails before men and boys darted in with knives. Fifty of the cavalry had not made it out of the cantonment, and a trail of dead soldiers and camp followers marked the way to the river.

All discipline was at an end. The following morning the advance guard set off at first light although "no order was given, no bugle was sounded." Camp followers and pack animals pressed ahead, making a disciplined march impossible. Incredibly, the column stopped again at 1 P.M., giving the tribes in the passes plenty of time to organize an ambush for the following day. The only rationale for stopping was to keep the force together. But the delay depleted stores further as the Afghan cavalry took what it wanted, and the British lost three of their precious field guns to marauding tribesmen, who pressed down from the hills on all sides.

On January 8, crossing the narrow five-mile defile of Khurd Kabul, the British put up their only determined fight, fortified by the contents of a cask of spirits broached early in the day. Effective deployment was impossible because of the confusion of thousands of camp followers, but both infantry and cavalry fought off several assaults as the column made its slow progress.

Lieutenant Sturt had to prevent drunken cavalrymen undertaking a suicidal charge into the massed ranks of Afghans. Lady Sale sat on her horse observing events as if she might have been out on a hunt in England, stirrup cup in hand. "I felt very grateful for a tumbler of sherry, which at any other time would have made me very unlady-like, but now merely warmed me." At the narrowest part of the gorge, Afghan warriors poured withering fire down from behind low stone walls. As Lady Sale rode through, she was wounded in the elbow, and three other balls went through her sheepskin jacket.

More than 2000 camp followers were now dead as well as hundreds of soldiers. Many of the surviving sepoys burned their clothes to keep themselves warm, leading to instant death the next night, as only four tents had survived. "An immense number of poor wounded wretches wandered about the camp destitute of shelter, and perished during the night. Groans of misery and distress assailed the ear from all quarters." Akbar Khan appeared, demanding more hostages, more money and the withdrawal of Sale's force from Jalalabad—all conditions that were immediately agreed to, but the killing still did not stop. Sturt died of his wounds that night, tended by his wife and his mother-in-law, and was buried in a shallow grave scraped out of the frozen mud.

But most of the dead remained unburied; "the sight was dreadful; the smell of the blood sickening; and the corpses lay so thick it was impossible to look from them, as it required care to guide my horse so as not to tread upon the bodies." Lady Sale and the other women and more of the senior officers fell into Akbar Khan's hands, and the first thing they saw in his camp was a force of 500 of their sepoys who had deserted to the Afghan side. Lady Sale retained her notebook in a bag round her waist and continued to chronicle the loss of an army.

By January 9, the fourth day out, "there was not a single sepoy left of the whole Kabul force." East India Company coins, looted from the retreating army, have been handed down from generation to generation in the pass since then, and an argument still runs in one Afghan family as to whether their ancestor killed 13 or 14 in the melee. Tombs of martyrs from that period are revered, and there is a persistent Afghan legend that a company of British soldiers could not cut down an oak tree when they tried to destroy a holy site, the Seh Baba tomb, in retribution, when their army returned in 1842, despite pulling it with elephants and horses and chopping with axes and sabers.

Woven into local folk memory are frequent accounts of British women taking Afghan warriors as husbands to save their lives, and a story of a boy, John Campbell, brought up in an Afghan house before running away after 15 years. The truth is more prosaic. The British women and children taken into Afghan captivity were gathered together and mostly well treated, and one English girl sold as a slave was reunited with her family several months later. However, women taken alive from among the Indian camp followers faced rape and forced marriage.

At last Elphinstone took decisive action, ordering a march through a "fine and moonlit" night, reaching the shrine at Seh Baba by midnight, and turning sharp right toward Jagdallak, the last major pass before the plains of Jalalabad. The column regrouped at daylight, eating raw meat from a bullock to keep alive, before marching on until the midafternoon, 30 hours after setting out from their last desperate snatched sleep in the snow. Of the 16,000 who had set out, the survivors consisted of 150 men of the 44th Regiment, 16 dismounted horse artillerymen and 25 from the 5th Cavalry. Each had only a handful of ammunition. Several hundred camp followers were still with them. They stopped behind some walls to rest, and Akbar Khan sent a message saying he wanted to see their senior officers.

Elphinstone, Shelton and another officer left the force, and became engaged in a macabre negotiation for the lives of the British soldiers, with Akbar Khan still pretending to be brokering peace and lying when he said food and water had been sent over to this pathetic remnant of an army. The mountain chieftains insisted they could not let them through unharmed, and Elphinstone offered further cash. They swore to kill the feringhees, until Akbar Khan hinted they should switch to speaking Pashtu, which the British could not understand. Then he disappeared, after giving orders that the officers should not be allowed to rejoin their men. When he returned at sunset, there was the sound of shooting across the wasteland, and Elphinstone and Shelton were still prevented from going back.

Elphinstone had managed to get a note to the force: "March at once; there is treachery!" They set out into hell. As the British climbed to the top of the Jagdallak Pass, they found the way blocked by a double barrier of thorn branches, laced together six feet high. Dr. William Brydon was mounted: "The confusion became terrible, all discipline was at an end, and the shouts of 'Halt, halt. Keep Back the Cavalry,' were incessant. I made my way with great difficulty, to the front." As the infantrymen tore a gap through the branches with their bare hands, under continual attack from all sides, the cavalry forced its way through and the infantry believed they were being abandoned. A survivor, Sergeant Major Lissant, wrote, "The men in front then said the officers seemed to care for themselves." Some accounts say the infantrymen shot at their own officers.

It was now every man for himself. A dozen or so mounted men rode on toward Jalalabad while those on foot made their way to a hill at Gandamack. There was another attempt to negotiate safe passage with a local chief, but when the British soldiers resisted being disarmed, the whole force was cut down. Captain Souter, who had wrapped the regimental colors around his body and must have looked a grander figure than the rest and so worth a ransom, was among the few survivors from the 44th to be taken prisoner.

On January 13, a week after the retreat from Kabul began, a sharp-eyed sentry on the ramparts at Jalalabad saw the exhausted figure of Dr. Brydon, crossing the plain on a pony given to him by a wounded Indian cavalryman after his own died under him. He was bleeding from one hand and had a bad head wound, surviving a blow from a sword only because he had put a copy of *Blackwood's Magazine* under his cap. As soon as his pony was taken into a stable, it lay down and died.

Brydon told a tale of treachery. Those on horseback had been offered food and shelter in an Afghan village once they were clear of the mountain passes, only to be set on as soon as they dismounted. Half of the party were killed there, the others cut down by pursuing Afghan horsemen. He was attacked by three more groups of Afghans, riding through the first with his reins in his teeth, "cutting right and left with my sword as I went through them." Soon afterward he encountered another group, and had to jab at his pony with his sword to make it gallop. A round fired from a jezail at close range broke his sword and wounded his pony.

Seeing a third party on horseback with the British fort now in sight, he rode toward them believing them to be British, only turning away when he realized his mistake. One of the Afghans rode after him and slashed at him, but was put off at the last instant as Brydon threw the broken hilt of his sword at the man's head. Still the blow cut into his hand. Unaccountably the man rode off, and Brydon went on, unarmed and badly wounded, into safety.

General Sale ordered a fire to be lit at the Kabul gate of the Jalalabad fort and lights maintained all night, with buglers playing every quarter hour to guide in stragglers who might be trying to cross the plain under cover of darkness. But none came. "The sound of those bugles I shall never forget," wrote Captain Seaton. "It was a dirge for our slaughtered soldiers, and heard through all the night, it had an inexpressibly mournful and depressing effect."

The massacre of the Kabul garrison sent shockwaves across the region that still reverberated into the twenty-first century, as a lesson was learned that would always boost Afghan morale in a battle: The British could be beaten. The amir of Bokhara now had the confidence he needed to execute two British captives, Colonel Charles Stoddart and Captain Arthur Connolly, without fear of retribution, and Britain's sometime ally in Herat, the tyrant Zaman Shah, was murdered in time-honored royal style, smothered with a pillow by his wazir, Yar Mohammed. Shah Shuja, betrayed after trying to negotiate his way out of the Bala Hissar, was cut to pieces by a mob. The king who had once worn the Koh-i-noor and a nine-inch-high diamond crown had his last bag of jewels cut from around his waist and tossed into a field. The man who picked them up assumed them to be worthless colored rocks but had them stolen in the bazaar by someone who knew better.

Retribution from British forces in India would surely follow, but first the Jalalabad garrison had to face an assault of unprecedented ferocity by tens of thousands of Afghans whose blood was up. When he had set out to "thrash" the rebel tribes in October, Sale had led his force through the same passes that later filled with British dead. He sustained 40 dead the first night and lost some stores, but his force was much better led than Elphinstone's army. Sale fought off successive assaults by the ruse of keeping his men quite still in the dark, even taking casualties from rounds fired blind from jezails, until Afghan raiders were within bayonet distance, when he ordered his men to open up with sustained volleys of fire.

Pressure on Sale's force did not stop after they moved into the Jalalabad fort, and the attackers were driven by the compulsion of jihad—novel to British troops then, it would become more familiar in wars in the region later. Dost Mohammed had "persuaded the Moolahs to preach a religious war against us...this had raised the whole country, and roused their fanaticism." A mullah living inside the fort was ejected after his house was found to be mined.

The fort was very large, and Sale's force worked hard to improve its defenses, but a month after the massacre in the Khurd Kabul pass, a sound rolled across the Jalalabad plain like thunder, "as if a thousand heavy wagons were driven at speed over a rough pavement...the ground heaved and set like the sea, and the whole plain appeared rolling in waves towards us." A severe earthquake destroyed every building. "It seemed as if some gigantic hand had taken up the houses, and thrown them down into the fort in one confused heap of rubbish...worse than the effects of 'a month's cannonading with heavy artillery."

The British officers exchanged their uniforms for clothing woven from camel hair—the first combat fatigues, several decades before they were routine wear. They slept where they worked, joining gangs with their men, working in the "toughness of digging, felling, moisture, dirt and mud" around the clock to rebuild the defenses. Captain Seaton earned the undying gratitude of the officers in his mess by setting up a still to give them a glass of spirits each a day.

They rebuilt the defenses just in time as Akbar Khan arrived in strength only a week after the earthquake. The British force ran very short of both food and ammunition. To replenish their supply of musket balls, they set a figure on a short pole dressed up in a "cocked hat, red coat, painted face" When it was hoisted up, Afghan snipers fired at it, and the garrison reaped a ready harvest of thousands of rounds of lead.

Keeping their horses alive was more difficult. The gangs of grass cutters sent out to forage were sustaining heavy casualties every day, and were hard to protect. Akbar Khan tried to press home his advantage by finding flocks of sheep to graze all the grass within a day's ride of Jalalabad, but when one of these flocks came within sight of the fort, Sale sent out cavalry to shepherd it in, supported by lines of infantry in a brilliant pincer movement. Alongside the value in food, the operation raised morale. This garrison was behaving very differently from the one in Kabul.

When news came through that the first attempt to send a relief force through the Khyber Pass had been repulsed, Sale took things into his own hands, mounting an all-out assault and destroying Akbar Khan's camp itself. One casualty was Brigadier Dennie, the hero of Ghazni in 1839, dying three years after he had written, when Kabul was taken: "The war may now be considered at an end."

The attack had the desired effect of weakening the support of the tribes in the Khyber Pass for Akbar Khan: The swirling weathervane that detected which way the wind blew in Afghanistan was swinging back to the East. The next attempt to force the Khyber by what the British called the Army of Retribution did succeed in getting through. But it was not until September that its commander, General Pollock, could issue orders that the Union flag should fly over the Bala Hissar in Kabul, in a spot where it was "most conspicuous from the city." General Nott, who had succeeded in holding Kandahar, marched north, retaking Ghazni on the way to join Pollock's army.

The force was in Kabul for only two weeks. Thousands of civilians—men, women and children—were killed in an orgy of destruction, and the Kabul bazaar, where Macnaghten's and Burnes's dismembered bodies had been put on public display, was blown up and burned to the ground. Many people had fled the city, but the sword of retribution fell indiscriminately on all those who remained, including some who had previously given protection and help to the British, to Mohan Lal's horror: "all their families, which had once given our people shelter, were pillaged of all their property, and driven from their houses."

The bazaar, perhaps the finest in Asia, had been built around four tall arched spaces gazed on in wonder by Lal when he had first arrived in the city 10 years before. "The parts of the bazaar which are arched over exceed any thing the imagination can picture. The shops rise over each other, in steps glittering in tinsel splendour, till, from the effect of elevation, the whole fades into a confused and twinkling mass, like stars shining through clouds, and the people themselves, not so big as beetles, seem as if a pigmy race." Its destruction would slow the recovery of the Afghan economy.

The slaughter and rape was not confined to the capital. The town of Istalif north of Kabul was destroyed and everything of value pillaged. An officer, Neville Chamberlain, who later played a crucial role in the frontier story, wrote that men under his command had become "licensed assassins." Returning to Istalif the morning after its sack, he recorded what he saw with some shame: "Furniture of all description, wearing apparel, provisions, books, arms, everything made by the hand of man and for his use, lay scattered and destroyed, trampled into the mud, soiled and broken. Here and there the crackling of fire was to be heard." A wounded Afghan woman, crawling toward a stream with a water pot in her hand, refused Chamberlain's offer of help with a curse. He was left "disgusted with myself, the world, and above all, with my cruel profession."

General Sale was put in charge of an altogether different mission: releasing the British captives, including his wife, whom he had left nine months before, expecting to be reunited "after three days." He took his force north toward Bamiyan, where the captives were gathered together—about 70 men, 12 women and more than 20 children, some born since the flight from Kabul. Elphinstone had died in captivity, but the other man most to blame for the Kabul catastrophe, Shelton, had survived. His pompous and insufferable character was on show even during the February earthquake. After escaping from a collapsing building, he turned to a junior officer in captivity with him to complain, with great sternness, that the man had gone down the stairs ahead of him, to receive the cheery response "I'm sorry; it's the fashion in earthquakes."

The captives had been able to receive mail and some newspapers, and the key intelligence of the arrival of the Army of Retribution had been transmitted to them by a simple code, picking out letters from random news articles. As news of the British relief force filtered through to Afghan chiefs, power subtly shifted. When the captives offered pensions to local Afghan chiefs, most accepted, which gave the chiefs an incentive to keep the remnant of the Kabul garrison alive as an insurance policy.

Leadership to the end came from Lady Sale. When Afghan weapons became available, not a single British soldier agreed to carry one, fearing the worst if they were seen armed. Morale had been crushed. Lady Sale sealed her formidable reputation when she said, "You had better give me one, and I will lead the party."

She did not record her reunion with her husband—such things were simply not for public consumption—and when it was alluded to by another officer, General Sale "tried to answer, but his feelings were too strong; he made a hideous series of grimaces, dug his spurs into his horse and galloped off as hard as he could."

The retreat from Kabul, with Lady Sale waving a sword, became a popular theme for military displays in rural England. One told of how "the heart of the Briton, even amidst the snows of India's icy clime, still beats warmly for his native home upon the sea-bound isle." A country able to weave heroic myth from the worst disaster, Britain turned the last stand of the 44th and Captain Souter's protection of the regimental colors into icons of fortitude. Meanwhile, the British in India could console themselves with the success of the reprisal campaign. A bullish military analyst said after Kabul was retaken, "It is a comfort to be able to look at a native in the face again with confidence. Now all is right. How easily achieved!"

But the Select Committee of the East India Company, which ran India, was more concerned. It questioned the whole legal basis of the war. Apart from the loss of life and sheer cost, its angry report listed other consequences: "chilling the affections of the native army, and the disposition to enlist; loss of England's character for fair-dealing; loss of her character of success; the Mussalman population is rendered hostile; causes of rebellion developed by the pressure of taxes and the withdrawal of troops."

As the blame game began, claims were made that the record of the negotiations in Kabul carried out by Burnes had been doctored. Leading the attack in Parliament was a bright young Tory MP, Benjamin Disraeli, trying to make his name, and backed by the public outcry over the calamity and the death of the hero Burnes. In contrast to the situation after the attacks on Afghanistan in 2001 and Iraq in 2003, Parliament debated the war fully in 1842, before the Army of Retribution had even reached Kabul, and MPs wanted to see all the papers. The defense of the "Secret Committee" was that they had altered Burnes's papers only to keep their real intentions secret from Russia—the Afghan war was always about the wider picture, never about Afghanistan itself.

The Tory government, responsible for sending in the Army of Retribution, had not started the war, and its leader, Robert Peel, could rail about the "presumptuous and reckless folly of others" in launching it. His choice for governor-general of India was Lord Ellenborough, who had been involved in Britain's frontier policy since the 1820s. However, against the wishes of both government and opposition in London, who wanted to keep troops in Afghanistan until a deal was done guaranteeing India's security, Ellenborough ordered a withdrawal two weeks after Pollock took Kabul and destroyed much of the city.

On October 1, 1842, Afghanistan was abandoned with a proclamation issued by Ellenborough in the same room as the Simla Manifesto that had begun the war exactly three years earlier. Ellenborough talked smugly of how revenge had "again attached the opinion of invincibility to the British arms." Cannons were fired at the Tower of London and in Hyde Park, and Queen Victoria was told that the campaign had "established the supremacy of British power."

In London, the head of the Secret Committee, John Hobhouse, complained: "Ellenbororough seems positively to have ordered the retreat from Afghanistan, and he is...justly abused for that dastardly policy." In Calcutta, the other members of the Indian government said they had not been told of the decision and lodged a complaint against Ellenborough.

The row over the withdrawal weakened the case being made by Tories in Parliament against the decision to go to war in the first place. Palmerston defended himself against the Tories with sarcasm, saying that perhaps now Britain would need protection: "We could prevail upon our dear Friend the Czar to take us under his wing."

Ellenborough further damaged his reputation by ordering the removal from Afghanistan of some gates supposedly seized from a temple at Somnath in India 800 years previously by Sultan Mahmud of Ghazni. Ellenborough wanted to send them on a triumphal tour to demonstrate how much Britain had done for India and to show "the happy union of our two countries." The gates he ordered to be seized were, however, later copies, not the real thing, and the decision offended just about everyone. Christian ministers of religion opposed it; Muslims saw it as encouraging Hindu triumphalism; and Hindus could not see what good it would do, since Indian history had changed and Somnath was no longer a Hindu site; its Hindu remains, a "crumbling edifice," had long been in the hands of Muslims.

The first account of the war, written by a journalist J. H. Stocqueler in 1843, called the action a "monstrous piece of folly," and said the decision to remove the gates was "ridiculed by the press of India and of England; laughed at by the people of his own party in parliament." The gates were left to rot in Agra, and the triumphal tour abandoned.

As for Afghanistan, Ellenborough's proclamation of 1842 declared: "The Governor General will leave it to the Affghans themselves to create a government amidst the anarchy which is the consequence of their crimes." Dost Mohammed, the man the war had been launched to remove, was allowed to make his way back to reclaim the throne he had lost.

This disastrous war set the tone for the British approach to Afghanistan for decades to come. A generation of empire-building Indian civil servants and soldiers believed it was not ready for civilization and could not be treated in the same way as other places. "The people of these countries are far from ripe for the introduction of our highly refined system of government or of society," wrote Sir Claude Wade, whose prescient analysis could have informed any of the subsequent foreign interventions in Afghanistan. "There is nothing more to be dreaded or guarded against…than the overweening confidence with which Europeans are too often accustomed to regard the excellence of their own institutions and the anxiety that they display to introduce them in new and untried soils."

British India retreated behind the Indus to lick its wounds, placing "the barbarous tribes of Affghanistan…between the British army and an enemy approaching from the West."

That enemy was coming uncomfortably close.

PART TWO

RUSSIAN MOVES AND THE SECOND ANGLO-AFGHAN WAR, 1842–1880

RUSSIAN EXPANSION

STEPPES

SEA of ARAL

KHIVA

Syr Darya River

Oxus River

TASHKENT

KHOKAND 1875

BOKHARA 1875

SAMARKAND

MERV 1884

PANJDEH 1885

MAZAR I SHARIF 1920

HINDU KUSH

KABUL

KANDAHAR

HERAT

1863

1864

1884-5

ASTRAKHAN

CASPIAN SEA

BAKU

CAUCASUS 1800-1833

BLACK SEA

TEHRAN

PERSIA

4

The Great Game

The Afghan will bear poverty, insecurity of life; but he will not tolerate foreign rule. The moment he has a chance, he will rebel.

—"The Lawrence Memo," 1867

While Britain was being sucked into an Afghan quagmire, Russia had been trying to extend its influence south across the chartless wastes of the steppes.

The region that would later divide into "the stans"—Kazakhstan, Uzbekistan, Turkmenistan, Kyrghystan and Tajikistan—was then a lawless desert where clan and tribal customs ruled, and bandits and slavers made frequent raids into Russian lands. In 1836 an old man arrived in the Russian southern garrison town of Orenburg at the end of a journey of 1,000 miles across the empty wasteland. He told of how he had been released after *55 years* in captivity as a slave, with 20 or so others, in a rare gesture of friendship from Khiva, a nation with a reputation for banditry. Thousands from Russia's border area were still held as slaves—Caspian fishermen, Volga boatmen, traders and farmers. Russia could not even buy them back, as the local ruler, the khan of Khiva, threatened a death sentence to anyone selling a slave to Russia: Slavery had the backing of the Khivan state.

The expeditionary force sent by Russia to deal with this was its first maneuver in a drive south across the high steppes of central Asia, a region of epic size bigger than Europe, that would in four decades take them to the Oxus River, the border of Afghanistan. But the first Russian military move in the Great Game would end in catastrophe.

In the years before the retreat from Kabul of 1842, the activities of British spies, horse dealers and adventurers, probing into the region north of Afghanistan, were already causing "serious alarm to the Russian government." They turned up in Bokhara, Samarkand and even the savage bandit territory of

Khiva, although a Russian official report worried nervously that it never quite knew what they were doing because its own spies were "unreliable Asiatics."

Since Moorcroft's epic journeys in pursuit of new bloodstock, Burnes had been north twice. Even while Russia was planning the expedition to deal with the slavers, another Briton, James Abbott, turned up in Khiva—a reminder that it was relatively easy for the British to reach the region from India compared to the obstacles facing Russia. The Russians did not believe Abbott's assurances that he had gone to Khiva to free slaves; they thought his real aim was to win a treaty in Britain's favor. But still they waited. Russia's military move against Khiva was put on hold until the British army had become more deeply involved in Afghanistan in 1840, so that Britain would have less excuse to complain about Russia's aggressive intentions. Delay into that summer proved fatal to the success of the mission.

Crossing the steppes with an army required first setting up caches of food along the route. The Russians requisitioned every camel they could find, more than 10,000 in all, but the attempt to take Khiva was doomed from the beginning. The advance party set out in the heat of July, when there was not even a thorn to eat along the way, and one-third of the horses died. The steppes were not a level plain, but rough ground with treacherous gullies, deceptive pits of deep soft sand and dried salt flats.

By the time the main expedition began, it was winter, and they quickly lost dozens of horses, killed as they tried to eat frozen weeds. After three months it was clear they would run out of food if they went on, so the force turned back. Amid the chaos, hungry camels gnawed at bark boxes and sacks, spilling precious rations onto the ground. Eight hundred men, and most of the camels and horses, died. The Russians realized too late that they should have learned the lessons of the ancient conquerors Genghis Khan and Tamerlane, who both crossed the steppes with faster, more mobile forces, traveling only in the late winter and early spring, after the ground thawed, but before it became murderously hot.

Russia concluded that it should advance its border permanently to the other side of the treacherous and inhospitable steppes, to secure access to the Aral Sea, the east shore of the Caspian and the rivers Sri Darya and Amu Darya— the Oxus itself. The rivers were lifelines that would take Russia south across the wasteland of central Asia. Russia's long-serving foreign minister, Prince Aleksandr Gorchakov, justified the expansion as similar to the move by the United States across America, Britain in India or France in Algiers—the search for a border with another settled state because nomads did not make good neighbors. "The position of Russia in central Asia is that of all civilised states which find themselves in contact with half-savage, nomadic tribes...it always happens that interests of security of borders and of commercial relations demand of the more civilised state that it asserts a certain dominion over others."

By 1864, when Gorchakov made his statement, Russia had taken an area the size of Western Europe in just three decades, planting a flag on the southern side of the steppes. But Russian troops still faced unsettled and unruly tribes, and threatened to move on—Gorchakov's logic would take them to the Hindu Kush and beyond. Russia had big elbows, stretching out at the same time to grab vast areas of northern Asia all the way to the port of Vladivostok, taking advantage of China's defeat by Britain in the Opium Wars.

At the heart of the Great Game was trade. Russia's commerce had advanced across the region ahead of its armies and diplomats. Other than trying to secure the release of slaves, the crucial factor for Russia in launching its first failed assault across the steppes had been the decision by the khan of Khiva to tax merchants from Russia at a far higher rate than those from other Asian countries.

In Kabul before the British occupation, Mohan Lal had calculated that Russian goods were worth 200,000 rupees a year compared to 300,000 rupees for British goods. And north of the Oxus, in the old Silk Road town of Bokhara, he saw Russian merchants trading in its bustling market alongside thousands of Jews and Indians. "Every article neatly laid in the shops of Bokhara had a beautiful appearance, and gave an idea of the influence of trade which is gaining ground in Central Asia." Guns, knives, sugar, paper, lace and horses came from Russia; cotton cloth, silk, spices and tea went the other way from India and Kashmir; and European goods, especially French china and glassware, were just beginning to make an appearance.

On his way north to Bokhara, Lal tested a report that the men of the region would share their wives and sisters with travelers. "To ascertain the existence of so peculiar a fashion, I exerted my curiosity as far as decency permitted, but did not quite succeed." He rather ungallantly concluded that he had not missed much. "The females possess no attractive features."

At the same time as Gorchakov was justifying imperial expansion as the sensible good housekeeping of civilization, the thinking of British India was moving in the opposite direction. The losses in the First Anglo-Afghan War led to a strong desire to have nothing to do with Afghanistan at all—a policy defined as "masterly inactivity" by the viceroy of India in the late 1860s, John Lawrence.

Lawrence remembered watching the Army of the Indus set out with high hopes in 1838, the hubris of every army that has ever tried to take Afghanistan: "I never heard a word uttered of doubt as to our success, or of anxiety as to the movements of Russia." The Lawrence family was to have a more decisive impact on British frontier affairs than any other in the middle years of the nineteenth century. John Lawrence's brother George had been Macnaghten's military secretary in Kabul, with him when he was killed at the meeting on a rug in the

snow, and one of the handful of survivors held prisoner for months after the
debacle. George Lawrence remembered an Afghan coming to their camp and
predicting they would lose, saying "Yours is an army of tents and camels; ours
is one of men and horses."

John Lawrence believed the biggest mistake had "consisted in occupying
Afghanistan at all. There was no escaping the evils which flowed from that
policy... To endeavour to hold such a country firmly, to try to control such a
people, is to court misfortune and calamity. The Afghan will bear poverty, insecurity of life; but he will not tolerate foreign rule. The moment he has a chance,
he will rebel."

Lawrence believed that if Russia did send a force into Afghanistan, then
Britain might do better as a liberator, since the Afghans would see Russia as the
aggressor. "The shoe pinches the wearer only. The side which held Afghanistan
is the one against whom that people would probably join." He would have pulled
Britain's main defenses back east of the Indus if he could, with a large army
threatening the frontier region from the plains.

But by now this was no longer an option. Britain had taken over Punjab after
two sharp wars with the Sikhs following the death of Ranjit Singh, and these
had brought land west of the Indus up to the foot of the Suleiman Mountains,
including the former Pashtun "capital" Peshawar, under British control for the
first time. Britain now occupied the line of the whole of the Afghan frontier
from the Indian Ocean to the Himalayas, completing the process by annexing
Sind in the south almost by accident—"a good, honest, useful piece of rascality"
in the terms of the time. As confirmation of Britain's south Asian supremacy,
the Koh-i-noor diamond fell into the hands of the Raj.

It was an attack by Persia on Herat in 1856 that led Britain to make its
first overture to Afghanistan since the withdrawal of the Army of Retribution
in 1842. Persia had watched Britain and Russia clash in the Crimea, and took
advantage of a power vacuum in Herat to carry out its long-standing threat to
seize the city. Britain declared war immediately, not risking another army in
Afghanistan, but attacking Persia with a ship-borne invasion force. In a tangled
tale of love, intrigue and war, a fleet was already in the area to back up diplomatic efforts to release a woman whose name had been romantically linked with
that of the British ambassador. She was the sister of the shah's principal wife,
and Britain had threatened to break off diplomatic relations and take military
action after she was imprisoned.

The war was a success, and Persia withdrew from Herat, but as so often,
Afghanistan was just another piece on the board—there was no need or desire to
engage with it on its own terms. Britain's sole aim in talking to Dost Mohammed
after the war with Persia was to secure assurances that he would not assist Russia
in an invasion of India.

John Lawrence was then the senior British official on the frontier, and sent a clear and emphatic recommendation about the proposed talks to the government in India, with two brief points: "(1) you will never be able to get the Afghans to make a treaty, and (2) if they make it, they will not keep it." But he lost the argument and had to sign two treaties against his own judgment, first with Dost Mohammed's son and then a year later with Dost himself, who came through the Khyber Pass to Peshawar, a city he believed was his, but was now held by Britain, to sign an agreement, pledging to be "the friend of the friends and enemy of the enemies of the Honourable East India Company."

Britain wanted to open an embassy in Kabul, but Dost turned this down, allowing a mission to Kandahar instead—a disaster from start to finish. The British were surrounded by spies, making it impossible to gather information. At last matters got so bad they were glad to leave, concluding that any British mission was likely to be insulted or murdered, an episode that confirmed the view of those like Lawrence who believed that Britain should have nothing to do with Afghanistan.

The Kandahar mission had other lessons for future deployments in Afghanistan. It had set out with 1,500 cavalry, but only 500 were any good when they arrived because of the heat and the difficulties of the journey. And the British assessment of Kandahar in 1857 contained descriptions that would have been familiar to Russian invaders in the 1980s, or indeed British, Canadian and U.S. forces in the region after 2001: "Quiet and industrious communities are ground to the dust, and their rich and once cultivated lands fast turning to wilderness, while more turbulent races hold their own by sheer force...Add to this the fact of all classes being blindly priest-ridden by crafty, bigoted and supercilious ecclesiastics, and a true picture is drawn."

The treaty with Dost may not have given Britain a foothold in Afghanistan, but it was tested sooner than anyone had expected. It was the last international agreement to be signed by the East India Company, whose long control of Britain's Indian empire was to be replaced by a far more formal system of imperial government in the wake of the biggest challenge to British authority in India, beginning with the mutiny of much of its army.

If tribal warriors from the frontier, or an Afghan army, had intervened against Britain in the desperate days of 1857, that might have been the deciding factor in what was a very close-run thing. But Dost honorably kept his forces out, not knowing that Lawrence was ready to offer Peshawar and the west bank of the Indus to him to do so. These were desperate times, and Lawrence was prepared to hand over the land despite a single-line telegram from the governor-general of India, Lord Canning: "Hold on to Peshawar to the last."

The frontier region was to play a further pivotal role in 1857. In the long hot months when the future of India hung in the balance, most of the troops who fought for Britain on the Delhi Ridge, and won the final battle for the city itself, assaulting a much larger insurgent force dug in behind well-defended positions, were Sikhs from Punjab and Pashtuns from the frontier. They had been recruited by a group of maverick soldiers and political officers under the leadership of another of the Lawrence brothers, Henry.

The generation on the frontier that became known as Henry Lawrence's young men were encouraged to create their own militias and to train and fight like guerrillas. The names are evocative—Hodson's Horse, Daly's Horse, Coke's Rifles, and Lumsden's Corps of Guides—and all are still remembered officially in the regiments that succeeded these and became part of the armies of India or Pakistan after partition.

This was a unique group forged in the fire of the First Anglo-Afghan War. The best known, John Nicholson, was killed, leading from the front, in the battle to retake Delhi. He was not yet 35 years old and had been appointed a general in the irregular army of the frontier, although he was still down as a captain in the Indian army list. His career exactly bracketed the pioneer days on the frontier, beginning with the war in Afghanistan and ending on the Delhi ridge. Fifteen years previously, in his first campaign, he had been held for months in filthy conditions in an Afghan jail, after the garrison at Ghazni had accepted Afghan assurances and surrendered following the massacre in the Khurd Kabul pass. Nicholson had looked on helplessly as his Indian troops immediately were set upon, stripped and butchered by the Afghans against the terms of the surrender.

As he was making his way out through the Khyber Pass after his release from captivity by the Army of Retribution, a macabre coincidence led to Nicholson himself being the first to discover the body of his younger brother, naked and mutilated. Alexander Nicholson had been killed as the Khyber Pass closed behind the Army of Retribution, the last soldier to die in the war.

Years later, Nicholson still called Afghans "the enemy" and refused to attend the treaty-signing ceremony with Dost in Peshawar, although he was by then the deputy commissioner there. He said he could not trust himself if he met them "and might even be tempted to shoot one." But he distinguished between the Afghans on the other side of the mountains and the Pashtun tribes of the frontier that he had come to know. To Nicholson, even the Waziris were better than the Afghans. "I have always hopes of a people, however barbarous in their hospitality, who appreciate and practise good faith among themselves— the Waziris, for instance—but in Afghanistan, son betrays father, and brother brother, without remorse."

Generations of Britons recognized something that appealed to them when they crossed the Indus. Ahead lay Afghanistan, with its theft, horror and deceit; behind them, India's blood-red sky, sapping summer heat and complex faith with its myriad gods.

And in between were the Pathans, later more usually known as Pashtuns, who had a character the British thought they could deal with. The Sikhs may have been respected, admired even, as warriors, but they were not liked—their faith was not far removed from what were generally seen by the British as the absurdities of Hinduism. The frontier Pashtun though was different. "There is an air of masculine independence about him which is refreshing in a country like India." The British could look a Pashtun "between the eyes, and there they found—a man. Sometimes the pledge they made was broken; there were wild men and fanatics, and on one side the assassin struck, on the other the avenger. But the pledge held, the respect, the affection, survived."

The landscape had chiseled the contours of the Pashtun character, as Burnes acutely observed when he first encountered them. "It is . . . the strength of their country, and not their military power, which enables them to cope with the Sikhs." The Sikhs had sensibly left the frontier tribes to themselves, but British forces tried to settle and pacify them from 1849, when they took over the lands west of the Indus.

Henry Lawrence's young men, licensed to do things not by the book, set off into this hinterland to make it their own in a singular way. Nicholson ordered the body of a well-known robber to be nailed to a door in the market of a village so people would know that the British had killed him. He also cut off the head of a rebel and placed it on a table in his office, calling in tribal elders one by one to see if they had anything to say. He ruthlessly put down any stirrings of mutiny, hanging suspects without trial, and ordered the beard of an Islamic cleric to be shaved after he thought the man had insulted him. Nicholson's fame was such that a religious cult grew up around him, whose devotees pursued him to his intense and growing annoyance.

There were significant successes. Bandits were turned into British officers. When he was recruiting for his Corps of Guides, Joe Lumsden deliberately sought mountain men who could look after themselves, including those "notorious for desperate deeds . . . who had defied all authority, and had never been seen in the plains but for murder and plunder."

James Abbott, who had first come to prominence when he alarmed the Russians by turning up in Khiva in 1840, became the administrator of Hazara, a vast area to the north on the east bank of the Indus. He made himself popular with Pashtun elders by his simple decision to allow the *azan*, the Muslim call to prayer, to be heard—it had been banned by the Sikhs. When another of the young men, Herbert Edwardes, took over in Bannu, west of the Indus, he publicly flogged Sikh soldiers for looting from the locals, and then spent months persuading tribal elders that paying tribute to Britain was both fair and sensible.

This combination of diplomacy and determination—improvising when they could and killing when they thought they needed to—was buttressed by a

Christian certainty that the British were doing God's work. It worked, up to a
point, in the plains and even the hills of Abbott's Hazara region to the north,
but as Britain came up against the reality of the mountain barrier that had
dominated its military imagination for almost half a century, since Lieutenant
Macartney's map, it faced its own version of the Gorchakov dilemma.

Civilization demanded that fines were paid and criminals brought to justice. But when revenue officers tried to collect fines, and troops pursued bandits,
their way was blocked by Pashtun mountain tribes whose honor code guaranteed hospitality to guests, including criminals. The historian Charles Allen
put the problem simply: "Virtually every one of the scores of confrontations
between Government and tribe, that escalated into conflict in the course of the
next century can be traced back to this single issue of principle versus honour."
Britain's answer, involving frequent raids into frontier villages, was the policy
later to be characterized as butcher and bolt.

The Pashtun honor code protected guests, guaranteed hostility to strangers and led to feuds between families being carried on through generations—
the language even needing a specific word to define revenge between cousins.
When Pashtuns were recruited as British soldiers, their officers tried not to
send them on leave at the same time as each other, since they tended to pursue
ancient blood feuds and not return alive.

Hardly a year passed between 1849, when the Sikhs were defeated, and
Britain's departure in 1947, when there was not some military engagement to
try to subdue the frontier tribes. This was *the* dominant security concern for
British India but was underreported even at the time. A dispatch after one of
these bruising encounters said, "The hardships of the campaign told so severely
on the British troops engaged that it hardly deserved to sink into the complete
official oblivion which has shrouded it." In the half century before 1900 there
were about 60 separate military operations in this mountain range, and a general uprising in 1897—an intensity of conflict unique in the world. In contrast,
the Indian army was deployed just 23 times to other parts of India during this
period—nearly all small-scale skirmishes in Assam—and mobilized to fight
only 15 times in other theaters of war, including Egypt, Sudan and twice in
China.

The campaigns on the frontier required considerable use of force. Reports
to Parliament used words like thrashing, crushing and punishing. Force was
always the first thing tried, the only language understood. Punishment meant
the destruction of walls, particularly defensive towers, as well as the confisca-
tion of livestock and the burning of crops.

Taking reports from just the first four years: In 1849, 2,300 troops were
involved in collecting unpaid fines. In 1850, after some sappers were killed by the
Afridi tribe, who were paid for access through the Khyber Pass, 3,200 "troops

traversed the country, and the Afridis were punished." In 1851, after Afghans entered villages in an area Britain thought was theirs, 2,050 troops reestablished order and took hostages "for the good behaviour of the tribe." The same year in the Mohmand country farther, north several villages were destroyed after a series of raids; the operation involved 1,597 troops. In 1851, 600 troops went back into the same area and forced "submission." In 1852, 3,270 troops had to restore order in one part of the frontier while 2,200 troops destroyed all villages in another. After all that a summary to Parliament claimed, "Their punishment had a wholesome effect for many years." But the soldiers were back in the same hills traversing, forcing submission and punishing the following year, and it did not stop.

And now something else was stirring on the frontier, as impervious to the unconventional warfare practiced by Lawrence's young men as it was to the thrashing and punishing of Britain's conventional forces. Holy warriors, mujahidin, had emerged, with a social and religious agenda that would have been recognized by the Taliban 150 years later. These were directly related to the fundamentalists swiftly put to death by Shah Shuja in Ghazni on the way to reclaim his throne in Kabul in 1839, when he realized who they were. From the 1830s onward British intelligence uncovered a trail of Islamist conspiracies across India. Silk letters were found sewn into the lining of clothing worn by messengers apprehended at night; instructions were discovered rolled up and hidden in bamboo canes; and Islamist songs were learned in secret and passed from Muslim to Muslim. A prophecy told how British rule would end in 1857, but the Islamist rebels did not fade away after the mutiny was defeated.

The most audacious attack was the assassination of the viceroy, Lord Mayo, by a Wahhabi-inspired "fanatic" while he was visiting a British penal colony in 1872. On his appointment Mayo had expressed his determination to act against the Wahhabi sect—the fundamentalist offshoot of Islam that was later to be promoted by Osama bin Laden. A year earlier in Calcutta the acting chief justice had been murdered on his way to preside over a Wahhabi trial, as Islamic fundamentalism continued to stamp its mark on the story of south Asia.

The trail always led back to the frontier region, where as early as the 1830s the Sikhs had faced a determined assault by mujahidin from the hill, that threatened their control of Peshawar itself. The Islamists were forced back only when they overreached themselves by demanding that their Pashtun allies hand over their daughters to them in marriage. The tribes broke the alliance, turning on the alien "Hindustani fanatics" and killing many of them, including their leader, letting the Sikhs off the hook. Then, as later, the attitude of Islamist warriors to women would dominate their relationship to the outside world.

The "fanatics" regrouped in the rugged and remote spot of Sittana, concealed in the folds of the mountains among the pine forests at the eastern end of Swat. These were the ghazis that Dost Mohammed had encouraged on the frontier against British forces. The willingness of Pashtuns to follow extremist religious leaders had been noticed by travelers for many years. Elphinstone himself said they were "remarkable for their religious zeal and intolerance, for their attention to all forms of devotion, and for the profound respect which they bear for Moolahs. The tyranny of these priests is there carried to an intolerable pitch." And Dr. Henry Bellew, a surgeon with the Corps of Guides, said that the tribe he worked among in Swat were "entirely controlled by their priests, and are at all times ready for a jihad."

The austere lifestyle of the ghazis drew its inspiration from the singular strain of Islam founded by Mohammed ibn Abd al-Wahhab, who was born in Arabia at the beginning of the eighteenth century. The sect that bore his name, Wahhabism, sought to strip Islam back to its fundamentals, the basic texts from the seventh century. Wahhabi leaders rejected the view of many Muslims that jihad was just about inner spiritual struggle: instead they understood jihad as imposing the duty of fighting a holy war against unbelievers. From the early nineteenth century, Wahhabism spread across India, leading to the foundation of the Deobandi school of Islamic thought.

Wahhabis did not just oppose British rule but their way of life. A remarkable insight into the mind of those drawn to this exclusive and austere cult came in the autobiography of a man jailed for being part of a network that linked the fanatics on the frontier with insurrection elsewhere in India. Mohammed Jafar believed that his contact not just with English people but with their *language* had threatened his soul, since English "is so closely connected with materialistic life that it is not only harmful but dangerous for the spiritual life. If a young man, before learning Quran and traditions of the holy Prophet in detail, learns English and reads English books of various types and different disciplines as I used to do, he will become an unreligious, uncultured person with excessively free ideas... Such knowledge will certainly make a person unreligious and atheist."

This made it essential for the fanatics to found their own schools and follow a separate way of life. Any contact with non-Wahhabi culture, including some Islamic culture, could be damaging to the purity of the faith. The most radical fringes of the Deobandi tradition taught that there could be no compromise at all with non-Islamic culture.

By 1849, the year that Britain began its attempts to control the frontier region, Wahhabi fanatics had secured enough support among the disparate tribes scattered in the hills to the north of the Vale of Peshawar for their leader to be named the *padshah*, or king, of Swat, where "the inhabitants, a semi-civilised race, are fanatical Mahometans."

One of the most serious attempts to take on the fanatics, the Ambeyla campaign of 1863, almost ended in disaster for British forces, as the Pashtun tribes came out in force against them, mobilized by the *akhund* of Swat, a revered figure with both political and religious influence, whose loyalties were never clear or consistent. The British advance was slow with a long line of elephants and bullock carts, carrying carpets, furniture and crockery, and after a week of fierce fighting the force was pinned down. Tribal fighters, including among their ranks many ex-British soldiers who had fled to the region after the 1857 mutiny, continued to pour in to reinforce the rebel forces. The British commander, Brigadier Neville Chamberlain, who owed his advance to Henry Lawrence, was no longer a young man but a highly respected leader, reputed to have been injured more than any other man in the British army. He wrote an urgent dispatch in which he stated that even tribes that had been opposed to the fanatics previously were now allying with them against Britain: "Old animosities are, for the time being, in abeyance; and under the influence of fanaticism, tribes usually hostile to each other are hastening to join the Akhoond's standard."

Many of the British regiments in the field had been locally recruited and were fighting against their own tribes, one soldier recognizing his father among the dead in front of his position after an engagement. After suffering large losses—36 officers and 800 men—Britain sent reinforcements in enough strength to persuade the fighters to disperse to their homes. The Bunerwal tribe offered to destroy the fanatics' camp themselves, providing the British forces then withdrew from the area. A small detachment of British soldiers accompanied them and found the Islamists' hideout to be far larger than had been anticipated, "containing several large edifices amongst which were the Moulvie's [mullah; religious leader] hall of audience, barracks for the soldiers, stabling and a powder manufactory." It was an exact forerunner of camps for international al-Qaeda fighters set up in a similar area in the 1990s, inspired by the same Wahhabi vision.

The destruction of the camp was resented by some local people who now crowded around the small British force, threatening to kill them. But one of their hosts said that the British had been invited in by the Bunerwals and would be escorted out by them—the honor code of the Pashtuns in action. A young officer, Frederick Roberts, already a holder of the Victoria Cross for his exploits on the Delhi Ridge in 1857 and later to achieve fame in Afghanistan, said it was a "plucky speech" by their Bunerwal host, who was no friend of Britain.

The British believed that 700 fanatics had died, but body counts, then as in the war against the Taliban in Afghanistan after 9/11, were useless in judging the success of an operation against Wahhabi warriors. Jihad was in the mind, and could not be snuffed out in combat. Only five years later, in the next major attempt to put the warriors down, 12,500 British troops were needed for an assault on tribes that supported fanatics living in the Black Mountain area farther east of Sittana—more troops than had been sent from India to China to take Peking in 1860.

Russia's commander on their southern frontier, General Konstantin Kauffman, appealed to Britain to make common cause with Russia against Islamism, since this was "the only danger to British rule in India, the others being merely imaginary." This was typical shadow boxing, with Russia denying its own aggressive intentions. But Russia faced its own problems with Islamic fundamentalism. In Bokhara mullahs tried to stop foreign trade, and there were religious police similar to those imposed by the modern Wahhabis in Saudi Arabia and by the Taliban in Afghanistan. "The men are stopped in the midst of their work by officers to see whether they can repeat their prayers: ignorance is followed by a whipping."

Bokhara came under the tsar's control in 1869, bringing Russian soldiers onto the Oxus River facing Afghanistan for the first time. In the 1870s they consolidated their position, as the great trading towns of the Silk Road—Tashkent, Samarkand and Khokand—came into their hands, as well as Khiva.

Russia had fulfilled the prophesy of that earliest British Forward policy advocate, John McNeill, with a relentless move that had been going on for a century, "varying the means, but never relinquishing the purpose." Back in 1836 he had asked why Russia would expend so much "blood and treasure" to take the south bank of the Caspian Sea. "These acquisitions can be valued or valuable only in as much as they afford facilities for arriving at some great end which would, in her estimation, remunerate her for all that might have been expended in attaining it."

The Russian advance was not only southeast toward the Afghan border but directly south toward Persia, across the giant barrier of the mountains of the Caucasus to the west of the Caspian Sea, where the bright uniforms and set-piece maneuvers of European warfare were no use in the treacherous forests, mountains and deserts. A Muslim guerrilla leader named Shamil was as famous an enemy in Russia in the middle of the nineteenth century as Osama bin Laden was to become for the United States at the start of the twenty-first.

Decades of warfare, particularly in Chechnya, informed the generation of writers who came to define Russia's soul, after traveling or fighting in the Caucasus, as Russia imposed its will on people who, Lermontov wrote, had "thieving in their blood." Pushkin wrote of "the splendid chain of these mountains; their icy summits, which from afar, on a clear dawn, seem like strange clouds, many-coloured and motionless."

Tolstoy may be best remembered for his vast novels about Europe during conventional conflicts, but the wild otherness of the Caucasus, beyond civilization, obsessed him and inspired *Hadji Murat*, the book he was working on in the last years of his life. He compared a guerrilla leader to a thistle with a beautiful and strange flower. Anyone who tried to pick it would be hurt—but the plant would be damaged beyond repair too, since it could not be picked cleanly.

And the way Tolstoy described how the Chechens felt about Russian invaders has a clear parallel with the strength of Afghan feeling against foreign invaders: "It was not hatred, but the refusal to recognise these Russian dogs as people, and such revulsion, disgust and bewilderment before the ridiculous cruelty of these beings, that the desire for their destruction, like the desire for the destruction of rats, poisonous spiders and wolves, was just as natural a feeling as the feeling of self-preservation."

The hold of this region on the imagination of Russia has continued. Nearly all of the areas in central Asia taken at such cost by Russia in the nineteenth century achieved independence during the collapse of the Soviet Union in the early 1990s. But Chechnya had been given a different legal status, annexed as part of Russia itself, and has been held by force by Moscow in two of the most ruthless wars seen anywhere in recent years; Hadji Murat's descendants were ground under tank tracks.

Back in 1873, Britain and Russia signed their first agreement over Afghanistan. After dancing around each other for 40 years, both agreed to remain out of the boxing ring—it was to be a buffer state between them. The Oxus was defined as Afghanistan's northern border, while the western desert was to be mapped and surveyed before being carved up. Britain agreed that the mountains at the northern end of India's North-West Frontier were Afghan, particularly a long finger of land running up to China, as it sought to keep Afghan land between its troops in India and Russia. As usual, Afghanistan was not consulted about its fate.

———   ———   ———

The death of the "Great Amir," Dost Mohammed, in 1863 had coincided with the promotion of John Lawrence to the post of viceroy in India. Britain's policy of "masterly inactivity" turned into studied indifference as the routine bloody power play between princes began in Kabul to choose a successor, each knowing that British recognition would bring guns and money.

Five years after Dost's death, and following fighting across the country that cost thousands of lives, one of his sons, Sher Ali, emerged from the bloodbath as the next amir. He owed the British nothing, and blamed them in part for the intensity of the struggle for succession, since they did not reply to his first demand for recognition when he took over a mostly united country as Dost's anointed successor. Britain had also recognized the claim of his half-brother, Afzul Khan, after Afzul had swept from the north to take Kabul.

Armies led by Yakub Khan and Abdur Rahman, sons of the two claimants, had played key roles in a swirling conflict marked by epic violence. After one battle Abdur Rahman claimed to have cut off the heads of 3,000 enemy dead and made a tower from them to discourage others, and he blew 50 bandits from the mouths of cannons to try to control the North. But he lost the fight, fleeing north across the Oxus to take refuge.

Even after Shir Ali took power, he complained of the duplicity of the British, believing that they were promoting the interests of one of his sons over another as heir apparent. This unique relationship, in which Britain sought to exert authority over Afghan external affairs by remote control, led to constant friction and misunderstanding. British Forward policy hawks did not believe they got much for their gifts of guns and money, since they could not send even a single squadron of cavalry into Afghanistan to scout the frontier. On the other side it was the constant complaint of succeeding Afghan amirs that they had to renegotiate terms every time; the deal was with an individual, not with the country.

So when Shir Ali emerged victorious and came down to the plains of India to claim his prize from the viceroy, he was not surprised that he was not offered the treaty terms he sought. He was left instead with vague offers of friendship and the standard gift of guns. His diplomatic reserve cracked when he saw the honor guard of Indian sepoys, who did not look like warriors to his Afghan eyes. He laughed openly at them, and said they were fit only to "feed the kites and enrich the earth as they were unsuited to the purposes of war."

In London, the Liberal party still tended toward the Lawrence view, restricting engagement, while the Tories urged the more aggressive Forward policy. The approach seesawed as power changed hands, with British officials in India forced to steer a consistent course between these opposing positions as orders from London changed. In 1876 Lord Lytton was appointed viceroy by the Tories, with a far more aggressive mandate than any before him. He believed Amir Shir Ali to be a "savage with a touch of insanity." Lytton's provocations would lead to war.

5

"AFGHANISTAN AS A WHOLE COULD NO LONGER EXIST"

A non-recognition of their failures and a considerable and often ridiculous exaggeration of their successes constitute the characteristics of Englishmen. They like to exaggerate the scale of the enemy, the low casualties, and the hardship: "The affair was brilliant, obstinately contested and bloody" is the usual description which they give to their engagements.

—Major General L. N. Soboleff, former chief of
the Asiatic Department of the Russian General Staff, 1885

Russia and Britain ground against each other, like forces of nature, two huge tectonic plates moving under the surface of the late nineteenth-century world. Sometimes the surface above was calm, sometimes it burst open, as in the Crimea. In Asia the movement felt as if it would erupt into an earthquake, and British officials cynically prepared to let Afghanistan fall through the resulting fissure in the earth. "Afghanistan as a whole could no longer exist" was the stated policy of the secretary of state in London in a letter to the new viceroy, Lord Lytton.

More than half a century after Lieutenant Macartney first drew the attention of empire builders in India to the various options for defense, the political generation whose caution was based on the catastrophe of the First Anglo-Afghan War had moved on. The Forward policy's time had come.

Disraeli's government had no regard for the details of a pass here or there in the Suleiman Mountains. Its mental map, on which Afghanistan "would no longer exist," turned India's defensive wall through 90 degrees. Control of the passes through the Hindu Kush, not the Suleiman range, motivated their policy. They saw British forward positions bristling with guns, facing Russian forces over the Oxus, not waiting for them on the Indus. Political memories in London were short, and belief in the power of British arms to prevail was spurred on by the newspapers, which could not understand why Afghanistan was so hard to conquer. Those in Simla and Calcutta who still whispered caution were side-lined, as the laying of a cable under the Red Sea in 1870 brought the government of India under more direct control from London. For the first time instructions could be sent instantly by telegraph, rather than taking weeks by sea.

An outbreak of war between Russia and Turkey in 1877 took a British fleet to the eastern Mediterranean; the tectonic plates overlapped and crashed under the waves as warships brought troops from India. Tension rose for six months in the Dardanelles, as Britain and Russia glowered at each other across Constantinople, but a year later at the Congress of Berlin the European powers agreed to step back from war.

Afghanistan was a crucial part of this jigsaw. Russia had moved farther south, taking a belt of land north of the Oxus, from Khokand in the east and threatening the oasis at Merv in the West, and there was no certainty as to where the Afghan border lay. Russia could now sweep down to the Hindu Kush at any time, certainly more quickly than Britain could mobilize from India.

Even while British politicians were returning from Berlin with a treaty that they could call "Peace with Honor," Russia raised the stakes with its most auda-cious move yet in Afghanistan, sending a diplomatic mission to Kabul, against the terms of the 1873 agreement with Britain that the country was to be a buffer between them. Russia wanted control of all of the land down to the Hindu Kush, and in return offered to help Shir Ali secure Peshawar and the former Afghan territories on the other side of the Suleiman Mountains. The dream of reunit-ing the Pashtun lands—Pashtunistan—lured Shir Ali to the Russian side.

Shir Ali had no affection for the British. He thought them duplicitous, and resented what he saw as his one-sided relationship with them in which they made demands and gave little concrete in return. The death of the son he had chosen to succeed him, Abdullah Jan, in August, closed Kabul for a brief period but only delayed the inevitable—the arrival of a letter from Britain announc-ing that it too would send a mission to Kabul. On September 21, 1878, a British military force accompanying an envoy attempted to march through the Khyber Pass—a formal charade, the equivalent of a duelist dropping his gauntlet at the gates of a rival. They were refused entry, as they knew they would be, and war was declared on Afghanistan.

The mission turned back at the Khyber was led by General Sir Neville Chamberlain, now almost 60 years old, who remembered coming the other way out through the pass 36 years before, when it was still "strewn with skeletons of men and animals...our gun-wheels ground to dust the bones of the dead. In some places the Affghans...had placed the skeletons one in the arms of the other, or sometimes sitting or standing against the rocks as if they were holding a consultation."

Disraeli's viceroy Lord Lytton had never seen the Khyber Pass, but he viewed war with Russia as inevitable, and wanted it on ground chosen by Britain. He wrote of the

> immense importance to us of the triangle formed by Kabul, Ghazni and Jalalabad, with the possession of the passes over the Hindu Kush. Defensively this position, behind a rampart of mountains, and with its communications unassailable directly commands the central group of roads, while directly threatening both the eastern and western group. Offensively it gives the power of debouching at will on the plains of the Oxus, and threatens every point of Russia's extended frontier. It is difficult to imagine a more strategical position; and whenever the moment of collision with Russia arrives, it must find us in possession of it, as friends and allies of the Afghans if possible, but firmly established there in any case.

British politicians anticipated victory, quoting military intelligence reports predicting that "in case of war with the English, most of the troops at each action will either come over to us or else disperse." The most significant opposition to moving forward came from senior army officers, who knew the hazards and the costs. But a rumbling of consensus for war began to roll through the clubs and drawing rooms of the rulers of India as well as among Tories in London. A member of the Council of India, Sir Henry Rawlinson, argued that Afghanistan had no right to independent existence at all: it was geographically and politically a part of India, so that dealt with abstract questions about the legitimacy of interference. Furthermore, it was "affectation to apply the nice distinctions of European diplomacy to a barbarian chief like Shir Ali Khan."

The British mission to Kabul was headed by a frontier political officer with an exotic background and name—Lieutenant Colonel Sir Pierre Louis-Napoleon Cavagnari—born in Parma in Italy to an Irish mother. He looked out the accounts from the First Anglo-Afghan War to find out the going rate to be paid as the toll for an invasion force through the Khyber Pass, and offered the same as before, 87,000 rupees, to the Afridi tribe, who had run the protection racket in the Khyber for centuries. To his surprise, there had been no inflation in invasion tolls—his offer was accepted. But despite the payment, British soldiers had to fight their way through from the beginning, in a complex and deceptive war where nothing, even victory, was as it seemed, and the geography and people of the frontier and Afghanistan once again confounded the optimistic expectations of the invader.

— — —

The first shots in the Second Anglo-Afghan War were fired on the afternoon of November 21, 1878, during a skirmish in the Khyber between Afghan cavalry and Britain's frontier specialists, the Corps of Guides. The Guides had been marching all night with one only day's cooked rations in their knapsacks. "The night was dark, the road tortuous, rocky and broken, passing for a considerable distance through heavy grass and jungle up the bed of the Lashora stream." The Guides took casualties and were pinned down without supplies for another day, but first light on the morning of the twenty-third revealed that a defensive fort and its surrounding positions had been abandoned, and they moved through the Khyber to Jalalabad. It was a pattern repeated throughout the war—a tough fight, then an absent enemy and an easy march forward—violence, deception, feint. Everything was an illusion.

Two other columns in an invasion army of 45,000 moved into Afghanistan at the same time, along the three navigable passes through the solid wall of the Suleiman range. The central column moved toward a high pass known as the 'Camel's Neck', south of the Khyber, while further South a force moved toward Quetta on military roads built through the mountains by the British invasion force in 1839. As in that earlier campaign, the lack of food and water on the route took an enormous toll of animals. Almost 12,000 camels died in the first move on Kandahar, and by the end of the war, a third of the camels available in the whole of Punjab had died in Afghanistan. But on the southern front the journey was harder than the fighting. In their only battle in the flat plain before Kandahar, Britain suffered a handful of wounded for about 100 dead of the enemy. And after the battle, some Afghan cavalry asked to join the British force—just as the intelligence assessment had predicted. It was beginning to look easy.

The governor of Kandahar fled. As the British took the town, most shops remained open, and large numbers of people came out to see their arrival. "Their attitude was perfectly impassive," in the words of the official army account of the war, "showing neither fear, hostility, nor pleasure." There were some subsequent isolated attacks on British officers in Kandahar, but the first serious military engagement in the South was at the town of Sangin, one of the most hotly contested towns when British forces returned to the area in 2006. In the cavalry battle that followed the first contact with the enemy at Sangin, the British calculated that one-third of the 1,500 men opposing them were ghazis, or "fanatics."

Shir Ali failed to retain the support of tribal elders and fled north with the Russian delegation he had welcomed to Kabul. However, Russia did not deliver the alliance he thought he had been promised, and he died, a disappointed man, in Mazar in February. His son Yakub Khan claimed the throne, and although his hold was precarious, Britain agreed to deal with him, demanding considerable involvement in Afghanistan's internal affairs. Yakub Khan's reply said that Britain's emissary to him had "strung one by one on the thread of description

the pearls of your friendly hints," although spies intercepted a quite different message from Yakub to tribal elders, inciting rebellion and the murder of
British soldiers.

The meeting took place at Gandamack in May, scene of the disastrous last
stand of the 44th in 1842, that had been transformed in the British national
memory into a moment of glory. The reddish stones near the bare summit
were said to be stained with the "blood of the English." The hill is still called
Feringhee Ghunadi—the mountain of the foreigners.

A British account described Yakub Khan as "peevishly" refusing everything
at first, before changing his mind and agreeing to everything. A crucial element
of the deal was that for the first time an Afghan ruler accepted British control
of all the main passes through the Suleiman Mountains, including the Khyber,
"and of all relations with the independent tribes of the territory directly connected with these passes." The new amir also agreed to conduct relations with
foreign states only in accordance with the "advice and wishes" of the British
government. Britain agreed to support the amir against any foreign aggression
and pay him 600,000 rupees annually.

There was a vote of thanks in both Houses of Parliament to all involved,
and even congratulations in the Russian press for Disraeli: "By a bold stroke, for
which thousands of Indian militiamen have paid with their lives, he obtained for
his country a commanding position in Central Asia—a position we have strived
to secure for fifteen years."

By now the expeditionary force had been in the field for longer than planned,
and as the summer of 1879 reached its hottest months, cholera broke out in the
Khyber Pass. "In this particular year and at this particular time, the choice is a
choice of evils," wrote the surgeon general with the British force. "If the troops
marched into India, they marched into cholera; if they remained, it advanced
on them." The decision was taken to move, but dozens died, the worst hit being
medical staff. There may not have been much fighting, but the war was taking
its toll: "Their clothes were stiff and dirty from the profuse perspiration and
dust; their countenances betokened great nervous exhaustion, combined with a
wild expression, difficult to describe; the eyes infected and even sunken, a burning skin, black with the effects of sun and dirt; dry tongue; a weak voice; and a
thirst which no amount of fluids seemed to relieve."

Heading in the other direction with a small escort force, Sir Louis Cavagnari
was the first British emissary to Kabul since Macnaghten. He was given a substantial house behind the defensive walls of the Bala Hissar itself, close to Yakub
Khan's palace. But as soon as he arrived in Kabul, Cavagnari's position looked
precarious. The official British military assessment of what happened next was
similar to what was commonly said in Kabul about Hamid Karzai, the leader
installed by the U.S.-led invasion force in 2001. "Yakub Khan's authority was

small beyond the walls of his capital, while the Mullahs and the anti-British party lost no opportunity of exciting the people towards the British alliance."

In the same way as Macnaghten had missed the warning signs before he was butchered, Cavagnari believed everything was fine until the end. On August 30 he wrote, "I personally believe that Yakub Khan will turn out to be a very good ally, and that we shall be able to keep him to his engagements." But a Pashtun officer in his escort, Risaldar-Major Nakhshband Khan of the Guides Cavalry, thought they were never safe. He saw Afghan soldiers from the South arriving in town, abusing British soldiers as they passed. His debrief by British intelligence after he fled was full of rumor: "I heard shortly afterwards from a friend of mine that he heard from a friend of his, who was present at the time..."

Cavagnari died after the old game of playing different forces off against each other. He paid money directly to a number of Afghan leaders, angering the amir, who had not disbursed the money he had received from Britain. When he was asked why he had not fulfilled his Gandamack pledge to pay the sirdars, the amir answered, "This is Afghanistan. We cannot get on here without practising deceit." According to Khan, another tribal leader present said that if that was the case, then "we may look upon Afghanistan as on the way to ruin; it will go out of our hands."

So the soldiers from the irregular militias who now filled the streets had not been paid, and although it was the amir and their own chiefs who owed them the money, they blamed the British embassy. And there was a rumor that Bibles printed in Arabic to evangelize the country, along with Korans, had been seen in the baggage of one of the members of the British party. According to the source of this story, the Koran in Afghanistan was only ever printed on expensive paper from plants grown in Kashmir. It was sacrilege to print it on European paper. "The Kabul Mullahs, who are renowned for their fanaticism, were in a state of frenzy when they saw the obnoxious books...The regiment, excited by the Mullahs, was of course soon brought into a state of mutiny."

Early in the morning of September 3, Risaldar-Major Khan was recognized and almost pulled from his horse as he rode from his lodgings toward the British residency. He managed to get away and concealed his horse in the stables at the house of an Afghan friend. From an upstairs window he saw a crowd heading up the hill to the Bala Hissar from the town. They were repulsed when they tried to rob the British-Indian cavalrymen, but an hour later they returned armed, and fighting began.

This did not look like a mindless mob; it appeared to Khan that officers in the Afghan army were directing events. The rebels looted the magazine in the fortress, although they did not try to take the treasury, where 500 of the amir's men remained at their posts. At one point he ordered his horse to be saddled, but he never mounted it, and never intervened, as the events unfolded in front of him.

At around 9 A.M., Cavagnari and the other British officers led 25 of their men out of the residency, charging the rioters on the rough ground in front. "When charged, the Afghan soldiers ran like sheep before a wolf." But the position was hopeless, and despite three other sallies, the residency was on fire by midmorning. There was little shooting heard from it after 3 P.M. Cavagnari's body was never identified. The only survivor of the mission, Risaldar-Major Khan, fled Kabul on a borrowed pony at night, disguised as a grass-cutter, the lowliest of camp followers, and made his way southeast toward the pass out of Afghanistan at the Camel's Neck.

General Roberts, who had commanded the central column in the invasion, was with the viceroy in Simla when news of the slaughter came through, and headed back toward Afghanistan straightaway. This was to be the campaign that would make his name—literally, as Lord Roberts of Kandahar. Yakub Khan knew what was coming and sent a pleading letter: "Some of the cavalry I have dismissed, and night and day am considering how to put matters straight. Please God the mutineers will soon meet the punishment they deserve, and my affairs will be arranged to the satisfaction of the British government. Certain persons of high position in these provinces have become rebellious; but I am watching carefully and closely every quarter." The viceroy replied that the British army was coming to support him—a response similar to Moscow's justification for the Soviet invasion in 1979.

Roberts calculated that the pass at the Camel's Neck was the best hope to reenter Afghanistan, since the tribes at the Khyber Pass were known for their treachery, and managed to get his force over the pass before it was closed by snow, despite transport difficulties that were "greater than I ever remember." Every surviving camel and horse available in the region was pressed into service. Roberts sent a blunt message to Kabul: "Be it known that the British army is advancing on Kabul to take possession of the city...all persons found armed in or about Kabul will be treated as enemies of the British government; and further, it must be clearly understood that if the entry of the British force is resisted, I cannot hold myself responsible for any accidental mischief which may be done to persons and property, even of well-disposed people, who may have neglected this warning."

But intelligence, that most basic need for any military campaign, was lacking. What Roberts did not know was that the leaders of several tribes thought his force could be beaten, and had formed an alliance. By October, less than a month after the deaths of Cavagnari and his party, as British troops approached Kabul from the south, a large Afghan force was coming together on the three-mile long ridge ahead of the city called Charasiab. At the same time Roberts learned that his supplies were under attack back at the high pass in the mountains, where British agents had tried to play brother against brother in the family that controlled the pass.

Roberts could not retreat, and needed to advance to Kabul quickly. But with just 2,500 men, he was outnumbered perhaps 5 to 1 by an enemy who had the advantage of high ground. After a feint attack at the end of the ridge at Charasiab nearest the road, the most direct route to Kabul, a joint force of Highlanders and Gurkhas assaulted the other end, storming the high ground before the Afghans could reinforce it. Most of the Afghan force retreated, leaving hundreds dead.

This decisive victory in the biggest battle of the war left Britain with 20 pieces of Afghan artillery, including one identified as a recent British gift, and opened the gateway to the capital. The speed of the advance and the ferocity of the fighting—the British force fired 40,000 rounds in the battle for Charasiab—left Kabul defenseless.

Yakub Khan abdicated, telling Roberts he would "rather be a grass-cutter in the English camp than ruler of Afghanistan." He went under armed guard into exile and a British pension in India. The acknowledgment on November 19 that he had abdicated was the first dispatch on a new telegraph line completed to Kabul from India, almost a year to the day since the first shots had been fired in the war. Shortly afterward—it was unclear whether by accident or design—the magazine exploded in the Bala Hissar, causing huge destruction, killing more than 20 people and forcing the British out of their temporary quarters. The Gurkhas were dispersed around other camps, some clad in greatcoats given them by grateful Highlanders for their support in the battle for the Charasiab Ridge, a gesture of comradeship that could be understood "only by those who know the coldness of the nights here."

After swift trials, 49 Afghans were executed on a gallows set up in the ruins of residency for their role in the uprising. Roberts also ordered that the remaining buildings in the Bala Hissar should be pulled down as an "act of retributive justice," and the material used to build barracks in the cantonment at Sherpur, outside Kabul, taken over by the British force.

For a period there was a strange atmosphere in Kabul: It was under martial law; and the residency building was still a charred shell, with human bones lying in the ruins; but British soldiers seemed to be able to move about freely, and organized cricket, horseracing, and boating on Wazirabad Lake. "Towards the afternoons the main bazaars present a most lively and animated appearance, and are densely and incongruously crowded: camels, elephants, mules, horsemen, Afghans and Englishmen all jostling along in a busy stream."

But every morning, posters would appear in Kabul urging jihad against the British occupation. Dissent began in the mosques. A mullah with the unlikely name of Mushk-i-Alam, "fragrance of all the world," led the opposition. He signed his letters Imam-ul-Mujahidin-i-wal Muslimin—"leader of the mujahidin"—the sort of title that would become much better known in Afghanistan in later conflicts. He was financed by the women of Yakub Khan's family, who literally gave away the family jewels to try to turn the tide against Britain.

The fate of the British occupation force depended, as always in Afghanistan, on whether the tribal chiefs—the sirdars—would mobilize against them. Strength tended to go with strength, while any show of weakness could be fatal. Roberts had been decisive, beating a large Afghan army on the field at Charasiab, to give him a breathing space. The sirdars acquiesced to British rule, even if they did not support it. And they owed nothing to Yakub Khan's son, who was just five years old; they were happy to take his family's money while they waited.

Roberts knew his intelligence was weak, so he had no idea of the strength of any forces against him, nor who would lead them. The winter came early that year, in mid-November. Roberts kept his inkstand under his pillow so the ink did not freeze, and three elephants died of cold on a hill east of the city, where they lay stinking for months as the ground was too hard to bury them and there was not enough wood to burn them.

Despite the apparent lull and Britain's military success, General Roberts himself made a list of what the Afghans might be able to complain about: "The prolonged occupation by foreign troops of the fortified cantonment which had been prepared by the late Amir Shir Ali for his own army; the capture of the large park of artillery, and of the vast munitions of war, which had raised the military strength of the Afghans to a standard unequalled among Asiatic nations; the destruction of their historic fortress, the residence of their kings; and, lastly, the imprisonment and deportation to India of their Amir and his principal ministers." All of these concerns might be exploited to "excite into vivid fanaticism the religious sentiment, which had ever formed a prominent trait in the Afghan character."

On December 8 Roberts ordered a parade to be held as a show of force at Sherpur, the fortified cantonment taken by Britain. This was an enormous site with low walls around a four-and-a-half-mile long perimeter, flanked by the Bemaru Hills. One corner covered the ground where General Elphinstone's cantonment had been before the destruction of his force in its retreat to the east in the winter of 1841. But the parade had to be abandoned as Roberts heard of large Afghan forces coming from the south and the west, and quickly sent troops out to engage them. British forces took heavy casualties in a series of running battles.

The hostile force quickly numbered about 100,000 men. A correspondent for the London *Daily News* reported, "The enemy fought desperately, and many of the inhabitants of the city joined his ranks; the villagers too, cut up any soldier who got separated from his comrades, even though he happened to be under the very entrenchments of our camp."

One of the main leaders of the uprising was Mohammed Jan, written off in a British intelligence assessment as a "drunkard and smoker of hemp." He turned out to be a good commander and an impressive artillery officer. One cavalry engagement cost 27 British dead, about one-sixth of those engaged, and more than 50 horses. Roberts ordered a retreat into Sherpur and prepared its defenses for a siege.

The first snow of winter had fallen, and Roberts paid exorbitant prices for sheepskin coats brought in from Persia to protect his force from the cold. For almost two weeks the British came under intense attack. As in 1841, the Afghans made good use of the high ground to fire into Sherpur, and were now equipped with British-origin Snider rifles as well as jezails. British attempts to break out were repulsed. On December 23 the Afghans made their most concerted assault. A General Hugh Gough was hit by a bullet, but saved by the suit of chain mail he had thought to bring from home—in what must surely have been the final use of medieval armor on a British battlefield. The following day the assault was abandoned and "The city lay before them undefended," in the words of the Kabul historian Nancy Dupree. "The British emerged from behind the walls of Sherpur to find the mountains and the plains which had bristled with thousands of hostile tribesmen now quiet and serene."

The disappearance of the enemy was as sudden as their appearance. They melted away just as they had in the Khyber Pass in the first engagement of the war more than a year before: violence, deception, feint. Everything was an illusion. Reports that a British relief column was on its way played some part in the abrupt ending of the second siege of Sherpur, but there was another process at work, which the British army at the time missed altogether.

Afghanistan was refusing to be dismembered, dropped down a fissure through the ground as if a casualty of an earthquake. For a century Britain had fought across the subcontinent, beating the great powers of the time—Tipu Sultan's southern forces, the Mahrattas, the Sikhs. They did not see that the Pashtuns, and the other tribes quarried from the landscape of Afghanistan, were different. They would not be annexed, in a "piece of rascality," like Sind. Even Russia had paused at the Oxus, after buying or beating, cajoling, but ultimately conquering, all of the peoples they saw as barbarians in Central Asia along the way.

In the twenty-first century, as military strategists again tried to grapple with Afghanistan, the slaughter of the First Anglo-Afghan War was often quoted as a lesson in the consequences of failure. An analysis of the events of December 1879 in the second war would be far more instructive. Roberts and his staff may have waged a successful military campaign, but they did not understand how power worked. They saw the amir's family as savages, the sirdars as duplicitous, the mullah with the fragrant name as a joke and the rebel leader as just a hemp smoker; they went sailing while a rebellion swirled around them, missing the signals that a storm was about to break over their heads; and they missed the significance of the sudden peace.

The Afghan leaders, "warlords" in modern terminology, were using the ancient tactics of mobile indigenous forces, inflicting harm where they could but avoiding confrontation, wearing down their opponents—tactics noted by the historian Herodotus as long as 2,500 years ago to explain how the Scythian nomads of central Asia beat King Darius, whose belief in the power of his military forces matched that of Britain in the nineteenth century or of the United States in the twenty-first. Darius's conventional army set off into Scythian territory but never saw its enemy, who constantly retreated into land they knew well, harrying where they could, until Darius gave up, suffering heavy losses as he retreated.

In the same way, the Taliban changed their tactics after suffering heavy casualties in set-piece engagements in 2006, the year the insurgency against the U.S.-led invasion of 2001 first intensified into open warfare. The Taliban moved from massed attacks to classic small-scale guerrilla raids and asymmetric techniques such as suicide attacks in a shifting alliance with other factions and interests, including the opium trade. They would take ground if it was offered to them, as in the town of Musa Qala, which they held for a year, but they never needed to win engagements on the ground as long as they kept up the pressure. Winning was not about tactical military advances but support in the villages and, always the most important thing in Afghanistan, the *perception* of victory—which way the wind of war was blowing. Force was threatened much more than it was used.

Victory on the battlefield was not the point. The Afghans in 1879 learned in the one set-piece confrontation on the Charasiab ridge that they would not defeat the British army in open warfare. So they avoided it. They were quarrelsome and confrontational with each other—weaknesses in conventional war, but qualities that gave them flexibility and unbeatable power in an insurgency. Their disunity generated centrifugal forces that made the country ungovernable and gave them a sinuous strength when they came together.

Of all of the foreign attempts to control Afghanistan in the two centuries after Elphinstone's first meeting in 1808, the Soviet invasion in 1979 was the one that came closest to success. And when the Soviet-backed government finally crumbled, the disunity of the forces that had ousted it flared into open civil war. Power had spun out of Kabul and could not be drawn back. In Afghanistan, the imposition of power from the center has always been temporary—like gathering together sand or water—since local loyalty outweighs any other. However strong the weapons of foreign forces, they have always achieved less than local forces, which can gather and disperse at will, as General Roberts experienced in the siege of December 1879.

A Russian analysis of British problems in the Second Anglo-Afghan War assessed this well: "English commanders understood that they had not gained possession of all of those strips of country over which the troops had passed, but only of the actual ground on which their forces were encamped."

General Roberts took over in Kabul again, but the insurgency had done its job, sending a signal well beyond Sherpur. In India and London, Forward policy hawks were now rethinking their options. The length of the military operation, the savagery of the death of Cavagnari and his escort, the cost of occupation and the sudden twists and turns of the war led to new instructions going out to an experienced frontier officer, Sir Lepel Griffin. The British no longer wanted to dismember or annex Afghanistan; they wanted to hand it over.

— — —

In March 1880, with the country still leaderless, Abdur Rahman made his move, crossing the Oxus River after 11 years in exile in Russian territory, initially supported by only a small force. As he moved south gathering strength, Britain corresponded with him, probing what he could deliver as amir. By the time he was strong enough to cross the Hindu Kush and camp in Charikar, north of Kabul, the government had changed in London, and with it British policy over Afghanistan. The Forward policy, already facing searching questions because of the failure of the war, went into sharp reverse.

The replacement of Disraeli by William Ewart Gladstone in April 1880 had brought a new moral tone to Britain's handling of international affairs, of the sort that would not reemerge until the election of Tony Blair's New Labour government in 1997. Gladstone took the high moral ground over Afghanistan in particular. During an election tour when he attracted huge audiences in the Scottish region of Midlothian in December 1879, he highlighted military atrocities allegedly carried out by the column commanded by General Roberts during the first phase of the war a year earlier.

Several dozen villages had been burned in retribution for an attack on British forces in Khost in the East—not far from where the Osama bin Laden would later build his Tora Bora cave complex—and 130 prisoners killed. A locally recruited Pashtun officer had been cleared by an inquiry, but the incident was witnessed by a reporter for the London *Evening Standard*, traveling with the army, and led to questions in Parliament. Gladstone used the incident to talk of the "rights of the savage," recounting the slaughter in the snow in as emotional a way he could, since his audience included women who, he claimed, had little taste for "the harder, sterner and drier lessons of politics."

Now in government, he wanted a radical new approach, and the first dispatch from Lord Hartington, Gladstone's new secretary of state for India, to his new viceroy was scathing of a Tory policy that had led to "the assumption of fresh and unwelcome liabilities" for Britain "and a condition of anarchy" throughout Afghanistan. Some British soldiers had now been in Afghanistan for two years, and General Roberts himself wanted withdrawal as soon as practicable: "I feel sure I am right when I say that the less the Afghans see of us the less they will dislike us."

Sir Lepel Griffin continued to correspond with Abdur Rahman, even after letters were found to be passing between him and the rebel mullah Mushk-i-Alam, but contingency plans were also drawn up to put Yakub Khan back in power instead, as if the British had not learned from the first war that an amir imposed by Britain was bound to be mistrusted. Abdur Rahman understood this very well: "If I showed any inclination towards the English, my people would call me an infidel for joining hands with infidels, and they would proclaim a religious holy war against me." He added that it was hard for an Afghan leader to alter 50 years of mistrust when each side had called the other "treacherous, unreliable, and breakers of oaths."

By the late spring of 1880, as the snows melted and the water flowed off the Hindu Kush to turn the valleys to the south green on either side of the flat gravel-covered moonscape of the plain north of Charikar, Afghan power flowed to four small tents pitched close together in the center of a military camp. Abdur Rahman sat, in one of the four identical tents, waiting and planning, "an extremely able man, the like of him has never been seen in this country" in the words of a British visitor. Knowing that Britain had no other realistic choice for amir, he delayed agreement with them. He wanted to know what terms they were offering, whether he held Kandahar, and "what enemy of the British government am I expected to repel."

Abdur Rahman had been taught his military skills as a child by a British officer called Campbell, who had commanded the army of his father. It was a tough upbringing. He had been imprisoned for a year after falling out with a powerful figure in court. When he was released, his father's British-born commander was dead, and he took control of the army himself, winning his first major battle when he was only 20. In the 1860s, in the murderous tussle for power after the death of Dost Mohammed, his armies took land as far south as Kandahar, before being flung back north.

Defeated, Abdur Rahman had turned down the standard British offer of a pension and a bungalow in Rawalpindi. "I had never seen the benefit of English friendship. They were the enemies of my friends, whose enemies were my enemies." It was a specific rejection of the terms of the treaty signed by Dost Mohammed in 1857.

When he later made his only trip to India in 1885, Abdur Rahman was confirmed in his decision not to accept the invitation. He found himself lining up among other petitioning princes from different parts of India: "the poor things were all dressed like women, wearing diamond pins in their hair, earrings, bracelets, necklaces, and other pieces of jewellery usually worn by women. The straps of their trousers were jewelled, and little bells were hanging in front of their trousers as low as their feet. They were sunk in ignorance, laziness, and indulgence. They did not know what was going on in the world nor what was in it…they spend their time in drinking and smoking opium."

Instead, after his defeat as a young man, Abdur Rahman had traveled around Afghanistan, and his account of his journey during a long winter reads like a dream, half seen, half remembered, filled with myth, mysticism and visions of lost kings.

When he lost his last battle and fled, all his cavalry dispersed, except for 40 men, who remained with him all his life and became his most senior military leaders. While he was sitting at the campfire one night, cooking a piece of meat in a blackened and beaten saucepan, a dog tipped it over and grabbed the meat, running off into the snow. It was his lowest moment, defeated by a stray dog; only days earlier he had been able to command a kitchen that could feed an army. A friend sent 200 gold coins, but they could not be exchanged, so he and his men remained poor and hungry,

In the frontier region a figure dressed in men's clothing ran up. It turned out to be a woman taken by Waziris when she was 12 years old. Abdur Rahman pulled her up on his horse and took her away to freedom. In another village there was a surreal fight over a sheep that they had bought, killed and were preparing to cook. The man who had sold it wanted them to bring it back to life. While they were arguing, a "king" appeared—a tattered character with bells on his bridle, who called himself Shah Jahan (one of the early Mogul emperors) and led them past an abandoned village where he said "Dost Mohammed" lived, making a halfhearted attempt to rob them along the way. They headed on through heavy rain to a village where two small dancing boys greeted them. And then they plunged into a long journey across a desert where the "horses' tongues were as if they were made of wood."

North of his former kingdom, Abdur Rahman met the khan of Khiva, whose 60 gunners were "all negroes." Then after trekking up the Silk Road, he arrived in Samarkand and lived under Russia's wing for 11 years, developing respect for them. His first son was born there. From Samarkand he had watched perplexed as Shir Ali tried to court Russian support, abandoning his alliance with Britain and falling into the Second Anglo-Afghan War. "He had not sufficient sense to understand that property which is not saleable in one market was of no value in the other." On his return to Afghanistan, Abdur Rahman knew that gaining power required a deal with Britain, but he wanted it on his terms.

As the summer drew on, the precarious position of British forces across the country became increasingly obvious. Griffin feared severe trouble after harvest time in July. "In a country like Afghanistan...where the people are ignorant, and where popular opinion is formed and directed by the Mulla class, the most fanatical and inimical to the English—it is impossible to predict with any certainty in what direction the next outbreak may occur."

Elements of the Forward policy ambition for Afghanistan had lingered, with a call from the army that had taken Kandahar that the South at least should remain under British control, as had been the plan when they took it. But plans changed when a huge Afghan force was said to be mobilizing nearby, and rumors of war spread panic in Kandahar: "The rich citizens have quietly fled from the place with their families and property. The people are burying their money and ornaments. The Hindu merchants are so alarmed that they have closed their shops. The panic is still stronger in the Fort."

In late July, ignoring Abdur Rahman's lack of agreement over terms, Griffin held a *durbar*, a grand meeting for tribal leaders, in Kabul, and proclaimed him amir in his absence. Abdur Rahman pointedly had not even yet arrived in the capital. But Britain's war was not over just because it had found someone to run the country. A week after the durbar, news arrived in Kabul of the catastrophic defeat of British forces at Maiwand, near Kandahar, by an Afghan army from Herat.

Britain had never tried to garrison Herat. In the general disorder of 1879 after the British invasion, Ayub Khan, another of Dost's grandsons, had made the short journey from exile in Persia and seized the city. He had as good a claim to be amir as Abdur Rahman, and in the summer of 1880, he raised a large army and marched on Kandahar, gathering tribal support as he went.

In a doomed remnant of the policy of dividing Afghanistan that had taken Britain to war, Kandahar had been handed over to the next generation of the alternative Sadozai royal line, Shir Ali—no relation of the amir of the same name. The aim was to keep Kandahar out of the deal being offered to Abdur Rahman.

It was the last attempt by Britain to install a ruler in Afghanistan until 2001, and indeed the last moment of power for the Sadozais—descendants of the father of the nation Ahmed Shah Durrani. With a British sword of honor buckled around his waist, Shir Ali was anointed *wali* of Kandahar, and said he hoped he might have "an opportunity of showing his readiness to draw it in the cause of the British government." But when they heard of the size of the army coming from the West, his forces promptly abandoned the British side, whereupon the wali unbuckled his sword of honor and fled to retirement and a British pension in Karachi.

The British defenders of Kandahar, who did not expect the pace of the advance from the West, sent out a slow-moving column led by General George Burrows. The attacking force led by Ayub Khan had considerable support from qizalbashes, Persian cavalry, and was traveling over terrain it knew. Far more lightly equipped than British troops, the Afghans crossed the Helmand River and advanced on Kandahar. The British force arrived on the flat plain near the little mud fort at Maiwand to find a huge Afghan army in battle formation, with cavalry and artillery ahead of them, and thousands of white-shirted ghazis, flags billowing in the wind, to their right.

Poor logistics had caused the British to dump much of their ammunition into a river for lack of transport, and they ran out of artillery shells after the first exchange of fire. Much of the British artillery then withdrew, with consequent loss of morale. The British were then squeezed by the Afghans moving forward in a crescent-shape formation. Retreat became rout. The message flashed to the viceroy read: "Total defeat and dispersion of General Burrows's force." Almost 1,000 men died, more than a third of the force, the worst British defeat on the battlefield in Asia.

The battle of Maiwand gave Afghans a legend: They remember how a heroine, Malalai, urged on the troops, waving her veil as a standard before she was killed. Into the twenty-first century she was still used in battle by the Taliban with poetry telling of love or martyrdom: "My lover if you are martyred in the battle of Maiwand, I will weave a coffin for you from the tresses of my hair."

Two days after news of the battle reached Kabul, Abdur Rahman agreed to become amir on British terms, although they still would not put the assurances he wanted in writing. Once again an Afghan amir would depend on goodwill, while even after the scale of the defeat in the South Britain made demands on him. Clever at constructing a narrative of heroic victory in the aftermath of defeat, Victorian England thrilled to the account of the relief column put together by General Roberts, which marched 334 miles in 23 days and defeated Ayub Khan the day after its arrival in the South.

What the British narrative of Roberts's march south did not highlight were the orders given by the new amir, Abdur Rahman, that the column should be given safe passage and Afghan cavalry escorts. He was now in control of Afghanistan. By the spring of 1881, Abdur Rahman had taken Kandahar and Herat, defeating his cousin Ayub Khan and leaving Britain with not much to show for the war.

In the meeting with Griffin at which he finally accepted British terms to become amir, Abdur Rahman described the Afghanistan he inherited from them in terms that could have been written after the conflict in 2001. "The country is in a deplorable condition. Everything which belonged to the state is ruined and requires renewal. The people are, as you can see, most turbulent and untractable, and devour all they can."

There is a postscript to the Second Anglo-Afghan War with contemporary resonance. On Saturday, January 17, 1880, a religious student, a *talib*, made history.

In the words of an anonymous diary: "This morning a man who had been allowed to enter the outer gate of the citadel with a load of wood, threw it down and attacked Sergeant Miller, of the Engineers, with a knife. A Havildar of Sappers standing by hit him with a pickaxe before he had time to strike. The *ghazi* was not well known here, but his dress showed him to be a *talib-ul-ulm* of the country beyond Kelat-i-Ghilzai. He was of extremely small frame and very much emaciated."

It was the first recorded suicide attack in Kandahar.

PART THREE

MAKING THE FRONTIER: THE THIRD ANGLO-AFGHAN WAR AND AFGHAN REFORM, 1880–1933

ROSHAN
SHIGNAN
WAKHAN
KAFIRISTAN
GILGIT
CHITRAL
ASMAR
KHYBER PASS
SWAT
BUNER
KASHMIR
CHAKDARA
MALAKAND
HAZARA
SRINAGAR
KABUL
JALALABAD
WHITE MOUNTAIN RANGE
PESHAWAR
BLACK MOUNTAIN
ATTOCK
Kabul River
Kunar River
TIRAH
Kurram Valley
RAWALPINDI
Jhelum River
Chenab River
Sutlej River
WAZIRISTAN
Indus River
WANO
KHOJAK PASS
CHAMAN
QUETTA

NORTH-WEST FRONTIER
AFTER 1893

BOLAN PASS

6

THE OASIS WAR AND THE DURAND LINE

How can a small Power like Afghanistan, which is like a goat between these lions, or a grain of wheat between two strong millstones of the grinding mill, stand in the midway of the stones without being ground to dust.

—Abdur Rahman, amir of Afghanistan, 1880–1901

In 1885, in a battle for control of an oasis on a disputed border, Russia and Britain came closer to war than at any other time during the years of the Great Game. This was at a time when the two great powers realized they needed to draw a line around Afghanistan and mark out the ground, if neither was going to put troops inside the country. The oasis was in the unmarked sands to the west of Afghanistan, but it was the border drawn along the country's eastern flank—the Durand Line—that would see more continuing conflict across it over the next century than any other frontier in the world.

Russia had continued to probe south, especially when Britain's attention was fully occupied in Afghanistan. In 1879, in a repeat of the failure of the opportunistic Russian move across the desert during the First Anglo-Afghan War, an initial Russian advance on the deserts west of Afghanistan was defeated by agile nomad Turkmen horsemen, and suffered heavy losses. Russia's commander General Alexei Lomakin faced a problem familiar to British armies on the other side of Afghanistan: the death of 12,000 camels in three weeks left him unable to move.

It was the most audacious Russian attempt to take land after years of gradual advances across the desert toward the west of Afghanistan, where fine sand like powder, whipped by hot winds in the summer and the savage cold of fierce winter nights, made this one of the most unforgiving terrains in the world.

Two years after Lomakin's defeat, in January 1881, a much larger Russian force returned to defeat the Turkmen and threaten the substantial prize of Merv, with its oasis. This was one of the ancient cities of the world, the capital of Khorassan, an old name for Afghanistan. Russia wanted to ensure that Merv would not be part of the modern Afghanistan. The city controlled a large area of desert northwest of the Hindu Kush, a busy trading area in the ancient world, but now an empty quarter, where the winds blew sand onto the ruins.

By the nineteenth century, Merv did not naturally fit anywhere. When Burnes had traveled to the region in 1832, it was held by Khiva. Fifty years later, Britain did not appreciate Russia's ambition, nor its ability to move that far that fast. In 1882, when Russia offered a meeting to draw up a border, the offer was ignored in London, and the chance to negotiate its future was lost.

In 1884 Russia made its inevitable move, annexing Merv and biting a slice from what Abdur Rahman called "Afghanistan's North-West Frontier." His warnings had been ignored. London knew a response was essential—politicians were hit by what one observer called "Mervousness." It had been three-quarters of a century since the East India Company analyst John Crokatt first noticed a "threat of immediate danger" to British control of India from Russia. None could now deny the immediacy of the threat. The seizure of Merv brought Russian forces and a railway line to within 200 miles of Herat, with no natural obstacles in between.

Russia procrastinated as Britain sought to negotiate. Both sides set off to map the desert, the British force led by the geographer Colonel Thomas Holdich, a laconic adventurer who was to play a crucial role in drawing the border of Afghanistan.

As he headed west toward Persia, Holdich believed that no Englishman had been even as far as Herat since Pottinger had helped to defend it against the Persians 50 years before. The whole of the ground west of Kandahar was unmapped—Helmand just an "open field." The account left by Alexander the Great was still the most recent guide available to him. Twenty-three centuries earlier the Greeks had brought their elephants down to southern Helmand in the winter, where it was warmer than on the high mountain plateau farther north. The place they had camped became known as Lashkar Gar—literally "the place of the warriors." It was to become the main headquarters of British forces in 2006.

Holdich led his force beyond Herat through the winter of 1884, drawing and surveying as they went. "Pheasant shooting and camel fights were our relaxation from the monotony of mapping." But there was urgency in the task. He knew that Russian officers in the field had much more independence than their British counterparts: Seizing ground made careers on the Russian frontier.

The British force numbered 3,000 in all, including camp followers. New, more compact horse feed made it easier to travel without the old armies of grass cutters. The expedition had been equipped not to fight but to impress the Russians, with "tents such as have never before been seen in Turkestan, mess equipment and mess tents, stores of wine and delicacies such as might serve the purpose of a royal banquet." The Russians preferred their own sweet sparkling wine to the French champagne carted across the desert by the British force, but did develop a taste for English ginger wine when the two sides met, circling around the subject of the frontier as they each sought out the other's true intentions.

Directly south of Merv, halfway to Herat, lay the next strategic oasis, Panjdeh. The first attempt by Russia to move in had led to strong protests from local Afghan leaders, and the Russian force withdrew. But there was silence from the Gladstone government, which was opposed to any further military adventures in Afghanistan. In India, Forward policy veterans muttered that the lack of a robust response would have consequences.

The Russians were led by a locally recruited officer, Colonel Ali Khan, his name Russified to Ali Khanoff. While his surveyors were enjoying English ginger wine, Khanoff probed again and again toward Panjdeh, knowing that control would give Russia another huge triangle of desert, access to water at a vital rail bridgehead, and make his name. When Khanoff pounced, Holdich himself was at Panjdeh, and believed the British should have gone forward to support Afghan defenses. But he was ordered to withdraw, and complained that he was put in a "false position...the sort of position that only an irresolute government could be responsible for producing."

Holdich concluded his last local negotiations with Khanoff at 3 A.M., and "the morning broke gloomily over the damp plains of Panjdeh." Clouds and drizzle concealed the Russian advance in the dawn. Outnumbered and outgunned, the Afghans were easily defeated and slaughtered in their trenches. As British troops withdrew, they tried to offer medical assistance to the wounded, but a local chief sent them a pair of dilapidated boots as an insult—a signal they should leave.

Khanoff now offered 400 rupees for the head of any British officer, and the British force tried to disentangle itself from the Afghan withdrawal, losing all its camels and dogs as it went. Holdich noted, "A rabble of beaten soldiery is not a nice rabble at any time, and it became a dangerous rabble when composed of Afghans all more or less prepared to lay their disasters at our door."

It was a bitter day, made worse by a freezing wind. The next morning the horses were covered in ice, "as if clad in iron." Holdich withdrew his force to assist in the defense of Herat, now a rich target of opportunity for an ascendant Russian commander who Britain had seen was willing to take chances where they lay. The British force assisted in the destruction of several blue-tiled minarets and a medieval mosque in order to give a clear line of sight against the

Russian threat: "The most glorious productions of Mohammedan architecture in the fifteenth century, having survived the barbarism of four centuries, were now razed to the ground under the eyes, and with the approval, of the English," wrote the travel writer Robert Byron, as he later surveyed the curious scene—a field of scattered minarets left isolated in a landscape where all the other buildings had been flattened.

If Khanoff's advance had failed, his actions would have likely been disowned by Russia. But Russia admired bold moves that were successful, and its newspapers took it for granted that Russian forces would continue forward and take Herat.

News of the fall of Panjdeh was broken to Abdur Rahman by the Indian foreign secretary, Sir Henry Mortimer Durand. The amir was making his only visit to India, to meet a new viceroy in 1885, when the disaster happened. He had a right to be disappointed, as his understanding of the terms he had been offered when he came to power compelled Britain to come to his aid. He later wrote contemptuously: "The English army and officials were so frightened and nervous, that they fled in wild confusion, not knowing friends from foes, and owing to the intense cold, several of their poor native followers lost their lives in falling from their ponies as they rode along."

But Abdur Rahman continued to seek protection from Britain, believing that ultimately Afghanistan faced a greater threat from Russia, whose border continued to move remorselessly south "like an elephant," crushing everything in its way: The Russian policy of aggression is slow and steady, but firm and unchangeable." Besides, he preferred British civilization. He had an English governess for his children, an English tailor, an Irish dentist and an irrepressible cockney engineer, Thomas Salter Pyne, whose whisky glass he personally filled, and whom he confided in, as long as Pyne continued to turn out high-quality copies of European guns in his Kabul factory.

Success in warfare was becoming dependent on engineers like Pyne. Better guns, and railways to carry troops, had changed the strategic map of Asia. Russian railways were being hammered into the sands in territory that had traditionally been subject to Afghan influence to the north and west, while British railway tracks continued to spin their spider's web across the map to the east.

Abdur Rahman had never accepted British influence in the Suleiman Mountains. To him the frontier region was "the hereditary property of Afghan kings, being part of their country" all the way to the Indus River. A railway line to Quetta, the route into Kandahar and the south of Afghanistan was just like "pushing a knife into my vitals," he wrote in a letter Durand called "embarrassing, stubborn and impertinent." And Abdur Rahman knew Britain had plans to go further. His spies brought news of a shed full of railway tracks marked "For the line to Kandahar." He proposed instead that the frontier mountains should remain under Afghan control. If Russia attacked, then he, the amir, would be able to recruit the frontier tribes to fight for Britain and not against. Prophetically he wrote, "If you should cut them out of my dominions, they will neither be of any use to you nor to me; you will always be engaged in fighting and troubles with them, and they will always go on plundering."

Durand was sent to Kabul to sort out the border issue once and for all. Britain sought control of all of the land around the strategic passes into Afghanistan. Durand approached the negotiations with the instincts of a bureaucrat, as if tidying up a few final details. But he felt there were few men in India now who really *understood* the frontier. As Abdur Rahman pushed across the mountains into areas close to British forces, the British response—holding back and trying to talk—would make another war with Afghanistan inevitable. Why could they not see it? But India was run by men who did not know a "Pathan from a Poobah."

Durand, a stiff, unimaginative, unclubbable man, saw Abdur Rahman as a "brutal savage" and thought he had the measure of him. "The Amir is not the Emperor of Germany, and to treat Afghan filibusters with diplomatic tenderness is pure folly. What they understand and expect is action, not talk." He had turned down a job in Burma because he wanted to remain and sort out the frontier question. But he felt himself surrounded by men who had never "seen an Afghani or given study to frontier questions. Their arguments fill one with despair." He was short of money and could not afford to go to England for a break. "As for me, I can do no good now, and I am afraid that the present state of things must end in a smash, while my own position is most unpleasant."

Durand had other personal preoccupations as well. His father had been criticized in a new book for abandoning his post during the Indian Mutiny, and while trying to clear his father's name, he was also writing to everyone he knew to help his son get into officer training at Sandhurst. He feared the boy would not pass the exams and might need a helping hand. Durand could feel the sands of time shifting under his feet. The India he knew of adventurers and empire builders was changing. In a private letter he wrote, "Englishmen are being excluded in favor of natives in all directions."

Durand had a naive belief in the indomitable power of British military might in all circumstances. He admitted that he had once been a "Lawrence man," wary of entanglement beyond the Indus, but by now was a committed believer in going Forward. Ignoring the evidence of decades of military intervention with no victory, he believed that once the frontier tribes were under the British, they would soon fall into line. "I am quite sure that these tribes are very much overrated, and that we have shown an unnecessary and unwise timidity in shrinking from the task of controlling them."

Among his papers Durand carried a copy of the last messages of Macnaghten from Kabul in 1840, to remind him of the dangers of getting it wrong. Britain now had its own history in Afghanistan—memories that did not rely on the campaigns of Alexander the Great. The military geography of Afghanistan had not changed since it was laid out so clearly in Lieutenant Macartney's map, but the Russian border was now much closer to India than it had been then.

Durand also carried an intelligence overview of the whole border question, by a Major Robert Warburton. "The Russian Warning" was a Forward policy manifesto of the most extreme sort: a rabid call to arms, frothing and foaming with warnings of how "socialism" was being given a foothold now that Indians were being educated. Warburton had learned none of the lessons of the Second Anglo-Afghan War. After securing control of the passes across the Suleiman Mountains, he wondered if Britain should take Kabul and hold the triangle from Jalalabad to Kabul and south to Ghazni in order to command access to the Hindu Kush. Britain's policy should be based on one principle: "Never to give the Russians an entry into the plains of Hindustan. Every endeavour should be made to fight them in Afghan soil and outside British possessions."

Durand used Warburton's analysis of the 108 passes across the Suleiman Mountains. Only a handful had any military use, but Warburton believed it essential to own them all to guarantee control. The key ones were the Khyber Pass, the 20-mile avenue controlling the main access to Kabul in the North; the Bolan Pass to Quetta in the South; and the Shutar Gardan, the back door to Kabul in the crook of the Camel's Neck halfway between. Durand knew that his most difficult negotiations would center on Waziristan; control of the Waziris was crucial to Britain's security. But despite Durand's huge confidence in the ability of the British imperial will to prevail, the Waziris would never be controlled.

In Kabul Abdur Rahman, who now held more Afghan territory than any amir for a century, was making elaborate preparations for the visit. A house in its own grounds was made ready for the party, away from the center of the city, since he wanted to reduce contact between his people and the British delegation. In his palace he prepared a room for the meetings with a curtain concealing a secret scribe who spoke both English and Dari to keep minutes for him, and he wanted all of the meetings to be held openly with witnesses present. There was to be no backstairs twisting of arms.

The Russians were not idle. Another of their frontier young bucks, Colonel Vannovsky, had taken his troops into Roshan, a tiny kingdom in the northeast of Afghanistan that Abdur Rahman had seized a decade before, along with the neighboring area, Shignan. Vannovsky was no maverick border adventurer; this was a calculated move by St. Petersburg to put pressure on the talks in Kabul. The two mountain statelets straddled the upper reaches of the Oxus River. Just in case no one had noticed, Vannovsky sent a messenger to Abdur Rahman to say he was there.

The amir sent the Russian letter on to Durand, who received it in Jalalabad, on his way to the talks. It seemed "civil enough," and he sent a "colourless answer" back to the amir, trying not to stoke up the fire. He was certainly not going to send troops to protect Afghan land, as the amir wanted. In fact, the Russian move may have played directly into British hands. Durand wanted permanently to secure a sliver of Afghan land pointing like a finger directly up to the northeast to the Chinese border. The Wakhan Corridor, 218 miles long but only 11 miles wide at its narrowest point, was a natural geographical barrier of high mountains with few passes. He wanted it to be a political barrier too—keeping Russia out of the vast, almost uninhabited wastes above British India.

The disputed kingdoms, Roshan and Shignan, were north of the Wakhan corridor, and in order to be able to sell the deal to Russia—in the spirit of creating an Afghanistan that was a true buffer zone—Durand needed Russia to have a stable border too. Across most of northern Afghanistan, Britain believed the best border was the Oxus River, which flows from the Wakhan region westward in a great arch forming the northeast tip of Afghanistan and then cuts directly west, wide and deep, gathering strength as one of the world's great rivers, before ceasing to be the Afghan border and sheering off to the north to drain into the Aral Sea. Where it runs through Roshan and Shignan, the Oxus is just a narrow stream, but it was still a much better border than any other.

South of the Wakhan Corridor lie the huge snow-covered wastes of the western Himalayas, including the world's second highest mountain, K2. This was the land immortalized in Rudyard Kipling's Great Game novel *Kim*, concerning a conspiracy of "five confederated Kings, who had no business to confederate," in Chitral, Gilgit, Hunza, Nagar, and Dir. British policy toward this trackless region was still evolving in 1893, and Durand's brother was one of the officers who moved between the "Kings," so he would have known the problems as well as anyone. In his letter to the amir, Durand made it clear that Britain would not deploy forces against Russia. He feared that the letter would upset him, and he warned the viceroy Lord Lansdowne, "You must not be astonished if, to use Rudyard Kipling's elegant expression, 'the hand begins to play.'"

A week after the British delegation arrived on Afghan soil, Abdur Rahman sent Pyne to join them on the last leg of the journey to Kabul. He would prove to be an invaluable intermediary between the stiff-collared Durand and the suspicious amir. He had a natural charm. While mocking his cockney accent in asides, Durand thought Pyne a "genial wine-bibber, with a real fund of anecdote and an acute sense of the ridiculous...real common sense in certain ways and self-restraint. There is no doubt that he is a man of unusual character." Pyne woke up the whole camp one evening by shooting a hole in the roof of his tent with his revolver.

Pyne's key message on his arrival in the British camp was the amir's concern about the Russian incursion. He said that Abdur Rahman was "sick with anxiety" and not happy with the British advice to let the Russians pass through without incident. Pyne told Durand that he should give Abdur Rahman guns or the "promise of guns thereafter" to show they trusted him and to provide him with the ability to parade his strength. Durand replied, "I don't carry guns about in my waistcoat pockets, but I suppose we should be ready to give him a few hereafter."

All the ingredients for the summit were now in place, with the parties displaying their opening hands while keeping their aces concealed. Britain had been harassing Abdur Rahman's officials in the frontier regions for the last couple of years, and the viceroy had choked off his gun supply, so Durand would have something to give in return for the amir agreeing to the new border. Russia was at the table, in spirit if not in fact—exerting pressure short of conflict. And Abdur Rahman had something to complain about, loudly—the Russian incursion—while saying nothing about the much bigger border questions in the South.

On October 1, 1893, with the weather still warm, Durand caught his first glimpse of the Bala Hissar across the Kabul plain. He had been a political officer attached to General Roberts's Army of Retribution in 1879 and found it "intensely interesting to see all the old places again." They made camp ahead of a formal arrival in the city the following day close to a "rather ghastly illustration" of the amir's methods. An iron cage by the roadside contained some human bones, "the remains of a noted highwayman who was caught and left in the cage to die." He had survived for 16 days.

Abdur Rahman had changed since Durand had last seen him in 1885, "with his new white teeth from O'Meara, and his ready smile and joke, quite different from the Afghan wild boar of '85 with his scowl and his tusks." Abdur Rahman was very short, but had a large head and penetrating eyes. He succeeded in embarrassing his Victorian guest: Durand confessed that the amir "held my hand so long and was very affectionate that I began to feel quite uncomfortable."

It was clear that Abdur Rahman was in no hurry to get down to business. For days, instead of an invitation to talks, the amir sent gifts and visitors to the British house—cucumbers, apricots, a squirrel-skin blanket and a barber, "an awful old ruffian, who looked as if he would cut one's throat for sixpence." Durand tried not to show his anxiety for progress as Pyne kept him entertained and showed him his gun factory. He told Durand that Abdur Rahman thought of nothing else. When someone gave him a telescope he said, "Oh, blow the moon. What's the use of the moon to me? Can't you make a gun of it?"

Five days after their arrival, Abdur Rahman sent across a map. It was a bold opening gambit, conceding nothing, and handing the Wakhan Corridor to Russia. Durand was relaxed about it, although he confided his fears to Lansdowne that perhaps the amir had done a deal with Russia, dropping his claim to Wakhan in return for retaining all of Roshan and Shignan, including the areas east of the Oxus. None of this mattered compared to Britain's territorial ambitions in the main Pashtun areas farther south—they were shadowboxing ahead of the main fight.

When they finally got down to talking, the atmosphere was good-humored. Abdur Rahman said he had a cold and, miming the pouring of a bottle, said he could not warm himself as they could, since he was a Muslim. Durand told him that the British demand to delimit the border relied on the 1873 agreement, which made Afghanistan a buffer zone between Britain and Russia—an agreement that Shir Ali had come to Simla to sign. Abdur Rahman sighed and said that Shir Ali had been a fool, and during the days that passed with no more meetings, he asked for the British copy of the agreement. Durand sent it along with the treaties signed by the Afghans in 1884. This "leaves him not a leg to stand on. But he may elect to stand on his head."

More days passed, with more requests for letters and maps coming from Abdur Rahman, while cold winds blew the fine Afghan dust into everything, bending double the forest of poplars outside Durand's house. Indian camp followers were now visiting the Kabul bazaars every day, and Durand was afraid of trouble breaking out between them and Afghans if the talks went on too long. He discovered that a draftsman working for the British side had been leaking details of their position to the amir, and feared that further delay could wreck the process. He began to dangle an offer of guns in front of the amir, at Pyne's suggestion, and realized how valuable it had been that Lansdowne had cut off the supply before the talks.

Durand wrote to Lansdowne, "I cannot help a sort of feeling of pity for him—standing there fighting his game out against Russia and England—absolutely alone. There is something rather touching about it." Durand was frustrated by the formality of the process and the snail's pace. "Alone with him I am sure I could convince him." Abdur Rahman's negotiating strategy was vindicated in this one sentence. He was never going to sit alone with Durand to "have things explained to him."

Finally, in the last few days of October, almost a month after their arrival, Durand began to get indications that a deal would emerge. As he rode toward a meeting with the amir, Durand saw the bodies of four people who had been executed "insufficiently buried" by the roadside, and farther on, the head and naked torso of a general, sticking out of the ground, still alive in the perishing wind, half buried as a punishment.

Now the negotiations became crude—one disputed frontier region, Chageh, was bought for 100,000 rupees. But the amir still resisted handing over Chaman, where Britain wanted to build its railway in the South, Asmar, in the North, and Waziristan itself. He warned again and again of the perils of partitioning Waziristan. Who would deal with the divided tribes, or those that moved in summer and winter between what was now going to be British and Afghan territory? For Durand none of this was of any concern. His map was not about the people who lived in these areas but the military geography. As long as Britain controlled access to the Shutar Gardan Pass, the Camel's Neck, then the question of summer and winter pastures was of no interest. His overwhelming belief in the civilizing power of the empire blinded him to the trouble he was inviting. "After all," he said to the amir, "you will only be losing a little population and a little wealth."

Abdur Rahman held Durand's gaze for a long time in response, and then answered with just one word—*Nam*—honor.

The next day a request arrived for a large sum of money in return for the partition of Waziristan. Durand derided it as a "rather stupid letter," but if all they were haggling over was the price, he knew that the negotiations had effectively ended. The maps passed to and fro during the next two weeks until, on November 12, almost six weeks after the talks began, they had a deal. Durand had secured the Wakhan Corridor as an Afghan buffer zone sheltering the roof of the British Indian world, control of all the passes across the Suleiman Mountains, and had conceded only an area north of the Khyber Pass that Britain believed to be of little strategic significance—the Asmar Valley, and the area of Kafiristan that went with it. In return, Britain agreed to raise its subsidy to the amir by 50 percent, to 1.8 million rupees; as for trade, all that Abdur Rahman asked for was the right to sell Afghan brandy and opium in India. As Durand took the quick way home, a raft down the Kabul River, he heard intelligence reports that the amir was already writing "fiercely" to people, "informing them that we have now given him a clear line round his country, which neither the Russians nor we will overstep."

Durand never saw what he had done in dividing Pashtun territory. He thought it meant Britain now had "our hands free on the frontier." Rather than freeing them, however, it tied British hands in the North-West Frontier region in ways that he could not have dreamed of. When the Sikhs had controlled the land west of the Indus in the 1830s, they had stopped short of going into the mountains with good reason. By insisting on control of the passes, and pushing the border into the Pashtun mountain fastness of Waziristan, Britain ensured permanent instability in the frontier region, with consequences lasting until today.

The one concession Durand made to Abdur Rahman—ceding the Asmar Walley and dividing Kafiristan—caused a storm of protest in Britain. The Kafirs were a strange mystical tribe, with their own religion that had enough similarity to Greek mythology to lend credence to the legend that they were left over from the days of Alexander the Great. Kafirs had traditionally been taken in the region as slaves, and as soon as the border was drawn Afghan forces moved in, looting, murdering and forcibly converting the population to Islam as they went. The British antislavery campaign went into top gear, protesting and petitioning parliament. Sir Lepel Griffin, the official who had first offered Abdur Rahman the throne, was now retired and led the campaign. He wrote in the *Saturday Review*, "A tragedy is now impending, for which, if consummated, England will be directly responsible, and of which no time will ever suffice to efface the stain. The country of a lion-hearted race, which for 1000 years has successfully resisted Muhammedan conquest, is about to be invaded by the trained army of the Amir of Afghanistan. This will be done with the sanction and in the name of England."

The new viceroy, Lord Elgin, was contemptuous. He saw no virtue in the Kafirs and no merit to the notion that they were related to the Greeks (whose treasures from the Parthenon his own ancestor had so enthusiastically taken to London). "They appear...to be an ignorant, idolatrous, and slave-dealing race...with no national sentiment, and always feuding with one another."

The viceroy was already facing problems of his own in the areas that Durand had put on the British side of the contentious new border.

7

"TRIBES GENERALLY
ARE RISING"

*The next expedition to the Black Mountain will I hope be a very long time hence, and
Bajaur and Bunar will cease to have any terrors...I trust that we shall now take
annual revenue from the Waziris.*

—Sir Henry Mortimer Durand, architect of the agreement defining
the Afghan border, writing in 1895. Within months
the whole frontier—including these regions—was in flames.

The geographer sent to mark Durand's frontier on the ground, Colonel
Holdich, had also commanded the unit that had come close to war
with Russia over the Panjdeh oasis in the deserts on the western side of
Afghanistan. From the moment he first set eyes on the complex mountains that
would become India's North-West Frontier, he knew that this would be a far
harder task. And he could see immediately that the Pashtun tribes in this region
would cause trouble, noting wryly that the boundary had been drawn "between
them and some of their pleasantest summer resorts." When he climbed to the
top of the "Throne of Solomon," the mountain that gave the Suleiman Mountain
range its name, he could see 40,000 square miles in front of him. The curtain
of ice and snow that he had climbed was only one of a complex array of similar
peaks above 15,000 feet, not aligned in three distinct ranges as in the imagination of Lieutenant Macartney, but pitching and tossing against each other like a
frozen sea above the world, a backdrop hanging from an impossibly blue sky.

It was 1894. The British now had many years experience of dealing with
Afghanistan, but Holdich mused that they still did not know much about the
terrain. High as he was on the Throne of Solomon, a snow-covered saddle amid
the peaks, nothing grew. Lower down, looking across into Afghanistan, he

could see small firs dotted across the hilltops, sparsely as no rivers rose in the limestone range, and farther still the brown of the lower hills like dust cloths dropped from the peaks, folding one over another to the horizon. Any one of a thousand valleys could conceal an army.

North of where he stood, the Suleiman range pointed like an arrow into Afghanistan. At the end of the arrow was the high pass known as the Camel's Neck, still the British army's preferred route into Kabul. Beyond the Camel's Neck, the mountains bent back around to the straight line of peaks running east–west that formed his horizon—the Safed Koh, or White Mountain—the defining heights of the whole frontier region, flanking the range that was cut through by the Khyber Pass to the north. And the Khyber was the last useful gap before the mountains curled east around the top of India, higher and higher, beyond endurance, into the Himalayas.

In the creases and folds of the earth in front of the White Mountain lay the hidden villages of Tirah—remote, forbidding and hostile to outsiders—whose boast was that they had never been penetrated by a foreign army. Holdich knew the true heart of the frontier lay directly to the southeast in Waziristan, where there were no passes of any value to an army, but only dozens of tracks known by a nomadic people who considered the mountains their own, and had no concept of a frontier: natural guerrilla territory.

Since the early 1870s Britain had not tried to impose its law beyond where the first shadow of the hills fell. The plains west of the Indus were "settled" and taxed like the rest of British India. But the mountain tribes were left to administer themselves, and British officials called on maliks, local elders, to arbitrate if they had a problem. Some places, in particular Waziristan, were beyond even this rough-and-ready law. The tribal leaders here were too weak or unwilling to play Britain's game, and even the usual remedy of force did not work.

Holdich noted "the extreme difficulty of administering a satisfactory thrashing to a mountain-bred people who have ever an open door behind them." U.S. forces might have used other language but undoubtedly recognized the truth of this observation as they tried to control the Afghan side of the frontier in the war that began after 9/11, when Taliban and al-Qaeda fighters could cross to and from the Pakistani side of the frontier with ease. Marking Durand's Line in the mountains did not close the back door.

There was a singular harshness in the land and the people, and a complex faith of ritual and magic bubbled beneath the surface. On their way down from the peak, Holdich's local guide suddenly stopped the party and spoke to the mountain. He addressed the rocks in ringing tones, saying that they meant no harm and asking that they should be allowed to travel unmolested. It was an arresting moment, dramatic, weird and otherworldly. No one laughed.

On November 3, 1895, before first light, an attack on the first major party sent from the British side to demarcate the frontier at Wano in Waziristan led to the deaths of 4 officers and 17 men. The raiders stole 23 Martini rifles and 15 horses. The ferocious attack had been led by a mullah, and it demanded retribution. British officers asked tribal elders to deal with it themselves, but they replied honestly that they would not be able to impose any sanctions, since they had no power over the mullah.

The leader of the Wano raid was Mullah Powindah, one of a network of fundamentalist mystics who by the summer of 1897 had incited tens of thousands of Pashtun tribesmen to believe that Britain could be beaten. This movement rippling up the frontier from the southwest headed toward another wave led by Wahhabi-inspired Hindustani fanatics moving down from the northeast. Where the two forces met, in Swat in 1897, the frontier ignited, leading to the most serious challenge during all the years of British rule of the region.

In Kabul, Abdur Rahman gave the rebellion significant backing. He was careful to conceal this in public, since he did not want to provoke another British attack on Afghanistan. Britain preferred to give him the benefit of the doubt, believing his assurances even when intelligence reports suggested that he was inciting mullahs on the frontier. Rahman had always skillfully used political Islam to his advantage.

Before he became amir, as he crossed Afghanistan during the fighting in 1880, he had left letters in mosques saying that he had come to "liberate Afghanistan for Islam from the English," and he declared himself *imam* as well as *amir*—priest as well as king—claiming spiritual as well as political leadership.

This gave Abdur Rahman the authority to declare that if attacked by the British, Afghans should take up a jihad to repel them. His book on jihad, passed from hand to hand on the frontier, was as bloodthirsty as anything later written by Osama bin Laden, and even quoted from the same passage of the Koran always used by bin Laden in his statements, which instructed Muslims to put the demands of jihad over their family, tribe or property. This was a particularly significant call for Pashtuns, who put their loyalty to family and tribe above all else.

Abdur Rahman's book specifically mentioned the effectiveness of night raids, like the Wano ambush, where horses would "generate fire when their horseshoes touch the flint of the rock, lighting up the night." And he defined in poetic terms the glory of eternal life promised to those killed fighting jihad, whose souls would be "placed in the throat of green-winged birds who circle in the air, and make their nests in the branches of the most blessed tree in paradise." Such images were an inspiration to poor and dispossessed frontier people, and stirred them to revolution.

Abdur Rahman was not a Wahhabi, nor were the mullahs he inspired, Mullah Powindah in Waziristan and the Mullah of Haddah—"the Light of Islam." But although they did not share precisely the same Wahhabi Islamist outlook as Mullah Sadullah in Swat—known as the "Mad Mullah" or Mad Fakir" by British troops—all could agree on the need for jihad against British rule.

The ability of Muslims with different views of jihad and various political ends to join against a common enemy would have profound importance when the frontier again became the front line, a crucible of violence, in the conflict that began in the late twentieth century. The frontier villages in Waziristan and Tirah that gave the best support to the Taliban and the foreign fighters in al-Qaeda were the same ones who had supported the mujahidin a decade before in the U.S.-backed fight against the Soviet Union. They had been quickest to rise against Britain in the nineteenth century then to find common cause against a common enemy: first Britain, later the Soviet Union, then the U.S.-led invasion.

There is another sinister similarity between the conflicts of the nineteenth century and later. Just as Amir Abdur Rahman incited jihad while claiming the opposite, receiving British guns and a salary all the while, so President Musharraf of Pakistan signed up enthusiastically for the "war on terror," receiving billions of dollars in military and other aid, while his intelligence forces continued to play a double game, supporting jihad in Afghanistan. These two Muslim leaders were playing the same game in conflicts more than a century apart as if on opposite sides of a mirror, promoting jihad across the same frontier while denying it at the same time. By 2001, Pakistan had been promoting jihad across the frontier for a generation, and it was hard to stop. The conflict had initially been assisted by billions of U.S. dollars in the war against Russia in the 1980s, radicalizing a new generation, leading directly to the rise of the Taliban, and turning Afghanistan and the frontier into a safe haven for those who wanted a global jihad.

Across this frontier, something bigger was always at stake in conflicts than power or land. For many in the field this was a duel between different world-views—a clash of civilizations. Britain in the 1890s characterized the mullahs as "crafty, bigoted and supercilious" men, preying on a credulous and superstitious people. But to the mountain tribes who followed them into war, they were a powerful political force that might rid them of the threat of alien rule.

At the end of the nineteenth century on the frontier, the enemy was not just British rule but British ideas, and progress. "The priesthood, knowing that their authority would be weakened by civilisation, have used their religious influence on the people to foment a general rising," wrote Winston Churchill, who had taken leave of absence from the Indian Army to work as a war correspondent for the *Daily Telegraph* during the 1897 uprising. "Embedding" as a correspondent then was a far more engaged business than in later conflicts—Churchill found himself drafted in as an officer to make up the numbers for one battle, and Lord Fincastle, correspondent for *The Times*, actually won a Victoria Cross for attempting to rescue a wounded officer. The man who died in the attempted rescue was another journalist, reporting for the *Times of India*, who had also taken leave of absence from his regiment.

With an extravagant disregard for what would later be called political correctness, Churchill noted a bloodthirsty impulse in Islam: "That religion, which above all others was founded and propagated by the sword—the tenets and principles of which are instinct with incentives to slaughter and which in three continents has produced fighting breeds of men—stimulates a wild and merciless fanaticism." On the frontier with its history of warfare, this became an explosive mixture: "the Mahommedan religion increases, instead of lessening, the fury of intolerance. It was originally propagated by the sword, and ever since, its votaries have been subject, above the people of all other creeds, to this form of madness. In a moment the fruits of patient toil, the prospects of material prosperity, the fear of death itself, are flung aside. The more emotional Pathans are powerless to resist. All rational considerations are forgotten. Seizing their weapons, they become *ghazis*—as dangerous and as sensible as mad dogs: fit only to be treated as such."

Churchill reserved special venom for men known as taliban, religious students: "a host of wandering Talib-ul-ulms, who correspond with the theological students in Turkey, and live free at the expense of the people." The way Churchill told it, the sexual morality of these taliban was rather different from the reputation of those who took over the government of Afghanistan exactly a century later: "they enjoy a sort of 'droit du seigneur,' and no man's wife or daughter is safe from them. Of some of their manners and morals it is impossible to write."

— — —

The problems in Swat, where the 1897 uprising ignited, went back to the building of a road. Roads brought progress and trade; to Churchill the Swat road represented the best hope of spreading the values of the empire: "As the sun of civilisation rose above the hills, the fair flowers of commerce unfolded, and the streams of supply and demand, hitherto congealed by the frost of barbarism, were thawed."

The road had been built to ensure stability in Chitral, the northernmost town of any size before the uninhabited high Himalayas. For 20 years the ruler of Chitral had been a quiescent British ally, but he died in 1892 leaving too many sons and an ambitious brother. With Abdur Rahman in Kabul playing off one pretender against another, and an anti-British tribal leader, Umra Khan, plotting from the east, sometimes in league with the Afghan amir and sometimes against him, the next three years were unstable and bloody for Chitral. As brother murdered brother in a Shakespearean orgy of violence, Britain found it hard to realize its three ambitions: influence Chitral, keep Russia at arm's length and demarcate a stable border between India and Afghanistan. In the winter of 1894, a small British force was besieged in Chitral fort, and Britain went to war to get its men out.

By then Holdich was inside Afghanistan negotiating where the frontier should run in the area north of the Khyber Pass. The first thing he knew of the siege was when a group of Chitralis came across the mountains to his camp on the Afghan side, demanding protection. They were "idle, good for nothing, and happy-hearted people, who have a deadly propensity for wholesale murder and family butchery...not a fighting people, but in a country such as theirs...a race of monkeys could make themselves respected as foes if they took to defensive tactics."

Holdich witnessed Afghan government support for the anti-British forces in Chitral. Abdur Rahman's commander-in-chief, Ghulam Haider, a close ally of one of the most political mullahs, was running guns through the camp, and an Afghan unit that Holdich had inspected as a formality on his arrival suddenly disappeared, he thought across the border in the direction of the conflict.

He also heard that the Afghan government was encouraging the frontier chiefs, maliks, to attack the British. They were "promised ammunition as well as compensation in kind for any loss of grain...special concessions have been promised the leading maliks who have property on both sides of the border." The camp became increasingly dangerous: Besides the Chitrali refugees, there were hostages taken by the Afghans from villages on the other side during the border demarcation, and forces loyal to the rebel leader Umra Khan appeared. When Holdich tried to send a Chitrali messenger across the mountains to the besieged British garrison in the fort, the messenger was shot before he had even left the Afghan camp.

The fort at Chitral was relieved before the arrival of the main British force after an epic march across the snow-covered passes from Gilgit in the east by a small force under Colonel James Kelly, a maneuver of extraordinary bravura, pushing mules laden with guns up mountains, across rivers and fighting all the way. A British officer in the fort, Sir George Robertson, said that when the relief force arrived, "All seemed to think, from Kelly downwards, that their march was a mere trifle, their hardships undeserving of reference." Meanwhile 16,399 British troops were sent through the Swat Valley to subdue the tribes all the way up the road to Chitral—a massive movement of men—and this was before the general uprising along the frontier broke out.

Britain installed a 14-year-old prince, Shuja al-Mulk, as leader in Chitral. But there were the same arguments as in Waziristan over how deeply they should become involved in the mountains. The engineers wanted to build a permanent road to guarantee swift movement of reinforcements, but pushing a road into tribal territory made it look as if it was being colonized, and incorporated into the settled areas of British India. The engineers had their way, and the controversial road was pushed across difficult terrain up to Chitral. Sir Lepel Griffin, now retired, wrote to *The Times*, "This policy consists in spending a quarter of a million annually on a post of defence and observation which defends and observes nothing, and on the maintenance of a road which leads nowhere."

The expense was not only in building the road and defending it; tribes along the route needed to be compensated for not collecting tolls—Britain was buying peace. Troops in the Malakand garrison on the new road also paid for the fodder and grain they obtained from local people, rather than seizing it, while their doctor treated 7,000 people, many from "the fanatical priestly classes."

The priestly classes had their own plans. The British force may have paid for rice, the fanatics could make it appear at will in a bowl to feed a crowd; the British military road carried ammunition to Chitral, the fanatics claimed to make bullets turn to water; and to match the British queen-empress, the fanatics produced a boy they claimed was the last survivor of the Mogul line, the Muslim emperors of India. Their leader, Mullah Sadullah, was not afraid. He could conjure up flags to appear with his forces in the field, and make them immune to gunfire. It was a win/win proposition: If his protection did not work, then as martyrs in jihad against Britain, his warriors had a special place in paradise, and he issued elaborate scrolls to say so.

The two British garrisons on the road from the plains, at Malakand, and the more remote fort of Chakdara guarding a bridge across the Swat River, were further fortified. But plans to send reinforcements up from the plains were put on hold, in case they only aggravated the situation. The scale and the ferocity of what happened next was beyond such rational military thinking.

The cry of jihad had been raised often on the frontier since the Hindustani fanatics had first mobilized the Swat tribes against the Sikhs 60 years before, but the Mad Fakir now led the most determined campaign for deliverance from the British. On July 21, 1897, he prophesied that by the next full moon, the British soldiers would have been driven back to the plains.

The way Churchill told it, Swati tribesmen watching polo were sporting enough to wait until the game had finished before leaving to arm themselves for the fight that they knew would start that night, even whispering a warning into the ears of locally hired grooms as they left. "They knew, these Pathans, what was coming. The wave of fanaticism was sweeping down the valley. It would carry them away. They were powerless to resist. Like one who feels a fit coming on, they waited. Nor did they care very much. When the Mad Fakir arrived, they would fight and kill the infidels. In the meantime there was no necessity to deprive them of their ponies."

Lieutenant Harry Rattray, the commander of the detachment at the small Chakdara fort, left the polo ground to return to his post when an urgent message arrived to say that tribesmen were massing around his fort. He rode back to take command before it was dark, straight through a group of local tribesmen who did not try to stop him. He managed to send a message to Malakand to warn them before the line was cut and every telegraph pole along the new British road burned to the ground. A brief telegram was sent from the headquarters in Swat to the viceroy in India: "Tribes generally are rising."

Rattray's fort was surrounded by high ground, and the enemy could fire into it day and night, joined by the irregular forces that Britain had paid to protect the road using their British-supplied rifles. A small relief detachment of cavalry arrived the day after the siege began, after a desperate ride from Malakand, fording a river and crossing paddy fields, where the horses sank deep in the mud while "the bullets of the enemy made watery flashes on all sides." After five days of fighting, Rattray sent a simple message by heliograph, the letters flashing from his signal tower: "HELP US." The signal tower was 200 yards from the main fort, and it was hard to supply the men there with water. He had also lost his hospital building to the enemy, who were using it as another firing position. Rattray estimated up to 14,000 surrounded the fort. When relief arrived at Chakdara after a week, 2000 tribesmen had been killed for the loss of 7 British dead.

The relief of Chakdara was carried out by a column from Malakand, itself under attack. Both the fighting and the weather had exacted their toll on the British forces. Twenty-one men in a detachment died of heat exhaustion after a forced march to relieve Malakand. There had been desperate hand-to-hand fighting as waves of tribesmen poured into the fort. A Sergeant Harrington saved his life by remaining motionless after dozens of Swatis broke into the hut he had been defending. They killed an officer, but although they felt along the walls, they never found him in the dark.

The political officer at Malakand, Major Harold Deane, saw the Mad Fakir advance toward British troops with crowds of unarmed teenage boys pushed ahead of him, among them "a boy aged thirteen or fourteen on whose head he bound a turban," perhaps the mysterious last prince of the Mogul dynasty. The boy was killed instantly. Some of the fanatics marched on British positions firing their rifles straight up into the air, believing they were invulnerable. Among the white cotton clothing of the Swat warriors, increasing numbers of black- and blue-clad warriors could be seen—men of the Bunerwal, Wahhabi Hindustani fanatics.

A British infantry officer wrote, "Bands of *ghazis*, worked up by their religious enthusiasm into a frenzy of fanatical excitement, would charge our breastworks again and again, leaving their dead in scores after each repulse, while the standard bearers would encourage their efforts by shouting, with much beating of tom-toms, and other musical instruments."

As Britain regained control of the Chitral road and the two forts, with a force of more than 11,000 men under the command of General Sir Bindon Blood, word came that the "Mad Fakir," Mullah Sadullah, had survived, although injured, and had fled to the west to join forces with another fundamentalist mystic, the Mullah of Haddah—the man anointed by Abdur Rahman as "the Light of Islam."

The tribal chiefs of Swat were now handing in a few weapons and swearing obedience to Britain again. Beaten in a fair fight, they could not understand why retribution should inevitably follow. "No black looks, no sullen reserve, marred the geniality of their welcome," wrote Churchill. "As we approached the first fortified village the sovereign and his army rode out to meet us, and with many protestations of fidelity, expressed his joy at our safe arrival."

The local slang term for British officers was *shikar*, hunter, since that was how they were first encountered, coming up into the mountains to shoot game. It led to a Pashtun saying: "You should always kill an Englishman. First comes one as a *shikar*, then two to make a map, and then an army to take the country, so better to kill the first one." But in the battles for the Chitral road, the shikari had won. Should that not be an end to it?

"It was not, however, possible to accept this sportsmanlike view of the situation," wrote Churchill.

They were asked where were the rifles they had been ordered to surrender. At this they looked blank. There were no rifles. There never had been any rifles. Let the soldiers search the fort and see for themselves. The order was given; three or four *sowars* drew their carbines, dismounted and entered the great and heavy gate, which had been suspiciously opened a little way.

The gate gave access to a small courtyard, commanded on every side by an interior defense. In front was a large low room of uncertain dimensions: a kind of guard-house. It simply hummed with men. The outer walls were nearly five feet thick and would have resisted the fire of mountain guns. It was a strong place. The Lancers, accustomed to the operation of hunting for arms, hurriedly searched the likely and usual places, but without success. One thing, however, they noticed, which they immediately reported.

There were no women and children in the fort. This had a sinister aspect. Our visit was unexpected and had taken them by surprise, but they were prepared for all emergencies. They had hidden their rifles and cleared for action. The two chiefs smiled in superior virtue. Of course there were no rifles. But matters took, for them, an unexpected turn. They had no rifles—said Major Deane—very well, they should come themselves. He turned to an officer of the Lancers; a section rode forward and surrounded both men. Resistance was useless. Flight was impossible. They were prisoners. Yet they behaved with Oriental composure and calmly accepted the inevitable. They ordered their ponies and, mounting, rode behind us under escort.

The British force moved up the Swat Valley in the later months of 1897, destroying defenses, burning crops and negotiating with tribal elders, but to Churchill's dismay they remained in Swat, rather than heading east to the lair of the Hindustani fanatics. General Blood was keen to press home the advantage, but with memories of the difficulties of the Ambeyla campaign in 1863, and a reluctance to push deep into the mountains, the government held back. Building the Chitral road had been controversial enough; now that it had been retaken, there was no reason to go farther.

The paradox at the heart of frontier policy was exposed: Britain could not successfully annex it, or leave it alone. The mountains and the men who fought in them had lost a battle—they always would in a straight contest against a large and technically superior force—but they were still free, and always would be. Fields could be replanted, walls rebuilt, tribes rearmed. Churchill expressed the frustration of the military men in the field, who felt they had done only half a job and that their failure to finish it would have consequences. "The news...spread like wild fire along the frontier, and revived the spirits of the tribes. They fancied they detected a sign of weakness. Nor were they altogether wrong. But the weakness was moral rather than physical."

In late August, a month after the Mullah Sadullah had first gathered his banners, there was a raid by warriors from Mohmand at the west of the frontier on a Hindu village within sight of a British fort near Peshawar. This was seen as a far more serious incident than the uprisings in Waziristan or Swat because it was an incursion from the mountains into the "settled areas"—British India itself. The telegraph crackled to Simla with a report to the government of India that called the raid the "most open and audacious violation of British territory which has occurred in the Peshawar District, or indeed in any Frontier district for many years."

Half of General Blood's Malakand force was sent west to Mohmand to "inflict severe punishment." They found themselves facing a far more competent enemy than the hordes of ghazis who had offered themselves for slaughter in front of their guns in Swat. The Mohmand tribesmen deployed classic guerrilla tactics: avoiding set-piece battles, withdrawing and then ambushing the better-equipped British force. In one engagement Churchill nearly lost his life and wrote that "the actual casualties were, in proportion to the numbers engaged, greater than in any action of the British army in India for many years.

Out of a force which at no time exceeded 1000 men, nine British officers, four native officers, and 136 soldiers were either killed or wounded."

The Mohmands were defeated, and among the rifles handed in was one identified as having come from the British army defeated at Maiwand. The uprising was now causing profound concern, and questions were asked about the wisdom of the past policy of paying subsidies to the mountain tribes and letting them govern themselves. When the revolt then spread to the Orakzai and Afridi tribes, it shook at the foundations of frontier policy. These tribes were not only loyal and the main source of Pashtun recruits to the British frontier regiments; the Afridis were also the guardians of the Khyber Pass.

The viceroy Lord Elgin wrote to London, demanding the right to inflict severe punishment: "the unprovoked aggression on Khyber pass gravely affects our position on the frontier, and is calculated seriously to weaken us in relation to tribes generally." The fall of the Khyber was the worst British miscalculation of the summer. Reports that the Afridis and Orakzais were rising were initially discounted because of their loyalty, so preparations to deal with the outbreak were slow and late. And even when there was no doubt that 10,000 Afridis were moving toward the pass, the British still hoped that a locally raised force, the Khyber Rifles would stick to their treaty obligations, so did not reinforce them with regular troops. Many Afridi British soldiers remained loyal, but they were rapidly outnumbered by those who changed sides. As the rebels swept down the pass, they burned British border posts behind them.

The British defense at Landi Kotal, the gateway to the Khyber Pass, was under Subedar Mursil Khan, an Afridi who had one son under his command and two in the attacking force. He led a small defense detachment of just 374 men, many of whom fled at the start of the fighting. The battle for the fortress went on for a day and a night, until the gates were treacherously opened from the inside. During the negotiations that followed, Mursil Khan was killed, and the fort and 50,000 rounds of ammunition fell into rebel hands. An afternoon's ride away, a relief column in Peshawar waited for orders. But no orders came. Churchill called it the "shocking and disgraceful desertion of the forts." At an angry public meeting in Simla, a civilian received considerable applause when he said that "the 23rd of August was a day of pain and humiliation for every Englishman in India. We had 12,000 troops at the mouth of the pass...marking time...and we allowed those forts to fall one after the other."

By October, General Sir William Lockhart had assembled a force of 43,703 troops to save the frontier. And this army, then the largest put together in Asia under a single British general, was still heavily outnumbered. The fall of the Khyber Pass had led to a general mobilization of tribal warriors in Tirah, the mysterious and enclosed region beneath the shelf of the Safed Koh. Lockhart inserted his force here to split the rebellion and prevent the union of forces from Waziristan and Tirah.

The battle at the start of the Tirah campaign in October was one of the most controversial of the war. Gordon Highlanders, with Gurkha assistance, and against little opposition, took a lofty ridge, the Dargai Heights. It was a commanding position, 5,000 feet up, and looked down from a series of ledges over open ground. But Lockhart abandoned the ridge, because he could not easily supply those who held it. When the British force next looked up there were 12,000 well-armed tribal warriors on top of the heights, who had no concern about supplying themselves. After a day in which every effort to retake the Dargai Heights was beaten back, the same two regiments, Gordon Highlanders and Gurkhas, fought their way up again, taking 200 casualties, including 39 dead. It was a reverse of the usual frontier battles in which British defenders would inflict heavy casualties on a tribal assault.

General Lockhart then fought his way into Tirah, proud to have broken the "boast of the tribes" that it was impregnable. And after his force spent months burning villages, and destroying livelihoods, they withdrew.

Experienced military voices were now asking whether all the punishing and crushing, pulling down towers and trampling crops under the feet of elephants, had done any good at all. Half a century of "butcher and bolt" had not brought peace. Lord Roberts, who left India as a field marshal in 1893 after 41 years, had seen much of this at firsthand. He wrote, "Burning houses and destroying crops unless followed up by some sort of authority and jurisdiction, mean...for us a rich harvest of hatred and revenge."

Retribution had been a central policy for Britain in controlling its Asian empire. Anyone who killed a British soldier had to know there would be a heavy price to pay. One of Kipling's darkest poems, "The Grave of the Hundred Dead," tells of how all must know that a "a white man's head must be paid with heads five-score." A locally recruited platoon count up the heads of rebels killed in revenge for one English officer: "Each man bearing a basket / Red as his palms that day...And the drip-drip-drip from the baskets / Reddened the grass by the way."

But after the 1897 uprising there was a growing realization that "blockades and small punitive expeditions" might not work anymore; the frontier tribes were flexing a new kind of strength, and among the rebels were men who had learned modern ways to fight as British soldiers. Reasons given for the revolt included concern over the Durand Line and an increased salt tax. But Britain understood the insurgency to stem mainly from the ability of the mullahs to gain a hold over "these ignorant, fanatical, bigoted, priest-ridden people, who absolutely believed that we should be driven out of the country." At the end of the nineteenth century, Britain had learned the power of a virulent strain of political Islam to mobilize revolution; it was a lesson forgotten until it had to be relearned at the end of the twentieth century.

After the uprising, the black-coated Wahhabi fighters, Churchill's "sombre-clad warriors of Ambeyla," were forced to move farther north, to an even more remote camp. But like their al-Qaeda successors, they were more than a camp, a base—they were an ideology, a mission, a mind-set—not to be defeated by force of arms. They continued to put out a newspaper, called the *Mujaheed*, which preached that it was the religious duty of all Muslims to wage jihad against the British.

The genie could not be put back in the bottle; something else needed to be tried. But the British did not know what that something should be. The decision to withdraw after taking the previously unconquered hills of Tirah led to another argument. The viceroy wrote, "We do not contemplate as the basis of settlement with Afridis...the annexation or permanent occupation of Tirah," adding, as if in an aside, "The Commander-in-Chief dissents."

Most were agreed that no "new responsibility should be undertaken, unless absolutely required by actual strategical necessities and the protection of the Indian border." But fierce political debates went on in London and India even over whether to continue to garrison the Swat road, let alone move farther into the frontier region.

There were calls for a more enlightened frontier policy, employing officers who spoke local languages and could avert the constant conflicts. By the turn of the century Britain could look back at two golden ages on the frontier—the time of Henry Lawrence's young men in the 1840s and 1850s, and Sir Robert Sandeman's control of the southern frontier area of Baluchistan, pushing forward to Quetta in 1879. Sandeman had stressed the need to "deal with the hearts and minds of the people"—an early use of the phrase that would come to define enlightened counterinsurgency strategy a century later. But some still wanted Britain to play no further role west of the Indus. In a debate in the Commons, one opposition Member of Parliament said that Britain had "no more right to be in Chitral than...in Timbuctoo."

Wars in Afghanistan and on the frontier book-ended Victoria's long reign. The First Anglo-Afghan War, within months of her coronation, scarred the reputation of the army in India for a generation; the second put an end to any thoughts of a garrison on the Hindu Kush. The 1897 uprising would pull British imperial ambition even farther back—to the eastern foot of the mountains, where the Sikh warrior-king Ranjit Singh had stopped in the 1830s.

The Marquess of Salisbury, prime minister when the queen-empress finally died, was confident that ultimately Britain would prevail: Control of "these splendid tribes" was an "inevitable conquest." But he was concerned about what might have been unleashed: "I do not underestimate the difficulty which all over the world we are feeling with the Mahomedan population wherever we come across them. There is an impulse stirring in them. A slight victory, an exaggerated victory, has recalled to them their past of a thousand years ago, when they were victors in every part of the world, and they cannot but believe that that glorious period of their history is to be repeated."

8

BOLT FROM THE BLUE

Considering how overtaken by surprise we were by what you rightly describe as a bolt from the blue I think that everything has gone off better than we had any right to hope it would.

—Sir George Roos-Keppel, British Commissioner in
the North-West Frontier Province, writing in 1919 as
an Afghan force attacked through the Khyber Pass and Waziristan

"His Highness asked me about his marital duties."

Times were changing. The sex life of the new amir was not what Major Robert Bird of the Britain's Indian Medical Service expected to be dealing with, but this was the twentieth century. Whatever he said, Freud would probably have approved. Two days later Amir Habibullah did not call Bird in until the afternoon, after spending the whole day in his harem, and said he felt "much better."

Habibullah had taken over as amir without opposition, on the death of his father, Abdur Rahman, in 1901. Afghanistan was entering a new century in which its ability to negotiate its way in the modern world—on sexuality and on so much else—would be tested, quite literally, to destruction. A century that would end in mutual incomprehension between the Taliban and the West began with the Afghan king consulting a British doctor about his sex life.

Habibullah was a short man, hugely fat, who enjoyed going slowly around his estate on a tricycle. He was moderate in sexual matters, since "his appearance gives no evidence of excess," whatever Bird meant by that as he obsessively recorded the sexual appetites of people he met. When the amir's senior adviser came in with a headache, Bird learned from an interpreter that his tastes were "far too connubial."

Bird had been initially called to Kabul in an emergency to save the amir's arm, injured when his gun burst while he was out hunting. In his diary the doctor was an unsympathetic observer of Habibullah's court. The palace was grimy and poorly maintained, and the water supply was contaminated, as the seals on the filters were broken. The cavalry drilled in a sloppy way, their uniform sashes worn the wrong way around; even on the amir's own carriage "the horses were unkempt, the harness dirty." Although the palace was beautifully furnished in an English style, with pure gold ornaments and fine carpets, there were inferior prints on the walls and, horror of horrors, "a Cadbury's advertisement book lying on the centre table. I told him this was hardly appropriate."

More seriously, Bird heard there had been food shortages for two years and an outbreak of cholera. Stocks of grain in the caves at the foot of the Buddhas at Bamiyan and elsewhere were low. There was hunger in the land, but Habibullah did not seem to notice. Like his father, he was preoccupied with guns and with strengthening Afghanistan against the inevitable Russian invasion. He thought Britain was ignoring the threat. "Afghanistan is the first step of the ladder," the amir told Bird. "The man who wants to strike must put his foot on something firm before he reaches over to strike with his sword." A Russian shadow was ever present. During the doctor's visit, three men who were believed to be Russian spies were discovered in Kabul; one was shot, one imprisoned and the third turned to work for Afghanistan.

When he came to power, Habibullah made the same complaint as every Afghan amir for half a century. Although Britain expected them to keep to their side of existing agreements, they had to renegotiate protection as a personal deal. It was a one-sided contract. Britain relied on the deal imposed on Shir Ali in 1873, which defined Afghanistan as a buffer state where Russia had no rights, and on the terms of the Gandamack Treaty, signed by Yakub Khan in the Second Anglo-Afghan War in 1879, handing over the right to manage Afghanistan's foreign policy to Britain, confirmed by Abdur Rahman before he became amir in a letter given to Sir Lepel Griffin in the tent at Charikar. One treaty imposed over the head of an amir, another extracted under the duress of war, and a signature on a letter by a man not even in power—these were the documents Britain relied on to control the foreign policy of Afghanistan. But the terms Britain would offer in return depended on the nature of the external threat, and needed constant renegotiation by succeeding amirs.

Afghanistan was paid handsomely for the relationship, and given weapons, but its unwillingness to open up further, allow foreign troops on its soil, or even a permanent embassy, was a source of constant frustration, especially as the amir was "unable to check the fanaticism" of his subjects, in the words of a new secretary of state for India, Lord Morley, in 1906.

It was hard to take this amir seriously. An invitation to India turned into high farce. The initial aim had been for Habibullah to spend a few days in Calcutta then join a shooting party in central India. But he was mesmerized by the nightlife and two English women in particular, ignoring the fact that one was married. At parties he was followed around by a servant carrying a velvet bag of gemstones, which he would hand out to women he fancied. He overstayed in Calcutta by weeks and missed the shoot, the main reason for the invitation.

His Afghan escort became restive, and after he visited a Masonic lodge, the decision was taken that he must leave following a rumor that he had become a Christian. Lord Kitchener, conqueror of Khartoum and commander in chief of the Indian Army, was recruited to bundle him onto a train late at night, threatening him with an uncomfortable boat trip instead if he did not do as he was told. Rumors of the amir's deviation from the Afghan norm in sex and religion led to a failed assassination attempt on the road back to Kabul.

By now the frontier region had been brought under the direct control of the viceroy rather than the neighboring Indian province of Punjab. But whatever political system was tried, Britain still felt the need to conduct frequent raids into the frontier region, particularly Waziristan. Lord Curzon, the most political of viceroys in this period, had long been opposed to the "infatuated nonsense" of the Forward policy. He wanted to put local forces in forward positions, with British troops in reserve to strike hard if needed—remarkably similar thinking to what was developed by British and Canadian forces in southern Afghanistan during the worsening insurgency in the war that followed 9/11. Afghan forces were to take the lead role in operations against the Taliban as far as possible, with the foreign troops and their heavy weapons in reserve.

Back at the beginning of the twentieth century on the frontier, whatever the policy was called—"close border," "modified forward"—for British soldiers, it was business as usual: "The sudden alarm, the long dust-choked ride through the stifling heat of a July night, clattering out to the stony glacis of the frontier hills, and away forty miles before dawn only to find as often as not that the birds had flown, leaving a trail of death and destruction behind them." Young officers on the ground became contemptuous of the military value of such missions, known to them as General Willcocks's Weekend Wars, "after General Sir James Willcocks, who waged them to the satisfaction of himself and of the government of India."

Curzon was brilliant, opinionated and impatient. By bringing the frontier under his direct control he thought he could shape a more consistent policy, less vulnerable to mood swings at Westminster. The region remained divided between the settled area, the mostly level ground west of the Indus, and the mountainous tribal areas beyond, which now came under central government influence but had more autonomy. The change emerged from Curzon's impatience that responsibility for what he saw as "most important sphere of activity" in Indian foreign policy was delegated to a regional government in Punjab, not controlled centrally. When he first became viceroy in 1900, he wrote a long memo, framed in the most undiplomatic terms, outlining the weaknesses of those who had run the Punjab government over the previous quarter of a century: "None had any substantial experience of the frontier."

Curzon liked to paint a sentimental picture of the frontier, where "young British officers have gone in and out among the tribes, lived with them, hunted with them...played polo with them." But the old arguments about the depth of engagement still went on. Moreover, direct rule did not persuade Kabul that the frontier area was permanently British, and the Durand Line remained an open wound. Whether for the vanity of individual commanders like General Willcocks or for any wider military purpose, constant skirmishing engaged another generation of British soldiers on the frontier.

At the most robust end of the spectrum sat Sir George Roos-Keppel, commissioner in the North-West Frontier Province, writing in 1916 after a quarter of a century on the frontier. There should be no more "butcher and bolt." The old policy of short expeditions "has had its day": What was needed was for the whole of the region to be crushed. Not taking control decisively when the Durand Line was drawn had been a mistake; the tribes needed to be militarily defeated *for their own good*. The frontier was seen almost as an unruly boy in a public school—in need of a good thrashing to bring him into line.

"I do not advocate the crushing and disarming of the tribes and the occupation of their country in any spirit of revenge—far from it—I look upon it...mainly in the interest of the tribes themselves—in fact as a scheme for the reclamation of a fine, manly and courageous people capable of great development and of becoming a source of strength instead of weakness to the Empire."

This scheme would be especially effective in Waziristan, "the plague spot of the whole frontier," and would end a situation where there were "hostile savages from one end of our border to the other...I would begin with the Mahsuds and Wazirs...I would go on to the Mohmands, Bajaur, Swat and Buner. There is not much fight in these people if they are attacked by a sufficient force and I do not think that these operations would prove very costly either in lives or money."

Whatever happened on the frontier, Roos-Keppel believed that war with Afghanistan was inevitable. As early as March 1916 he wrote "the belief is universal that we shall find ourselves at war with the Amir during the course of this summer." It would, however, be another three years before a joint force of Afghans and irregular tribal levies would pour down the Khyber Pass, crying "Death or freedom."

Although Habibullah was still taking a British subsidy, he had allowed a German mission to open in Kabul during World War I and even allowed Indian insurgents to set up a German-backed Provisional Government of India. Germany has the distinction of being the first foreign country to exploit jihad for its own ends in South Asia. Its agents spread an extraordinary rumor that the kaiser had secretly become a Muslim, so joining Germany's war against Britain was now an act of jihad. One German spy held meetings in villages, claiming to have the kaiser on the other end of an open two-way radio circuit while he negotiated with tribal elders, offering them extravagant gifts for support.

Germany's alliance with Turkey, home of the caliph, the historical leader of the world's Muslims, was central to this new alignment. Habibullah became increasingly concerned as several members of his family, and other leading Afghans, joined a War Party opposed to the continued connection with Britain. He had allowed the German delegation in for a while, and the Indian rebels to set up their provisional government, but he had gone no further than that and did not want to provoke Britain.

Habibullah's brother Nasrullah was a constant threat during his reign. As he operated on the amir in 1904, the Indian Army doctor, Major Bird, thought that Nasrullah's face expressed anything but brotherly concern. "I read it as expressing a fervent hope that something would go wrong. The moment I turned and caught his eye he squeezed out one tear, rather crocodilian."

But when an assassin finally did get Habibullah, while he was out hunting near Jalalabad in 1919, it was the amir's third son, Amanullah, then governor of Kabul, who seized his chance, took power and threw Nasrullah into jail, where he died soon afterward. War with Britain followed, partly to divert the attention of the tribes in case they blamed Amanullah for the death of his father. Amanullah's ally, the head of the armed forces, general Nadir Shah, had already moved out of Kabul. He was to play a crucial role in the war, leading his forces through the Camel's Neck into the Kurram Valley and encouraging a general tribal uprising in Waziristan on the British side of the Durand Line.

The war started with the distribution of a proclamation from Amanullah in Peshawar, appealing for a jihad against Britain. Afghan forces moved down the Khyber Pass, gathering tribal support along the way.

Exhausted by World War I, Britain found it hard to mobilize the forces it needed. Thousands refused the order to move up to the Khyber and remained under canvas in a mass protest that was not reported at the time. Those who would fight were often young and inexperienced, but within a week they had reversed Afghan gains in the Khyber Pass and pushed forward onto the plain toward Jalalabad, where British soldiers had been before. On May 9, 1919, south Asia saw its first air raid, as two war-worn Sopwith Camels dropped bombs on Afghan forces at Dakka. They did not have enough power to clear the surrounding mountains, so had the disconcerting experience of being shot down on as they flew along the Khyber Pass.

The planes had some psychological value, since tribesmen would flee from them, but the conditions were very tough. One plane mistook a dust storm for the ground, and landed on top of a tent; no one was hurt but the plane was destroyed. The only larger bomber available, a Handley-Page, bombed Kabul once. A convenient east wind blew it over the Khyber Mountains and by good fortune changed course to blow it home again after the raid.

There was mass desertion from British forces by frontier-recruited troops, but Roos-Keppel was surprised that there was not a more widespread revolt on the frontier. Other than "about a thousand scallywags," most remained calm. He wanted to go all the way to Kabul—another generation believing it could be done, brushing aside the lessons of history. "In the last forty years which have elapsed myths have grown up about the Afghan fighting strength and these are firmly believed by the people of India."

But the government in Delhi was resolutely opposed to such an entanglement, believing it would take more troops than were in the whole of India to occupy Afghanistan effectively. It ordered the main force not to push forward even as far as Jalalabad. Toward the end of May, less than a month after beginning the war, the amir sent envoys pleading for peace, but there would be three more months of fighting before the tribal regions were pacified again. Reinforcements of planes were sent from Mesopotamia, and by the end Britain had lost two shot down.

Over several rounds of peace talks Amanullah won the freedom he wanted. Britain's long and costly control of the foreign policy of a country where it could not even send its troops came to an end. The talks were prolonged while Britain sought a treaty to prevent Afghanistan falling straight into the hands of the new Soviet Union. Twice the British delegation set off homeward from Kabul following "absolutely final" treaty terms from Amanullah that were unacceptable, but each time they went back, while Turkey trained Afghan forces, and Soviet-backed Indian revolutionaries set up an office. The prospect of communist influence in a resurgent Islamic Afghanistan was potentially as bad as anything Britain had feared during the century-long Great Game.

The Russian Revolution had changed the dynamic in central Asia. Roos-Keppel saw it as a direct factor in the 1919 war: "I cannot help feeling that there is a great deal of Bolshevik influence in the Afghan lunacy." T. E. Lawrence, Lawrence of Arabia, while working in the region as a humble aircraft mechanic in the 1920s, thought that war between Britain and the Soviet Union over Afghanistan looked likely. "It's quite on the cards Russia may have her go in our time." But ultimately the Soviet Union needed better relations with Britain more than it needed Afghanistan. A Soviet delegation in Kabul in 1921 began by offering Afghanistan the return of the Panjdeh oasis and the slice of land taken with it as well as a large subsidy. But as the talks went on, the offer was withdrawn; once again the needs of Afghanistan were sacrificed to big-power politics, as newly communist Moscow looked over the frontier to British India.

As his Turkish-trained armed forces took shape, Amanullah was far more interested in an alliance with other Islamic powers and sent troops north across the Oxus to assist a Muslim revolt against Soviet control. But the rebellion fizzled out when its leader died, and Amanullah's dreams of expansion were further crushed when the Soviet Union seized control of Bokhara, pushing out its khan. The Soviet leader Joseph Stalin had begun by sending pacifying messages to the Muslim-majority regions of central Asia that Russia had gobbled up in its century-long push south, but then seized power by force where he could not foment revolution. Relations between Afghanistan and the Soviet Union became even more strained after Amanullah gave asylum to tens of thousands of Muslim rebels who had streamed south into Afghanistan across the Oxus.

The new amir had also been forced to give refuge to thousands of Indian Muslims who flooded along the Khyber into Afghanistan to live in protest at Britain's war on the Turkish caliphate. The "Khilafat" movement was designed to weaken British rule by draining India of people, but the rug was pulled from under this bizarre protest when Kemal Ataturk and his Young Turks founded the secular nationalist Turkish state that emerged from the rubble of World War I and terminated the caliphate. Shah Reza was reforming Persia along similar lines.

Amanullah was impatient for reform in Afghanistan too. Since 1911, a highly influential fortnightly magazine, Siraj-ul-Akbar (Great Light) published in Kabul, had been bringing Afghanistan into contact with the secular Islamic reform movement spreading worldwide. Founded by Mahmud Tarzi, who went on to become Afghan foreign minister, the magazine bound nationalism, religion and modern technological progress together in a way they had not been linked before, at least not in Afghanistan. Editorials extolled the benefits of schools, road building, chemists' shops and equality for women, alongside pieces about the need to reform Islam to take its place in the modern world. These were the earliest stirrings of a global Islamic movement—against imperialism and strongly anti-British.

The long years of plotting and reading Tarzi's reformist magazine could be put into effect once Amanullah was in government. Clothing took center stage in what became a battle over more than politics—it was a fight for the Afghan soul. Amanullah followed the lead of the reformers in Turkey and Persia to demand the opposite of what the Taliban would later try to impose: *Western* clothing should be worn as often as possible. To appear at court and in some other parts of Kabul men had to wear Western suits; turbans and lambskin hats were banned and replaced by bowlers and homburgs; women were encouraged to appear in public unveiled.

In a poor country it was not as easy to impose this as strictly as it had been imposed in Persia and Turkey. Visiting tribal leaders from outside Kabul were given Western suits when they arrived for meetings, suits that were solemnly reclaimed from them and folded up as they left town, to be given to the next visitor.

Amanullah was prone to walking about with a large pair of scissors to cut the clothes off anyone who did not follow his rules, but behind this clownish behavior was serious intent. In an effort to reform Islamic practice and reduce the influence of the mosques, he introduced education for mullahs and cut their government subsidies; a secular school of law was set up to replace Islamic judges; and in a direct assault on the Wahhabi tradition, any mullah trained in an Indian Deobandi college was disqualified from preaching.

Women were given freedom of choice in marriage, and there was support for women's associations. Extravagant spending on weddings was discouraged, and a minimum marriage age of 18 was stipulated for girls to get married. There was education for girls, and primary school classes became mixed up to age 11. Plans for hospitals, clean water, adult literacy classes, foreign language teaching and new newspapers poured forth. Slavery was banned and commerce encouraged. Whole factories were bought abroad and reassembled in Afghanistan. Amanullah looked beyond Afghanistan's Islamic allies, Turkey and Persia, which had inspired his reforms, for new links. Britain was kept at arm's length, but other European countries, in particular Germany and France, were encouraged to send engineers and archaeologists, as a museum was opened and Afghanistan's extraordinary past began to be unearthed.

But Amanullah's dreams were wrecked by the obdurate conservative tribal reality of Afghanistan. Only a few years later, in 1933, the travel writer Robert Byron would visit the shell of Amanullah's half-finished and now deserted grandiose new town at Paghman, in the hills near Kabul. He saw "a French municipal office, surrounded by a French municipal garden and entirely deserted. While below it, occupying the centre of the whole four mile vista, stands a German match factory in the ferro-concrete-farmhouse style...In each glade stands a house or office or theatre of such appalling aspect...that it is impossible to imagine where Amanullah could have found the architects to design them, even as a joke. But no, they are not a joke. Untenanted, shoddy and obscene, they defile the woods and streams and the view of the plain beneath."

The first uprising against Amanullah, in 1924, was led by mullahs from Khost in the East, who stirred people up holding a Koran in one hand and a copy of Amanullah's legal code in the other, and proclaiming that the country could not have both. The rising was crushed with the help of two planes bought from Britain and flown by German pilots, and the mullah seen as the main instigator was hanged. But at a national *loya jirga* (gathering of elders), Amanullah was forced to compromise on some of his reforms, in particular over women's rights.

His reform program regained impetus after a seven-month tour that took in several European countries in 1927–28. By the time Amanullah drove himself in a new Rolls-Royce back across the border from Persia into Herat, he had bought several more factories and had a clear plan for his country. He now called himself the king, not amir, of Afghanistan, and spoke for four days to a loya jirga, where he insisted on Western dress. A British observer thought the tribal chiefs "were an unhappy and pathetic sight. Clad in black morning coats and trousers, with white shirts, black ties, and soft hats, they looked very much more like caricatures of Nonconformist clergy than Ghilzai, Mangal, and other tribesmen."

Amanullah outlined a far more radical program than before, including the complete emancipation of women, monogamy and education for all. Just as the Taliban would later use the police to force women to cover up, so Amanullah employed them to persuade women to reveal more. Women in rural areas routinely went without a head covering for practical reasons, so they could work, and would put on a burqa to go to town. Under the new rules, in the new town of Paghman, women wearing any covering except for a specially designed flimsy veil would have it removed. The king's appeal to women to go bare-headed was answered by his queen dramatically removing her veil in public.

When the uprising that brought Amanullah down began months later, it was pictures of Queen Soraya in an evening gown taken on her trip to Europe, bare-armed and with a plunging neckline, that the mullahs showed to demonstrate how far things had gone. The spark for the revolt was the arrest and execution of five mullahs. As unrest spread, Amanullah desperately tried to rescind much of the reform program, and closed girls' schools. But it was too late, and he was forced to flee Kabul only six months after his bold schemes were outlined at Paghman. He rallied some support in Kandahar and in a desperate last move went to the shrine where the cloak of the Prophet was kept, declaring he was a good Muslim. By another man, the gesture might have seemed bold, but he was no Dost Mohammed, and his reign ended in bathos.

The throne was held for a while by a man known as Bacha Saqao, meaning "son of a water carrier," a Tajik bandit who had rallied enough force to take power. Afghanistan could never be ruled by a Tajik, but the real power brokers, the Pashtun tribal leaders, delayed giving their support to Amanullah's commander in chief, Nadir Shah, as he tried to restore order. It was only after Britain signaled quietly that "its" tribes would not be stopped if they wanted to cross the frontier to fight for Nadir Shah that the balance of power shifted decisively in his favor.

Bacha Saqao's forces were defeated on the ridge at Charasiab where British forces had won the decisive battle for Kabul in 1879. He barricaded himself into the palace, where his hostages included two members of Nadir's family, but the general did not flinch and ordered a bombing raid. Bacha Saqao's brief reign was over, and he was hanged.

They were perilous times. Nadir Shah knew the price he had to pay and allowed the tribes who had supported him to loot the capital, including the palace. Their loyalty was not to him but to themselves and their clans. And then, like the hordes that had appeared and disappeared, making and unmaking kings during Britain's attempts to take Afghanistan in the nineteenth century, they were gone. Nadir Shah, who was descended from another branch of the ruling Barakzai clan, took power for himself rather than trying to reinstall Amanullah, whose grandiose schemes had emptied the treasury.

Afghanistan's conservative tribal culture had defeated an invasion from abroad—not an invasion by foreign armies this time, but foreign ideas, particularly about the treatment of women. Of the Islamic countries that modernized in that unique window of opportunity after World War I, Turkey's secular path was the most robust, Persia looked determinedly westward for decades, but Afghanistan quickly turned back to what it knew. Amanullah's Western suits were put away, his new town abandoned. The boldest attempt to modernize Afghanistan had been made too quickly and chaotically to succeed, and without any attempt to build support outside a tiny Kabul elite.

Only four years later Nadir Shah was assassinated, but his brothers were now firmly in control. Afghanistan had peered over the precipice in the disorder that followed the death of Amanullah and backed the new dynasty. Nadir Shah's son Zahir, just 19, was put on the throne in 1933 and was to rule for 40 years of peace and relative prosperity.

PART FOUR

REVOLUTION AND THE SOVIET INVASION, 1973–1994

9

"MUSLIM REACTIONARIES"

When the highest political leaders of the USSR sent its forces into this war, they did not consider the historic, religious, and national particularities of Afghanistan.

—Postwar assessment of the Afghan war by the Russian General Staff

Congressman Charlie Wilson from Texas opened the door of his room in the Pearl Continental Hotel in Peshawar in January 1984 to greet one of the richest, and certainly the most influential, of Afghan leaders. Almost two centuries had passed since the first encounter between a Western emissary and an Afghan leader, but this meeting would have a more immediate impact on Afghanistan than when Elphinstone met Shah Shuja in the same town. Behind Wilson, climbing off the bed to greet the Afghan guest, was a former Miss Northern Hemisphere no less, known as Snowflake. Not wanting to expose too much flesh in this conservative Muslim town, Snowflake was covered up. Her version of modest was a pink nylon jumpsuit with a zip that ran from neck to navel, and the footwear she thought would put the Afghan visitor Gulbuddin Hekmatyar at his ease were combat boots, chosen because he was a warrior—the most prominent leader of the mujahidin, holy warriors, fighting the U.S.-financed war against Russia's invasion of Afghanistan.

Hekmatyar's dark expressionless eyes and thickset face, framed by the standard ragged Pashtun beard, showed no reaction, although he preferred his girls covered from head to toe by a burqa. As a student leader in Kabul in the late 1960s he had achieved notoriety by encouraging his followers to throw acid in the faces of girls whose heads were not completely covered. He was opposed to the drinking of alcohol too, but he would forgive Wilson anything because the congressman was bankrolling the war. Hekmatyar had become used to the whisky-drinking Texan having a different girl with him every time he came to town, and he was not going to complain.

Afghanistan's fate hung in the hands of a fun-loving buffoon and a psychopathic Islamo-fascist. And now the money was really beginning to make a difference. Only two years after this meeting, in 1986, a new leader in the Kremlin, Mikhail Gorbachev, would signal his desire to end the war, calling Afghanistan Russia's "bleeding wound."

Hekmatyar's progress, from acid-throwing student thug to someone the U.S. government would trust with billions of dollars, had begun in the early 1970s, as Afghanistan's longest period of stability under a single monarch began to unravel. Zahir Shah had been on the throne for 40 years when his cousin Daoud dislodged him in a palace coup in 1973, while Zahir was on a trip to Rome.

Afghanistan's long peace had brought some prosperity. During the cold war it was a member of the nonaligned group of nations, competed over by each side of the divided world. In Victorian times Britain had used guns and pensions; Afghanistan now found itself bribed by roads and power plants.

Development meant that in the 1970s, Afghanistan exported more raisins than California, mostly from Helmand in the Southwest, after the United States built a huge irrigation system, based on the model of the Tennessee Valley Authority; this was to come in useful later when opium poppies emerged as the staple crop in the region. Power for the capital came from a hydroelectric plant built by Germany, harnessing the force of the Kabul River as it plunged off the high central Asian plain and down toward the Indo-Gangetic lowlands to the east, while China put in the irrigation system that carried the melting snows of the Hindu Kush into the canals of the flat Shomali plain north of Kabul. Less than 5 percent of a country of deserts and mountains was irrigable agricultural land, so anything that carried water farther made a big difference.

But pressure for political and social reform had come with economic progress, and Daoud was impatient for radical change, wanting Afghanistan to join the modern world. He was from the tiny lucky elite that had received education abroad during the brief reform years under Amanullah in the 1920s and would govern as a president, not an amir.

About 15,000 foreigners lived in Kabul, mostly young people who had been in the vanguard of the social revolution of the 1960s, another tribe to add to Afghanistan's rich tapestry. In those far-off more innocent days before Iraq's collapse and the Ayatollah's revolution in Iran, it was possible to take a bus from London to Delhi across virtually open borders. Hippies brought in their lifestyle, and took back rugs and shawls and embroidered sheepskin jackets. (The travel writer Bruce Chatwin blamed them for introducing Marxist ideas—the first cause of the Afghan descent into chaos.) The influence of the modern world may not have made much of a difference to life out in the provinces, but it did in cities like Kabul, Herat in the west and Mazar in the north. Afghan women sought education and jobs. There was even a Miss Kabul competition—hardly the cutting edge of feminism, but a sign of change nonetheless in this traditional Islamic culture.

As part of his reform package, one of the first things Daoud did when he seized power from his cousin was to launch a crackdown on Islamic fundamentalism, then competing as one of several political ideologies. In Kabul student elections in 1970, Islamist activists had won a majority. Daoud rejected offers from the Saudi government to pump some of its colossal new oil wealth, gained in the price hike of 1973, into Kabul University. He knew it would come with Wahhabi strings attached, and wanted no part of it. The Saudis took their oil money to Pakistan instead, providing a fresh injection of cash to the fundamentalist system of education in Wahhabi madrassas, where boys learn the Koran by heart to the exclusion of almost all other teaching. After spending a year in jail for his role in planning the murder of a Maoist university student, Hekmatyar followed the money and ran away from progress in Afghanistan—one of the first in a wave of Afghan fundamentalists who fled across the border.

Pakistan quickly recognized the potential of the disaffected Islamists, recruiting and training them to fight against Daoud when he played the Pashtun nationalist card. Daoud was trying to gain domestic support by reigniting the old dream of Pashtunistan, which pushed the Afghan border east across the mountains as far as the Indus. The issue of the frontier still lay like rough sandpaper between the two sides, as much a cause of friction at the end of the twentieth century as it had been two hundred years before, with a new twist now that the Durand Line was almost 100 years old. Afghan Pashtun nationalists interpreted clauses in the 1893 deal that made it look as if it were good for only a century. It was now close to its expiration date.

The Afghan Islamist exiles were open to recruitment on Pakistan's side against the narrow nationalism of Pashtunistan: Their ideology ignored borders in favor of a wider global Islamic view. Afghanistan's-long unfinished nightmare began here, five years before the Soviet invasion, as the men the United States ultimately backed against the Soviet Union took up arms to oppose the mild social reforms of the Daoud government. Alongside Hekmatyar in the first Pakistani-financed three-month-training course as guerrillas in 1974 was another Islamist student leader: Ahmed Shah Massud.

Massud was not a Pashtun like Hekmatyar but a Tajik from Panjshir, a long oval valley not far northeast of Kabul. Panjshir means "five lions." Surrounded on all sides by high ridges, and accessed only by a narrow choked canyon where the river bursts out between winding cliffs to the south and a high pass in the north, Panjshir is a natural fortress concealed among the deceptive mountains of the Hindu Kush, as Massud would discover in the war that was to come.

Within a year of his training and still four years before the Soviet invasion, Massud had led an uprising in the Panjshir, exploiting rumblings of discontent against the president's reforms, particularly in relation to women. It was a disaster that failed to attract popular support. More than 100 of Massud's followers were arrested, and many were executed. The plan had called for simultaneous uprisings in several provinces. But none of the other Islamist student revolutionaries did what they had said they would, although there were several suicidal attacks on police stations across the country.

It is said that Massud never spoke to Hekmatyar again, blaming him for the failure of the uprising. The deep divisions between the mujahidin that would later cause so many Afghan deaths began at that time. Hekmatyar formed his own party, Hezb-i-Islami, the party of Islam, and a year later had Massud arrested in Peshawar on charges of spying. Massud was released, but a close friend was tortured and killed. The Panjshir uprising gave Daoud the excuse he needed for a much wider crackdown on Islamism. A radical mullah was executed, and Professor Burhanuddin Rabbani, the leader of the secret underground Islamist network, fled to join his ex-students in Pakistan. He would not return to Kabul until the chaotic postcommunist days of 1992, when he emerged as president of Afghanistan.

The Soviet Union looked on at the mounting chaos with increasing concern. There had been Soviet military advisers in Afghanistan since 1954, even during the long reign of Zahir Shah. The Afghan officer corps, pilots and tank drivers all trained in the USSR, the technical language of the military was Russian, and when Daoud ousted the last king of Afghanistan, he did it with Soviet help. But as the British Empire had found, buying guns for Afghanistan did not buy absolute loyalty. When Daoud sought better links with Western countries, the Soviet leader Leonid Brezhnev called him to Moscow for a personal warning. Brezhnev's approach to this troublesome client state was similar to that adopted by some Victorian viceroy.

In response, Daoud told the Soviet leader that his demand that Afghanistan break ties with other countries was an unacceptable intervention in Afghan internal affairs. "We will never allow you to dictate to us how to run our country and whom to employ in Afghanistan." His face was "hard and dark," according to a Soviet witness, and he had to be reminded to shake Brezhnev's hand on his departure. A year later he was dead, overthrown and murdered along with many of his family in the Saur (April) Revolution in the spring of 1978. Pressure for more radical political reforms had been growing for several years, and the revolution succeeded with the backing of a significant part of the army's officer corps.

Daoud was replaced by a communist regime that became more hard line as each day passed. The communists changed the national flag, painted schools red, encouraged education for girls and rights for women, canceled all rural debt and started to impose land redistribution measures that upset the clan and tribal system of the Afghan countryside. Much of this, in particular rights for women and rural land reform, would have been seen as progress in any other country, but the chaotic cancellation of debt backed by the use of force provoked an insurgency led by rural landlords that spread across the countryside. The repressive response of the government sparked a worsening cycle of violence.

Some estimates put the number of Afghans who were killed in fighting in the year *before* the Soviet invasion as high as 50,000. These reports may have been exaggerated by Moscow to justify its intervention; in the chaos no one was keeping a tally as hundreds of thousands of technocrats, intellectuals and political moderates as well as Islamists fled the country. Ninety percent of university teachers joined the exodus. A Soviet witness spoke of "mass arrests, shooting of undesirables, and the shooting of Muslim clergy." Hundreds of men in Kunar in the east were killed in one massacre, while others were thrown into the Oxus and drowned in reprisal for an uprising in a village. The revolution had split the army, where loyalties were severely challenged as the violence worsened. There was a mutiny at the Bala Hissar fortress itself in Kabul, still a key strategic location as it had always been, while outside Kabul some military units were down to one-third of their normal strength.

The Islamist guerrilla forces trained by Pakistan now had a clear target and a simple message. To them, both Daoud's gradualist approach to democracy and the shock tactics of the communists came to the same thing: a threat to their way of life. They went to war to defend traditional Afghan rural conservative values against democracy, progress, the education of girls and godless communism.

Hekmatyar led the first successful raid by the new mujahidin in January 1979, almost a year before the Soviet invasion, attacking the fortress at Asadabad, north of the Khyber Pass. A force of about 5,000 men under Hekmatyar's command left Pakistan via the pass and penetrated the Kunar Valley, the route used by Alexander the Great. There was no battle. In a pattern repeated often during the long war that was to come, the commander of the fort went over to the side of the mujahidin.

As events spiraled toward the Soviet invasion and a wider war in 1979, the most serious single uprising, in Herat, began with the deaths of several Soviet advisers and their families, killed when a group of army officers took control, dividing the government forces. Several thousand people were killed during the ground and air assault on the city to retake control for the government. One of the rebel army officers who fled when order was restored was Captain Ismail Khan, who later emerged as the key mujahidin leader in the West of the country in the fight against the Soviet occupation.

Following the Herat uprising, the new Afghan leader Nur Mohammed Taraki made the first of 20 Afghan requests to the Soviet Union to send troops. He suggested that they be disguised as Afghan soldiers, so they would appear as troops from neighboring Soviet republics, ethnically similar to Afghans from the North. He said this was the only way to "save the revolution." The Soviet prime minister, Alexei Kosygin, declined, although he was shocked by the violent death of the Soviet advisers and their families, since he had believed that the communist regime in Kabul was popular. When Kosygin and Taraki spoke on the phone, the Soviet leader asked what had happened to the thousands of Afghan soldiers trained in Moscow. Taraki said that most had become "Muslim reactionaries," and he could now rely only on "older secondary school pupils, other students and a few workers."

The conversation is a window into another world, the banal rhetoric of Marxist analysis, in which a large and complex country urgently needing development was not seen as ready for the historical processes required by a real communist revolution because it did not yet have a proletariat. Taraki admitted that "the working class in Afghanistan is very small, and it is a long affair to train them." Once again as so often in the past, Afghanistan found that foreign involvement in its affairs was shaped to fit a predetermined picture drawn abroad. Direct Soviet military intervention was ruled out for now. The Afghan leader flew to Moscow to be told to his face by Kosygin: "If our troops were introduced, the situation in your country would get worse." Soviet deployment "would immediately arouse the international community, and would invite sharply unfavourable many-faceted consequences."

Nine months later Soviet forces crossed the Oxus River. What changed was a rapidly deteriorating situation. A power struggle within the Afghan government ended in a shoot-out in the presidential palace between Taraki and his prime minister, Hafizullah Amin. Taraki's retirement "on health grounds" was then announced on Kabul radio. The truth is that he was killed, smothered by a pillow at Amin's orders. The Soviet leader Brezhnev, now old, decrepit and apparently understanding little of what went on around him, wept when he heard the news. In Afghanistan, the new leader Amin tried to change tack, admitting government mistakes and blaming the country's problems on Taraki. In November he arranged a public reading of the names of those who had died in prison in the 18 months since the Saur revolution that had ousted Daoud. There were 12,000 names recorded, but the reading had to be halted soon after it began amid scenes of chaos and public hysteria.

Soviet suspicions that Amin wanted a "more balanced" foreign policy— one less dependent on Moscow—were confirmed by the Pakistani president, General Zia ul-Haq, who later said that Amin constantly appealed to him for support; by December the appeals were "frantic." Amin was right to be concerned: The Soviet Union had given up on him, and a Politburo report described the Afghan leader as "an ambitious, cruel, treacherous person…insincere and two-faced." Amin had spent some time in the West, and Soviet intelligence reports suggested he was a Central Intelligence Agency stooge. The suspicion alone was a death sentence.

The Soviet Union turned instead to Babrak Karmal, one of the founders of Afghan communism in the 1960s, but now sidelined as an ambassador abroad after long-standing doctrinal and personal disagreements with the Afghan leadership. In the middle of December 1979 he flew in a Soviet plane into Bagram Air Field, not far north of Kabul, expecting to mount a coup against Amin, but it did not happen, and he returned to Moscow. Karmal's noncoup epitomizes the confusion of the period, as the Soviet Union moved like a sleepwalker into its longest and costliest military engagement since World War II. No one will admit to making the decision to invade, and in the rewriting of history that subsequently happened, those alive afterward found it easy to blame those who were dead.

By the beginning of December the Soviet Union already had the equivalent of two battalions in Afghanistan. The largest concentration of troops was a battalion of central Asian reservists who had been moved into position to hold Bagram Air Field. Elite Spetznaz troops guarded key Soviet positions in Kabul itself, but they were deployed only in a defensive capacity. It is clear that the Soviet military was opposed to a larger intervention. In an eerie repeat of the suicide of the Soviet envoy Vitkevitch soon after meeting Burnes in Kabul for Christmas dinner in 1837, a key Soviet military adviser shot himself when he returned from Kabul to Moscow and realized that his political masters had now changed their minds and were intent on a major military deployment.

The Soviet military was not even consulted about the operational implications of what was being planned. On December 10, only two weeks before the invasion, Nikolai Ogarkov, the chief of the General Staff, was summoned by the defense minister, Dmitri Ustinov, and ordered to prepare a force up to 80,000 strong for "a temporary introduction of Soviet troops into Afghanistan." Ogarkov called the decision "reckless," saying that the force would not be large enough to take the country, if that was what was wanted. He was interrupted by the defense minister: "Are you going to teach the Politburo? Your only duty is to carry out the orders." That evening he was summoned to Brezhnev's inner office, to meet the so-called little politburo—Defense Minister Ustinov, the long-standing foreign minister Andrei Gromyko, and the head of the secret police, the KGB, Yuri Andropov.

The fingerprints of these three men are on the decision to invade, although Gromyko, who survived long enough to be able to spin his version of history, always pointed to Andropov as the key figure: He said it was Andropov's KGB reports that tipped the balance. But even Andropov did not envisage a full-scale invasion. In mid-December he sent a memo to Brezhnev saying that he thought the two battalions already there should be "entirely sufficient for a successful operation" to install Karmal as leader.

It is certain that the whole Politburo did not preapprove the invasion. A remarkable handwritten document survives showing that there was no widespread consultation at this level. The final decision to invade was made on December 12, but some of the Soviet ruling body did not sign the "order" to invade Afghanistan until the twenty-sixth, once the country had fallen. The first that Brezhnev's foreign policy adviser heard about it was on the BBC after it happened.

The main invasion began on December 22 with the first of more than 350 flights by heavy Illyushin and Antonov transport planes, carrying paratroopers into Kabul and Bagram. Some of the troops took over the capital, while others went directly north to secure the Salang tunnel, the route through the Hindu Kush from the North for the armored brigades that were now pouring across the Oxus on makeshift pontoon bridges. There was little Afghan resistance amid contradictory orders; some officers believed the Russians had come to keep Amin in power. Soviet advisers had taken the precaution of removing the firing pins from the guns of as many Afghan tanks as they could get their hands on, with the excuse that they were to be replaced by "winterized" versions. President Amin's palace guard did put up a fight, but they were overwhelmed and he was shot dead by Soviet soldiers.

There was from the start a lack of clarity about the motives and aims of the military intervention, further muddied by deliberate propaganda. Broadcasts claiming to be from Kabul Radio, actually beamed from across the Soviet border while the invasion was taking place, denounced Amin as a tool of U.S. imperialism and reported that Karmal had taken over, as if this were all an internal matter. By the time the real Kabul Radio had fallen into Karmal's hands on December 27 and broadcast a request from Afghanistan to the USSR to send "political, moral, and economic assistance, including military aid," the invasion was over.

Karmal would later promote various versions of how he came to power. He hinted that he had been running an underground resistance movement for months, or alternatively he said that he had been invited to take over by the Afghan politburo, who had told him that Amin was planning to flee abroad with money "savagely plundered from our toiling people." He began to drink heavily, was seen to shake in public and tried unsuccessfully to resign. It was not an auspicious start to his rule.

According to a formal statement from the Soviet defense ministry, one key reason for the invasion was concern that instability would spread north across the Oxus to the predominantly Muslim republics that were then part of the Soviet Union. Apart from giving "internationalist assistance to the friendly

Afghan people," the intervention was designed "to prevent possible anti-Afghan actions on the part of the bordering states." There was no evidence, though, that the invasion was seen as having any historical inevitability. None saw it as unfinished business from the long nineteenth-century Russian push across central Asia and the Caucasus. Prince Gorchakov, the architect of Russian expansionism then, would not have understood the limited aims of the Soviet Union now. This was not an imperial grab, the long-feared move to allow Russian soldiers to "dip their boots in the warm waters of the Arabian Gulf"; rather it was portrayed as assistance to friends, as Soviet troops had deployed for example to Ethiopia and Angola.

The Soviet defense minister did not expect to have troops in Afghanistan by the following winter. He believed that the mujahidin would throw down their weapons when faced by the Soviet army, although he was warned by the Soviet General Staff that it was more likely that the rebellion would worsen. The troops were ordered to remain in their garrisons as much as possible, and not become involved in combat. Their stated aim was to help the local population with aid, not fight against an insurgency.

Decision-making machinery in the West was closed for Christmas when the invasion happened, and at any rate the United States had taken its eye off Afghanistan that year, even after the murder of its ambassador, who had been caught up in the political intrigue in Kabul in February. The Soviet invasion came out of the blue for Washington, and did not fit the pattern of behavior it had come to expect from Moscow. Spy planes had seen the troops gathering on the border, but the force was clearly not big enough for a full-scale invasion. Vice-President Walter Mondale said, "What unnerved everyone was the suspicion that Brezhnev's inner circle might not be rational."

U.S. military and diplomatic attention was focused instead on Afghanistan's western neighbor Iran, where a U.S.-backed regime had been ousted by the Ayatollah Khomeini's Islamic revolution. In November 1979 warships were sent to the Persian Gulf as the long ordeal began for U.S. diplomats besieged in their Tehran embassy by student zealots. And although President Jimmy Carter did speak out against the Afghan invasion—in a protest that he called the strongest of his presidency—promising to "make Soviet involvement as costly as possible," early measures fell short of arming the mujahidin. There was to be a boycott of the 1980 Moscow Olympics, a cut in grain sales to the USSR and some delay in signing a nuclear arms reduction deal.

Carter did not like secret wars and had tried to bring the CIA into line over the funding of guerrillas in Central America. In early 1980, however, he changed his mind and allowed covert operations to be funded for Afghanistan, to be launched from Pakistan. Even though they were at a very low level at first, this was a significant policy reversal.

The other main backers of the mujahidin made uncomfortable bedfellows for the United States. China had long had a strategic alliance with Pakistan, and the countries shared significant defense technology, naturally moving into joint support of the mujahidin. The new Islamic government in Iran opposed the Soviet invasion too; Afghanistan had traditionally been seen as Persia's backyard. It was no coincidence that the first major uprising against the communists, in the spring of 1979, well before the full-scale Soviet invasion, broke out in Herat, very close to the Iranian border. About a quarter of the refugees who had fled from Afghanistan went west to Iran, and after its Shia Islamic revolution Tehran allied itself particularly with guerrilla groups from Afghanistan's Shia minority.

In Kabul, Karmal's new government tried to win back support with a number of radical shifts in policy: scrapping the red flag and restoring the three-colored Afghan flag, funding the building of 2,000 mosques and granting state salaries to 16,000 Muslim leaders. The measures resembled Amanullah's desperate attempts to save his reform program in the 1920s, when he faced an Islamist backlash, and they were as useless.

The "official mullahs" were targeted by the mujahidin, and by the end of February there were mass uprisings in Kabul, initially led by students but then spreading city-wide. Civil servants defected en masse and normal government ceased to function, as the regime gave up any pretense of being part of an idealistic revolutionary movement. Any discipline that remained in the ruling elite was undermined by Soviet aid and the easy availability of consumer goods. In April 1980 President Karmal complained of "lawlessness, disobedience, embezzlement, bureaucracy, pilferage of public property, chauvinism and so forth," but given that his mistress was the education minister and his half brother also had a post in the administration, he was hardly practicing what he preached.

The communist reign of terror against dissidents continued. A Soviet observer said Kabul justice reminded him of Stalinist excesses: It "practically repeated ours, point by point, of the 1937–38 years." An Afghan academic, Mohammed Hassan Kakar, who was held in Pul-e-Charki jail near Kabul for five years, calculated that 150,000 people were arrested, and 50,000 of them executed there.

But no one, least of all Russia, really expected the ragtag, pajama-clad mujahidin to pose much of a threat. Violence between different communist factions killed more people than the mujahidin at the beginning, and for some years most of the rebels were equipped only with copies of British-era Lee Enfield rifles, not the AK-47 assault weapons that were later supplied in huge numbers. Funding came from individuals and some governments in the gulf states, but it was still small, and in the first two years, before Charlie Wilson became involved, U.S. support totaled less than $10 million.

The mujahidin nevertheless made progress as initially Soviet forces rejected Karmal's appeals to take them on; that was not their mission, despite extreme provocation, including a revolt in January 1980 in Kandahar, the main city in the southern Pashtun heartland, when Soviet citizens and troops were literally hacked to pieces. But at the beginning of March, as disorder spread, new orders arrived from Moscow: "Begin active operations for destruction of the formations of the armed opposition." The Soviet military had been drawn against its better judgment into an Afghan civil war.

Once it became clear that the mujahidin were not going to throw down their weapons, there was a fundamental shift in Soviet military policy. Far from being able to begin a withdrawal, the Soviet Union changed the makeup of its forces in Afghanistan, replacing reservists with regular troops, and dug in for the long haul. The Limited Contingent, as the invasion force had been called, had no training for counterinsurgency warfare, and was equipped with heavy armored vehicles designed for a different task.

The Soviet army began operations against Hekmatyar's forces in the east in March, just as the melting snows of the Suleiman Mountains opened the mule tracks for the mujahidin.

10

CHARLIE HORSE

Well if that's your only problem, I can have my Israeli friends put Swastikas on the guns.

—Congressman Charlie Wilson's response when the CIA told him it could not be seen openly to source weapons for Afghanistan from Israel

If it was an unpromising start for the Soviet side, the situation could not have been more favorable for the mujahidin. They had textbook conditions to mount an insurgency: support in the Afghan villages, a safe haven across the mountains with access by narrow tracks that suited them but were impassable for the Soviet forces and a ready supply of young men willing to die. Death in this holy cause was considered an honor, followed by swift burial in the soil of Afghanistan and a shortcut to paradise as a *shaheed*, a martyr—a narrowly focused aspiration for a generation, with an inevitably degrading impact on other cultural values.

The mujahidin had a unique, mad courage: some were able to travel wounded for days without complaint, and a reporter saw a man put his hand into a fire when his honor was challenged, and not withdraw it until the fat from his flesh was dripping into the flames. Best of all for their cause, Afghans, and Pashtuns in particular, never forgot an insult but would seek *badal*, revenge, through the generations.

In a system of recruitment based on patronage that would have been recognized by the Durrani nobles of the eighteenth century, clans would provide men for the war effort. The fighters were not paid but would spend up to four months in the field before being replaced by a brother or cousin and returning to melt into the civilian population until called on again. In the beginning there were dozens of different mujahidin groups, although the most successful leaders were the ones who knew how to attract funding and those like Hekmatyar, who were most ruthless.

From the start he imposed on the refugee camps in the frontier region the kind of Afghan society he wanted to see. Intellectuals, progressive reformers and women's leaders were murdered or jailed, and survival was impossible outside the mujahidin cause. To concentrate the military effort, Pakistan limited the number of insurgent groups to seven, and ration cards were issued only to those who belonged to one of the seven, so the refugees were radicalized and recruited for the war whether they liked it or not.

There was no room for free thought in this wartime economy. Many children, particularly orphans, went to the Saudi-financed madrassas, now well established in the frontier region as well as elsewhere in Pakistan. These schools preached an unreconstructed Wahhabi view of Islam similar to that of the Hindustani fanatics at the center of Britain's frontier war in 1897 and provided the ideological bedrock for those who would ultimately create the Taliban.

Hekmatyar continued to polarize opinion. His mujahidin comrades were suspicious of the personality cult that surrounded him, believing that his desire to control the camps took his focus off the fighting in Afghanistan, but he saw the big picture, encouraging the belief that Soviet forces could be beaten. This was a hard argument to win; the CIA then thought that the key battleground where they could destroy communism was in Central America, the backyard of the United States and a region it thought it understood. CIA Director William Casey said, "If America challenges the Soviets at every turn and ultimately defeats them in one place, that will shatter the mythology. Nicaragua is that place." No CIA operatives spoke Pashtu; the conflict in the Hindu Kush seemed remote.

It was not until 1982 that Congressman Charlie Wilson made his first trip to the region, intrigued by reports he heard of the mountain warfare against a communist invader. Moved by the conditions he saw in a hospital for wounded fighters on the frontier, he immediately donated a pint of blood and always did the same when he visited afterward. The trip changed Wilson's life and would transform the war. Until then the CIA had been cautious, following the advice of one of its officers who had spent three years in Kabul before the war: "Don't put white men in charge. Don't give the Afghans a lot of money. Don't trust them. It would be like throwing money into a cesspool. All they need is a little help and the Russians will be sorry they ever went into that country." But no one in the CIA thought that the mujahidin could ever defeat the Soviet army; all they hoped for was containment.

Wilson believed the mujahidin could do much more than be "a burr under the saddle, an extreme nuisance." Fresh from the frontier, he met the CIA station chief in Pakistan, Howard Hart, at an absurd meeting in an inner room at the U.S. embassy, with the *1812 Overture* playing loudly to mask their conversation from spies. Wilson came away unimpressed by Hart's lack of ambition: "He never envisioned killing the beast."

An instinctive cold warrior, six feet seven inches tall, and with ambitions as lofty, Wilson went back home to try to change things, playing the one game he knew really well: the political game on Capitol Hill. The mujahidin were heroes he could understand, from the same stock as the defenders of the Alamo. At last he had a cause, something to echo the work of his childhood hero Winston Churchill, who had saved *his* country from a threat others had ignored and, like Wilson, was fond of a drink. Wilson was on the Defense Appropriations Subcommittee, responsible for funding CIA operations. When he returned from that first trip to the frontier, he called to ask how much was allocated for Afghanistan. When he heard it was $5 million, he said "Double it." There was no executive order, no debate in Congress. No one noticed.

He was on the right committees and called in favors across the Hill, securing first millions and then billions of dollars from the federal budget for the mujahidin. The humiliation of Vietnam was still fresh, and he knew the names of every one of the 167 men from his congressional district who had died there. This was payback. "I love sticking it to the Russians. And I think most Americans do. They need to get it back, and they're getting it back."

The aid all went through Pakistan, where the United States now backed the military dictator General Zia, who liked to say that they needed to "keep the pot boiling" in Afghanistan but not let it boil over and spread the war back into Pakistan. Zia was already hosting more than three million Afghans, the world's largest refugee population. Like the British during their century and a half of domination in this region, he did not want the Russian army on his side of the Suleiman Mountains, and they were closer now than they had ever come during the British period.

Zia did a deal with his secret service, the ISI, one of the key power brokers in Pakistan, giving it carte blanche to run the war in Afghanistan providing it did nothing to upset his authority at home. Wilson was clever at finding new sources of non-U.S.-manufactured weapons: military aid to Afghanistan had to be deniable, so as not to provoke Moscow to retaliate elsewhere. Arms were bought with funds mainly from the United States and Saudi Arabia, shipped to Karachi and driven in trucks to a nondescript unmarked distribution site amid the sprawling encampments near Rawalpindi, originally built as the main British garrison town in northwestern India and now the headquarters of the Pakistani army. The ISI insisted from the start on direct control of the weapons supply.

The system could not have been better designed to encourage corruption: the CIA later calculated that 20 percent of the arms and funds destined for Afghanistan went astray. And apart from the leaks in Pakistan, the need for U.S. deniability led to shady deals with suppliers. On his trip to Peshawar with Snowflake in 1984, Wilson was testing the ground for a promising new source of weapons: guns seized by Israel from the Palestinians. The guns were of Soviet origin or design, so not traceable to the United States or Israel. Wilson was one of Israel's strongest advocates in the United States, and he knew that on the face of it, taking arms from the Israelis to fight an Islamic jihad in Afghanistan was unthinkable.

He wanted to short-circuit objections from both the CIA and Pakistan by asking Hekmatyar directly if he should buy them. The reply came swiftly back, delivered without expression: "We take Russian weapons from dead Russians to use against them—I don't see why we can't take them from the Israelis. Allah has many mysterious ways of providing for his faithful." That evening Wilson and Snowflake hosted all seven leaders of the different mujahidin groups, and late that night one of them returned to present him with a captured Russian AK-47. He was their man.

Britain's answer to the hard-drinking, womanizing Texan Charlie Wilson came from a rather different background. Robert Cecil, Viscount Cranborne, from one of the country's grandest families, had recently been elected a Tory Member of Parliament. Like Wilson, he believed that Afghanistan represented a unique opportunity to challenge communism, against the prevailing wisdom at the time across the British political establishment. After Cranborne spoke out strongly against the invasion at a meeting in London, the Soviet ambassador grabbed him by the arm on the way out and said, "Why not let us do it? We will win and then you will look silly." At an Oxford seminar in early 1980, Cranborne urged the strongest possible response to the Soviet invasion and was ignored for the rest of the day.

But he had seen CIA intelligence demonstrating the weakness of the Soviet economy, and became part of a drive to shift domestic opinion, turning the Afghan struggle into a fashionable cause, aided by the visceral anticommunist instincts of the then newly elected prime minister Margaret Thatcher. Tory ministers began to idealize the mujahidin as noble warriors—not terrorists but freedom fighters—their struggle favorably compared to that of the French resistance in World War II. Neither U.S. nor British backers of the mujahidin knew what problems they were stirring up when they funded Islamic fundamentalism.

Although Britain could never match U.S. funding, it punched above its weight in other ways. British soldiers and spies were not prohibited from entering Afghanistan, as U.S. citizens were, and they collected intelligence as well as supplying high-technology equipment. They would also take direct action. The CIA operative who ran the war, Gust Avrakotos, said the Brits had "a willingness to do jobs that I could not touch. They basically took care of the 'How to Kill People Department.'" At a time when the CIA was facing strong criticism for providing an "assassination manual" to gangs in Nicaragua, this British support filled a useful gap.

Cranborne provided another key component in the war effort, by focusing on humanitarian aid. He had read his Chairman Mao. The Chinese leader had compared the civilian population around insurgents with the water that fish need to swim in. The refugee outflow to Pakistan was draining the pond, so if Cranborne could get food and money in, Afghans would be more likely to stay in their villages, providing the support the mujahidin needed to operate.

Soviet military planners had read Mao too, and from early on in the war the most intense application of military violence was applied to a wide strip of territory in the east of Afghanistan, in an attempt to create a *cordon sanitaire*, depriving the fish of water, and so making the mujahidin vulnerable when they moved supplies. This involved frequent armored assaults on the ground as well as bombing raids by fixed-wing planes and heavy use of Hind helicopter gunships—the Soviets' most feared weapon. But although Soviet tactics developed as the war progressed, they never had enough men or the right equipment to dominate the ground. Their strength was never more than about 100,000, one-fifth of the U.S. forces at the height of the war in Vietnam, in a country that was five times the size.

Soviet equipment was unsuited to the terrain. Tanks were not easily maneuverable in the mountains, and lightly armored troop-carrying vehicles were vulnerable to attack. Infantry found their heavy flak jackets slowed them down, especially when operating at high altitude, while 1950s-style backpacks were cumbersome. Soviet field uniforms did not provide good camouflage, and were restrictive and uncomfortable to wear, while their boots were noisy and not suitable for the mountains—commanders would issue sneakers when they could get hold of them. As the mujahidin became better equipped when U.S. funding began to flow on a large scale, Russian soldiers would try to steal their sleeping bags, since Soviet-issue cotton sleeping bags became heavy and useless when wet. Soviet army food came dried, and was hard to cook hygienically, while the tins reflected sunlight and gave away their positions.

It was not surprising that morale was low, and Soviet soldiers would sell their weapons and other kit in exchange for drugs and even food. An Estonian conscript remembered, "Often regular Afghan army soldiers exchanged their Russian arms for food and drink from peasants. So we did the same thing, because in the chaos of war to explain the loss of a weapon is easy. We used to buy all kinds of food and drink and even bread in exchange for our weapons." The conflict was violent and brutalizing both for the Afghans and the Soviet conscript army. Travelers found carrying large amounts of money at Russian checkpoints were "sent to Kabul," meaning taken around the back and shot so they could be robbed. A Russian ex-soldier told of an incident in his unit that led to a court-martial:

> One night, after drinking a lot of home-brewed beer, they decided that they wanted some hash and some lamb, so they set out for a neighbouring *kishlak* [village]. They ran into an old man on the way there, and they were so drunk that they struck the old man on the head so hard that a piece of the rifle's

stock fell off... Soon they reached the *kishlak* and entered a house. There was a
woman inside. They started raping her, and she started screaming. When her
sister darted out of the house, there was nothing left for the fellows to do but
to stab both of them. Then they entered the house next door. There were children inside, and the soldiers opened fire on them with their AKs. They shot all
of them but one who managed to escape... then the soldiers took a whole sack
of hashish and a lamb and returned to their unit.

They were caught after the boy who escaped reported the incident and identified them. At his trial the soldier turned to his accusing officer and said "When
I was knocking off twenty people at a time on your orders, you said, 'Well
done! Here's a man with excellent results in combat. Put his name on the board
of honour!' But when I got hungry—all right, I did get plastered, I was drunk
then—and went to get a, lamb because there was no food, I killed the same
people that I always killed. This time, however, it wasn't on your orders. So
now you've decided to try me?" The soldier remembered his commander saying
"Here's a case of three fools who got caught. Do whatever you want, but don't
get caught."

The Afghan army was an unreliable ally. It faced constant defections from
the start as not only individuals and units but whole divisions went over to the
mujahidin, taking their personal kit and rifles as well as tanks and armored
vehicles. When units were ordered to go on operations, there was always the risk
that they might defect. Ordinary logistical operations like the replenishment
of ammunition had to be calculated against the likelihood of defection, while
units left without ammunition were obviously useless if attacked. Conscripts
were often recruited by force, with the inducement of shorter military service
for those who signed up voluntarily and the threat of long jail terms for desertion. Some were signed up by deception. New university students without party
membership cards were told there was no place for them in Kabul, and they
would have to go to college in Charikar, not far north of the capital. When
they arrived they found no college, only a military training ground. They were
no choice but to sign up, and in return they would be promised a degree. One
student conned in this way remembered "the next day everybody started desert-
ing." Officers were rushed into the front line after just three months training.

Despite this, the Afghan armed forces did much better than predicted by
many Western analysts. Their commanders competed with the mujahidin for
regional support and respect, and the effective ones who emerged, like General
Abdul Rashid Dostam in the North, earned loyalty similar to that given to
mujahidin commanders by their fighters. However, in a dynamic that would
have been recognized by rulers right back to Shah Shuja, who tried and failed
to hold onto his throne in 1809, commanders waited to see which way the wind

was blowing. Units would defect to the mujahidin and then sometimes return to the Afghan army, as a classic Afghan struggle for power developed under the surface of the Soviet war.

Both the Soviet army and its Afghan allies were assisted by tactical weakness and division among the mujahidin. The downside of the regional loyalty that gave the mujahidin much of their strength was the unwillingness of fighters to move out of their area or cooperate with other commanders. Mohammed Yousaf, who led the Afghan desk of Pakistan's ISI for much of the war, became increasingly frustrated by the tendency of the mujahidin to wage heroic and preferably noisy warfare rather than utilizing the advantages of stealth and subterfuge. Gains frequently would be squandered as the mujahidin did not consolidate their victories but grabbed what they could before running for the hills, tactics condemned by the Pakistani spy chief as "typical tribal fighting for immediate tangible gains, localised in area, and with no higher strategic objective."

In one incident in 1984, Yousaf, aiming to destroy the Soviet oil pipeline that ran south from the Hindu Kush delivering fuel to Bagram Air Field, suggested a silent night raid to set explosive charges and even proved it could be done on an exercise in Pakistan. But the mujahidin insisted instead that they should carry out a full-scale assault, capturing guard posts and of course seizing what booty they could find, before finally laying a charge on the pipeline. A Pakistani plan to drive trucks loaded with explosives into the Salang tunnel—the crucial Soviet supply route through the Hindu Kush—was rejected as not being heroic enough. Worst of all from the ISI point of view, the mujahidin in the East refused to ferry supplies into Ahmed Shah Massud during the most determined Soviet attempt to take the Panjshir Valley in 1984—their seventh. It was a bloody encounter for both sides, with one Soviet battalion losing half its troops.

What Yousaf missed in his frustration was the fact that the success of the mujahidin against the Soviet occupation was partly explained by their disunity. They had fierce local loyalty, were achieving significant successes in a guerrilla war and, unusually for such a conflict, inflicting more casualties than they were taking. Even if conventional forces lose guerrilla wars, as they usually do, they tend to inflict far higher casualties than they suffer themselves.

By 1985, when Mikhail Gorbachev took over in the Kremlin, none of the three forces at play in Afghanistan looked as if it had the potential to be militarily decisive. The Soviet army was big enough to take the punishment; the Afghan communist forces were improving but believed not to be strong enough to fight alone; and the mujahidin had made the country ungovernable without having the capacity to take it for themselves. The deaths of two Soviet leaders in quick succession, Andropov and Chernenko, after the long illness and death of Brezhnev, meant that the USSR's Afghan policy had been drifting for several years. Gorbachev ordered an increase in troop numbers and intensified the conflict with the aim of winning or pulling out if the surge failed. But 1985 was also the year that the military balance changed against the Soviet Union, as the mujahidin took delivery of their first Stinger missiles.

Ever since becoming involved in the Afghan cause, Charlie Wilson had been looking for a weapon to bring down Soviet helicopters. As early as November 1982, on a trip to Israel, he tried to commission a design for an antiaircraft weapon that could be carried on the backs of mules. The pursuit of the weapon was such an obsession for him that the CIA code word for this project was *Charlie Horse*. Wilson went ahead with the trip to Israel although news that he was facing charges of using cocaine in a Jacuzzi in Las Vegas full of showgirls had just broken in the U.S. press. (Wilson would later say, "The Feds spent a million bucks trying to figure out whether, when those fingernails passed under my nose, did I inhale or exhale—and I ain't telling.") His escort in Israel, and then on to Egypt, was an American who specialized in belly dancing. She put on a private performance for the Egyptian defense minister, but it did not result in the antiaircraft weapon Wilson sought.

The following year, Wilson almost missed a flight he had arranged to take key members of the House of Representatives Appropriations Committee to Pakistan. The police believed he had been drinking and driving, and had left the scene of a car crash. He succeeded in escaping the cordon around his apartment, hungover and unshaven, only when an official government car arrived to take him to the airport. But the Texas-trash lifestyle did not damage his ability to make the money flow into Afghanistan—in 1984 it topped $100 million a year, the following year it was three times that figure, and it kept rising until it was almost three-quarters of the CIA's budget. Total U.S. spending on the mujahidin during the conflict was $3 billion; $600 million of that went to Hekmatyar. And the U.S. funds were matched dollar for dollar by Saudi Arabia.

More than a third of the money went to China to buy AK-47 assault rifles, now the standard weapon of the mujahidin, and the CIA was introducing new weapons into the battlefield every three months, including two-way radios, an early GPS system and a booby-trapped vacuum flask that exploded if you poured water into it. Moving all this materiel across the frontier was a huge job in itself, and the increasing intensity of the war led to a problem that had been familiar to the British army in Afghanistan in the nineteenth century: a shortage of pack animals. Mules imported from Brazil could not take the climate, while Egyptian mules were ensnared by vaccination and health issues. In the end Tennessee mules proved the best option, although donors were shocked by the stories that filtered back of the mujahidin eating and having sex with them.

By 1986 the CIA operation in Peshawar was headed by a larger-than-life character called Milt Bearden. There was little pretense at cover. Bearden was happy to meet journalists in the American Club in Peshawar and talk about "my war." And it felt as if the tide was turning when a lucky rocket destroyed the Soviet ammunition dump in Kabul. The mujahidin were making better use of booby traps and had improved their training, and their morale went up when a certain Engineer Ghaffar shot down three Hinds on his first outing with the lightweight shoulder-launched Stinger missile. The weapon Wilson had sought for so long was finally available: Charlie Horse had ridden into the war. Two hundred Soviet aircraft would be lost to Stingers in the weapon's first year of use. Soviet ground troops began to refer to Hind helicopter pilots contemptuously as "cosmonauts," as they took to flying high to keep out of range.

Soviet forces did make some significant advances, taking back Khost on the Pakistani border with major mujahidin casualties. Elite Spetznaz troops were employed as ordinary infantry for this operation, but this was fighting of an intensity that Gorbachev knew he could not sustain against an enemy that was well motivated, and now well funded, armed and trained as well. If the Soviets had retained air supremacy, Gorbachev's troop surge might have been decisive, but he now had other priorities. He believed that his project to reconstruct the Soviet state, perestroika, was threatened by Afghanistan.

Gorbachev wanted new leadership in Kabul, and in May 1986 Karmal was replaced by Najibullah, the head of the feared KHAD secret police, nicknamed "the Bull." A former boxer who had personally killed political prisoners by stamping on them, he was not an obvious appointment for a peacemaker. At his first attempt to reach out, launching a national reconciliation commission, he appealed for talks with the mujahidin as instructed by the Kremlin. But his invitation was hardly compelling as he called them "traitors and filthy vultures...in the service of sworn enemies of our people; reactionary imperialists and neo-colonialists."

Najibullah tried to court popularity and change his ways. He had previously used the shortened version of his name, Najib, in public, but now preferred the full version as it sounded more Islamic. And to try to pretend Afghanistan was not a one-party state, he carried out a kind of reverse rigging of the polls in elections for a new parliament to ensure that the opposition won seats. But they would not take up the seats allocated to them. The pretense that his own party was a functioning organization did not deceive Moscow, now that Marxist rhetoric had been replaced by the honesty of the Gorbachev years. A political analyst reported to the Soviet Politburo that the Afghan communist party was not a party of members but of membership cards: "a circulatory system without blood."

At a Politburo meeting in 1987, Gorbachev laid out the stark choices available to the Soviet Union. He said that the only way to win the war would be to double the number of Soviet troops in Afghanistan, but that would wreck the rest of the reform program he had introduced. His foreign minister, Eduard Shevardnadze, took the U.S. secretary of state, George Schultz, aside during a session of the Afghan peace process that was rumbling on in Geneva and said that the Soviet Union wanted a way out. The mujahidin continued to argue, refusing to talk to each other or present a united position at the peace talks, but the Soviet signal was heard in Washington. By February 1988 agreement had been reached for Soviet troops to leave Afghanistan within 12 months.

— — —

The last Soviet soldier to leave Afghanistan was General Boris Gromov, the commander of the 40th Army. He was a stout short man, of Napoleonic demeanor with light-colored eyes, who smoked long Astor cigarettes with a gold band around the filter, "more the kind that women liked," according to a Soviet journalist, Artyom Borovik. In an unusually frank discussion with Borovik days before the end, Gromov criticized the Soviet high command for the defeat. The overall commander of the region, General V. I. Varennikov, was a living link with another kind of war. He had been an infantry officer at Stalingrad and had gone onto the liberation of Berlin in 1945. But Gromov said the old man had not been flexible enough for Afghanistan and had never known how to confront the mujahidin. "If it hadn't been for him our troops would have caused five times more trouble than they have."

The war had a savage end in late January 1989, just as the snow began to melt. To clear a route for the retreat from Kabul north through the Hindu Kush, a whole Soviet division fired a concentrated barrage onto the mountain paths on either side of the road, using mortars to try to start avalanches and block tracks. Fighters and bombers streaked overhead. Borovik said, "The ground was torn up and shaking. The cliffs were crumbling." Thousands of men, women and children streamed onto the main road in terror. The mujahidin leader Ahmed Shah Massud later said it was one of the war's most brutal operations. Borovik could not report the story at the time as he was working under censorship. His political supervisor in Kabul asked him what he knew, and even before he could answer he was told, "Even if you do know something, you have forgotten it already. Right?"

Soviet control of Afghanistan was not all about military power. In its early years Afghanistan's industrial capacity went up by 50 percent, as new factories were opened and gas fields were exploited. There was a new textile mill in Kandahar, a new bridge across the Oxus and work had begun on a tramline in Kabul. Trade with other countries, including those outside the Soviet bloc, increased. The military effort was accompanied by a major aid push too, with volunteer teachers working across the country.

But the war devastated the countryside. Between them, the mujahidin and Soviet forces destroyed 1,814 schools, 31 hospitals and 11 health centers and tore up almost 9,000 miles of phone cable. Afghanistan began its descent into preindustrial squalor. About 1.5 million people died. Atrocities against civilians were committed not only by the Soviet side. The mujahidin left car bombs in Kabul that killed civilians and burned down schools a decade before the Taliban came on the scene.

U.S. funding of the Afghan jihad was aimed at the heart of Soviet communism but had an unintended effect that analysts later came to call Islamic blow-back—creating Islamic warriors who turned on the society that had trained and financed them. American analysts were robust in defending their priorities. The former national security adviser Zbigniew Brzezinski said: "What was more important in the world view of history?...A few stirred-up Muslims or the liberation of Central Europe and the end of the Cold War?"

After the defeat of Soviet forces in Afghanistan the "few stirred-up Muslims" had nowhere else to go—a network of jihadis without a jihad. The international appeal of the Afghan war for Islamists began in 1984, with a book by a warrior priest, Sheikh Abdullah Azzam, called *In Defense of Muslim Lands*. Although of Palestinian origin, Azzam maintained that Afghanistan was *the* principal Islamist cause in the world, even more important than Palestine, and fighting in the jihad there was obligatory for every Muslim. He traveled constantly, telling tales of a heroic dream world, where the bodies of dead mujahidin did not decay but smelled sweetly where they fell. It was after reading this book that Osama bin Laden was inspired to move to Peshawar, and offer travel and living expenses for every jihadi. Reporters traveling in Afghanistan learned to be wary of "Arab Afghans," as the new jihadis came to be called, although many were not Arabs but Chechens, Chinese or Indonesian; some were European. They would break cameras or attempt forcible conversions. This was the beginning of the network that became al-Qaeda.

Islamist radicalization went both ways—out into the world and deep into Afghan society. But like an ocean liner, the United States sailed serenely on, not hearing the distant muffled warning bell of an Islamist threat sounding in the darkness. There was no attempt to factor the corrupting effect of the dollars that sloshed their way through the North-West Frontier nor the politics of those who had been financed and trained, although the mujahidin made no secret of the kind of society they would like to see. Many were fighting to uphold a feudal way of life, and all wanted to reestablish the traditional subservient status of Afghan women. Their leaders had formed an Islamist underground in Afghanistan 10 years before the arrival of the Soviet army; and insurgents like Massud, later darling of the foreign press corps, had fought, beginning with that first failed uprising in 1975, against the "godless communism" of the mild Western-leaning reforms of President Daoud, which included some political representation for women. Western foreign policy, nudged along by the righteous fervor of men like Charlie Wilson, had ignored all this, because Afghanistan was "the only place in the world where the forces of freedom are actually fighting and killing Russians."

By the late 1980s it looked as if it had worked. A generation of politicians brought up in the certainties of the cold war was mesmerized as the Berlin Wall came down, Gorbachev transformed the landscape, closing a chapter of history when deterring a Soviet advance across Europe had dominated western policy. Reports by the few Afghan and Islamic experts in Western foreign ministries about what this might mean for Afghanistan lay unread.

By now CIA Director William Casey was playing a tape code-named "Mohammed the Conqueror" in his car on the way to work. It recorded three hits against Soviet helicopters by a lone mujahidin fighter on a mountaintop; the third had been full of elite Spetznaz troops sent specifically to deal with him. And that was even before Stinger missiles: "the conqueror" had been armed with a DshK antiaircraft gun carried up the mountain on the back of a mule. When people asked how the war was being won, the Pakistani leader General Zia would say, "Charlie did it."

After years of traveling to the region with different girls, Charlie Wilson had decided that one of them, a former Miss World contestant he called "Sweetums," was his one true love, and he planned an extravagant wedding in the Khyber Pass, accompanied by mujahidin commanders, the Egyptian defense minister and even his best Israeli contact, to be seated anonymously in the VIP stand. But shortly before the nuptials were due to take place, Wilson visited California as guest of honor at the annual Mule Day parade, to honor the role of Tennessee mules in the liberation of Afghanistan. When Sweetums called Charlie's hotel room early in the morning, it was Snowflake who picked up the phone. The wedding plans were canceled.

11

"FIGHTING TO THE LAST AFGHAN"

We prefer involvement in internal war rather than occupation by foreigners and foreign troops.

—Mujahidin leader Gulbuddin Hekmatyar 1992

The torture and murder of 30 of Ahmed Shah Massud's commanders in July 1989, ambushed on their way from a meeting with Gulbuddin Hekmatyar, shocked even seasoned Afghan observers. The way a free-lance cameraman Rory Peck, who was traveling through the region, heard the story was that as the men were overwhelmed, only one was killed instantly. The others were cut up while still alive by their captors, who "indulged in an orgy of blood letting, gouging the eyes out of one, slitting the nostrils of another, cutting the ears, lips, and tongue off a third, before riddling the lot of them with bullets." Peck noted in his diary, "Afghans can be extraordinarily cruel." The victims were not expecting an attack in a mujahidin-controlled area, where they had been invited to discuss tactics for a planned joint assault on the Afghan communists in the northern town of Kunduz.

The killers must have been sent by Hekmatyar, who had called the meeting. It was an outrage that broke every rule of behavior in any theater of war, partic- ularly in Afghanistan, where the code of conduct for safe passage and hospitality is of such importance. In revenge, Massud seized a couple of local commanders associated with Hekmatyar and hanged them in public—not giving them the dignity of a soldier's death by firing squad.

This incident, six months after the last Soviet soldier left Afghanistan, showed in stark terms the main reason why the mujahidin had not yet marched in triumph into Kabul. If anything, they were now in a worse military position than they had been when Soviet forces were in the country. Predictions that

Najibullah's communist-backed Kabul regime would collapse had proven wide of the mark. He still held the key airports and towns, and his supply routes were intact. The disunity of the mujahidin had boosted the morale of his forces, and in March, only a month after the Soviet forces left, the mujahidin suffered a catastrophic reversal when they failed to take the eastern town of Jalalabad.

The Jalalabad campaign had posed the hardest question for any guerrilla force—when to move onto the offensive and hold ground. If it was a tough call for a single commander, it was impossible for the Afghan mujahidin, who were not only disunited but fighting each other. The cautious approach—continuing to harass supply routes, grinding down the will of the Kabul government—was preferred by many commanders, but as so often in Afghanistan, the decision was taken outside the country.

Pakistan had a new prime minister, Benazir Bhutto. Later she would be assassinated as she ran for office again, but in 1989, her government financed and backed the largest single offensive by the fundamentalist mujahidin during the 13-year campaign against Soviet-backed government in Afghanistan, the assault on Jalalabad. The new head of the ISI, General Hamid Gul, believed it would deliver the swift collapse of the Kabul government expected by the world. The plans for the Jalalabad assault were made by Gul with U.S. support, but there was little input from mujahidin leaders.

The spring is the most beautiful time of year in the wedge of land in the east that lies lower than the high Kabul plain, like a footstep into Afghanistan. From the north the Kunar River, flanked by mountains rising in impossible folds, brings its waters down to join those of the Kabul River with all the urgency of a journey that has begun almost in the Himalayas. Despite years of intense Soviet bombardment, the mujahidin retained control here, mainly because Pakistan held the strategic high ground. The Pakistani spymaster Mohammed Yousaf saw why the border ran where it did: "All the dominating heights belonged to Pakistan, and we had good reason to thank the colonial administrator, Durand, who had so long ago drawn his line with such tactical insight."

To the south of Jalalabad, on the far side of a plain noted as "beautiful flat fighting ground" by Durand himself as he passed this way almost 100 years before, lies the barrier of the Safed Koh—the White Mountain range. Nearer Jalalabad are low hills, just beginning to show the new green fuzz of spring in March 1989. By the time the battle for the city was over, four months later, the scattered red of wild poppies among the green growth had come and gone.

The mujahidin assault began in waves down the Kunar Valley and along the straight road from the border at the Khyber Pass. Within a day they controlled the airport to the east of the city. It was to be their only significant advance during the long weeks of fighting to come; they had signaled their intentions too clearly to the forces defending Jalalabad, who were well dug in. Eight different mujahidin leaders commanded separate parts of the assault, and they refused to obey Pakistan's orders to control all the access roads and mount diversionary tactics elsewhere in the country, so Najibullah was able to resupply the defenders throughout.

A Russian journalist who spent a few days there said it was "like Stalingrad," with very high civilian casualties from the frequent rocket attacks by both sides and close-quarters fighting. With no overall mujahidin tactical direction, it soon became a lethal daily slog. Thousands of mujahidin died, and some units lost more men in this one engagement than in the whole of the war up to then, defeated by a determined conventional force on the only occasion they attempted an all-out assault using conventional tactics. Retreating, the mujahidin lost an important garrison at Samarkhel.

Jalalabad was the biggest set-piece battle since the Soviet invasion and the only significant battle involving tanks on both sides. It was also the only time that Osama bin Laden is known to have led his Arab fighters directly into battle in Afghanistan, other than in skirmishes around the cave complex at Tora Bora, on the other side of the plain to the south of Jalalabad. Eighty Arab-Afghans died, and bin Laden had a narrow escape, fleeing just ahead of a government assault, after the location of his field headquarters was revealed by an informer. Bin Laden was then based at Haddah, the location of one of the most effective of the mullahs who had incited the uprising against British control of the frontier in 1897.

By now the Afghan mujahidin had learned to be cautious of the Arab-Afghans, who were dangerous traveling companions as they invited martyrdom, sleeping in white tents with lights on at night, to make it more likely that they would be bombed. In another similarity with the ghazis who emerged in the nineteenth century, they would write elaborate letters to the families of comrades who were killed, celebrating the news. The Afghan mujahidin also learned to hide prisoners, because the Arab-Afghans would kill them immediately.

Victory at Jalalabad strengthened Najibullah's hand: He had governed with a measure of consent, particularly in the cities, where the prospect of mujahidin rule brought fear to many people. A woman in Kabul said, "All I knew of the Russians in those days was that we had a lot of nice, cheap things in the shops which came from Russia. I could not help thinking at that time that a people who made useful things which were so inexpensive for us must be nice too." Najibullah's troops were more confident and better organized, and they knew they were fighting for their lives now that Soviet forces had gone. Hundreds of weapons were handed out to Kabul residents to defend themselves, and the government even recruited a women's militia, giving training, arms and uniforms to the first 1,000 who answered the call.

Among them was a bank clerk called Ramia, who had no doubts about the cause as she excitedly donned military uniform, "The Muslim rebels slit my husband's throat with a knife and they kidnapped my 17-year-old son. Now at last I have found a way to take my revenge." Another woman swapping her civilian clothes for the brown woolen Soviet-made uniform spoke, as if the incident had been yesterday, of the example of Malalai, the heroine killed in the Afghan victory against Britain at the battle of Maiwand, 110 years before. To her, the mujahidin were just another alien force, as much a foreign invader as the British or Russians, to be combated by all patriotic Afghans.

The presence of thousands of Soviet women, who had done many different jobs during the years of occupation, had had a profound impact. Kabul women had seen them working alongside men as helicopter pilots, doctors, engineers and in other trades. And as well as job opportunities, some women now had expectations about cosmetics and clothing that they were prepared to die to defend. Many of the women joining up to fight feared the mujahidin would impose a strict clothing code if they came to power, including the burqa, and would limit their freedom in other ways. Repression of women in Afghanistan did not begin with the Taliban. Women's freedoms were already being curtailed in areas that the mujahidin took from Soviet-backed forces.

There was simmering discontent too about women's rights across the border in the refugee camps around Peshawar, and against the same threat: Islamic fundamentalism. For most people, the aim of the war against the communists had been to restore freedom to Afghanistan, not to hand it over to the fundamentalists. But the way the war had been financed and run had empowered the mujahidin view of Afghan society and discouraged political thought outside narrow Islamism. Despite the defeat at Jalalabad, mujahidin leaders believed that they would now win. They had seen off the Red Army, and as victory felt closer, the brutal influence of fundamentalists became tighter in the refugee camps, the crucible of the new Afghanistan.

Women in the camps had been warned for several years about wearing cosmetics, tight-fitting clothes or going out without being escorted by a male member of their family—Pashtun village values imposed on all refugees. Now there were stricter orders, instructing women not to "walk down the middle of the road" or even "walk with pride."

Tajwar Kakar, a schoolteacher who had been tortured and held in a Soviet jail in Kabul for a year, now received regular death threats for teaching girls in the camps that it was not compulsory to wear the burqa. "We women have fought hard for the freedom of our people and our nation. We have been imprisoned and tortured. Some of us have been killed. And we have been the shield for the men who carried on the jihad. The women helped fight the jihad, and now they don't care about us."

Mujahidin threats against those who promoted women's rights were real. In 1987 Hekmatyar's Islamist gunmen had shot dead Meena Keshwar Kamal, the founder of the women's group RAWA (Revolutionary Association of the Women of Afghanistan). Other activists were beaten and jailed in the refugee camps. And Hekmatyar did not target only women. One of the main spokesmen of the mujahidin movement, Professor Bahauddin Majrooh, was shot as he came to the door of his house expecting to greet the British fundraiser Viscount Cranborne, who was due to see him. Cranborne survived because he had been kept waiting by General Zia at an earlier meeting. When he arrived he found the urbane intellectual Majrooh, "a whisky-loving Afghan with a good line in obscene and very unfunny anti-mullah jokes," lying dead in the street. Majrooh had organized a survey of refugees that found almost three-quarters of them wanted the king back—enough of a crime to have cost him his life. Hekmatyar's men were also blamed for the deaths of several foreign journalists.

Only a week after the ambush of Massud's commanders in the North, Hekmatyar turned his attentions to the South, poisoning Abdul Latif, an effective mujahidin leader known as the "lion of Kandahar." Hekmatyar's bid for control of the opium trade spilled over into Peshawar as well, where he murdered a commander and five of his lieutenants. He helped to train Osama bin Laden's fighters and assisted Omar Abdel-Rahman, the blind sheikh indicted for the 1993 bombing of the World Trade Center. Hekmatyar's contempt for the United States was apparent as early as 1985, when he refused to shake President Reagan's hand, while "duty" mujahidin leader in Washington—the seven leaders took it in turns, in order to keep up lobbying pressure. He went on to support Saddam Hussein in both Gulf wars.

In many ways Hekmatyar, who received the lion's share of U.S. funding, was more of a revolutionary than the Taliban who came later. He was certainly no friend of the traditional clan-based rural hierarchy of Afghanistan. The most widely respected mujahidin leader, Sibghatullah Mujaddidi, called Hekmatyar "a true monster and enemy of Afghanistan...a man no self-respecting nation should support."

Human rights groups in the United States, as well as some members of Congress, began to single out Hekmatyar as a growing problem after the Soviet pullout. The chair of the House Intelligence Committee, Anthony Beilenson, said, "Supplying military aid to the Afghan rebels is no longer in our interest now that the Soviets have withdrawn." But these reservations could not overturn the effect of a decade of rhetoric that it was in the Hindu Kush that the Soviet system would be destroyed by force. It was easier for the United States to keep the funds flowing than to stop them, especially as a Soviet-backed leader was still in power in Afghanistan and still getting Soviet arms and money.

Proof of continuing Soviet support came in the battle for Jalalabad, when Najibullah brought a new weapon into play with terrifying effect: the medium-range Scud missile. Four hundred were fired from Kabul onto mujahidin positions, and several fell across the line into Pakistani territory. The Soviet Union may have withdrawn its forces, but the military establishment was powerful enough to ensure that its friends would not be let down, increasing military aid to Afghanistan to $1.5 billion a year.

This funding was not consistent with the political rhetoric of Gorbachev's reformist government. At the Geneva peace talks, there were personal appeals from the Soviet foreign minister, Eduard Shevardnadze, to his U.S. opposite number, George Schultz, for a mutual end to the funding of clients in Afghanistan. But the appearance of Soviet-financed Scud missiles on the battlefield made it easy for the United States to reject Shevardnadze's appeals. The U.S. administration would continue the conflict as long as Najibullah remained in power, however many lives were lost—a policy that began to be characterized as "fighting to the last Afghan" by its critics.

This brutal logic meant a fight to the finish, ignoring the reality on the ground that fighting against the Kabul government was less effective during this period it had been at any time for several years. Peter Tomsen, who arrived as the new U.S. "envoy to the mujahidin" six months after the Soviet withdrawal, surprised reporters with his analysis. He seemed to be unaware of the scale of the defeat at Jalalabad. "I am confident of a military victory. The pressure is growing on Kabul, the regime's control is receding, the lines of communication are under increasing pressure and they cannot recruit troops. Time is on the resistance's side."

The new U.S. envoy also appeared unaware of disunity among the mujahidin, although it was now having a serious effect on the progress of the war. Conflict within mujahidin ranks led to the main commander on the crucial Kandahar front in the South even instructing his forces to hold back, leaving government forces in control, as he believed there would be chaos and clashes between rival mujahidin if they took the town.

The disjunction between reality in Afghanistan and policy in Washington meant the war would come to a much messier end than portrayed in the movie *Charlie Wilson's War*, where Tom Hanks as Wilson is shown failing to raise small amounts to build schools in Afghanistan after the Soviet pullout. The truth is that, like a drug pusher, the system itself seemed to be addicted to sending weapons into Afghanistan. In real life Charlie Wilson's last $400 million appropriation for his freedom fighters came as late as 1991—a larger figure for one year after the Soviets had gone than the United States had paid out in total during the first five years of the war against the Soviet invasion.

The payments continued even after Wilson went to Russia and was impressed by talk of democracy as the country began to shake off its Soviet baggage. Andrei Kozyrev, soon to be the first foreign minister of the new non-Soviet Russia, tried to persuade Wilson to join Russia in a new common front against radical Islam. This was a similar pitch for Afghanistan against the same enemy—Islamism—as the one made to Britain by General Kauffman, Russia's commander on their southern frontier, in 1875. On his return from Moscow, Wilson did a softer press interview than normal, and soon found a CIA agent in his office, asking him if had traded his "hound dog for a poodle."

By 1991 there was no excuse for not knowing what was going on. The intentions of the mujahidin were beyond any doubt. They were not going to introduce U.S.-style freedom to Afghanistan but instead were increasingly fighting each other. Hundreds of U.S. doctors, nurses and other aid workers were in the frontier region. Their convoys were regularly attacked, the contents looted and women's programs threatened. Disquiet grew even among those who had been the most fervent backers of funds for the mujahidin. One of Wilson's key aides, Charlie Schnabel, went on a fact-finding mission into Afghanistan after the mujahidin recaptured Khost, just south of Tora Bora. He reported back that it was a ghost town, destroyed by indiscriminate attacks by the mujahidin.

There were also now disagreements within Pakistan. General Zia was willing to end the war, even if meant sharing power with Najibullah. But Pakistani intelligence chiefs wanted a fight to the finish as much as the CIA did. One said contemptuously of Zia's approach that "the smell of political expediency and compromise was in the air." Their influence was such that Zia followed their line, ignoring a commitment he had made in the Geneva peace deal to stop arms supplies. Shortly before Zia died in a mysterious helicopter crash, he told President Reagan that he would continue to lie about Pakistan's role in Afghanistan: "We've been denying our activities there for eight years. Muslims have the right to lie in a good cause."

In Afghanistan itself, commanders who had fought the war on the ground, not from the safety of Peshawar, had been demanding more say in the postwar settlement even before the Soviet withdrawal. As early as July 1987, Ismail Khan had convened a conference near Herat in western Afghanistan of 1,200 commanders. Khan was a legendary figure in the mujahidin since, as an Afghan army captain, he had played a part in the uprising against Soviet influence in Herat in 1979, nine months before the Soviet invasion. The commanders he convened in 1987 easily agreed to a stirring declaration that the future of the country could be sorted out only by the "heirs of the martyrs as well as the Muslims of the trenches who are struggling on all war fronts and ready to be martyred." But delivering this declaration on the political stage was harder to do.

After the Soviets left, Massud called two similar meetings in eastern Afghanistan and then traveled from the Panjshir Valley to Pakistan for the first time since the war started, to hold a high-level meeting with Pakistani officials at the ISI. He agreed to their request that he should patch up his differences with Hekmatyar. But nothing came of this either.

The concern of Pakistani intelligence, puppet masters pulling the strings of the mujahidin for so long, was that the power games beginning in Peshawar for jobs after the war was won would distract "their" commanders from the business of winning the war. Afghans who had fled farther abroad also wanted a say in the future of their homeland. There were meetings and conferences in California, Canada and Europe, the three main areas of Afghan settlement. But these initiatives were stifled at birth; the way the United States and Pakistan were running the war left no role for the return of those exiled during the fighting.

Three windows of opportunity to recover Afghanistan from the hands of Islamic fundamentalism were squandered before the attacks of 9/11, and this was the first. Long-term friends of the country, such as Viscount Cranborne, watched in dismay as money continued to be "shovelled into the ideological pockets" of men like Hekmatyar, while more pragmatic commanders were ignored, and no serious attempt was made to widen the political base for a new government.

Shuras, councils of Afghan leaders, had been meeting intermittently in Peshawar to plan the future since the late 1980s, amid fierce and sometimes violent disagreements. The influence of Pakistan and the United States over the process meant that by the time the shura met in earnest to appoint a government that might actually take over, in early 1992, it empowered only the seven leaders, to the exclusion of royalists, returning exiles, commanders in the field and other groups, such as Shias.

At the end of 1991, Moscow and Washington finally stopped arms sales. The Russian government that took over after the failed coup against Gorbachev in August took a much more determined line over ending involvement in Afghanistan. The new foreign minister, Boris Pankin, went as far as to condemn the invasion and Soviet behavior during the war in Afghanistan. It was almost the last act of the USSR, which dissolved 11 days after the final official delivery of Soviet guns south across the Oxus River. Afghanistan had played its part in bringing down the curtain on the 70-year political experiment of Soviet communism.

In Kabul, Najibullah still clung to power. He changed the name of his governing party to Watan—Homeland—and admitted that communism was not for Afghanistan. But time had run out for him. The United States might have signed its last arms check, but Pakistani and Saudi weapons continued to flow to the mujahidin. They had made no deal. As if throwing gas onto a fire, they carried on giving the largest share of funding to the more fundamentalist commanders, in particular Hekmatyar, who had rejected a peace plan brought back by other mujahidin leaders in their first visit to Moscow in 1990.

Kabul was comfortably within rocket range of Hekmatyar's positions to the south and east of the city, and he was now killing thousands of people a year in indiscriminate attacks. In April 1992, when the Russian president Boris Yeltsin discovered that the Russian military had managed to keep 200 advisers working in Kabul, he pulled them out, further destabilizing Najibullah, who belatedly agreed to a United Nations' plan to stand down in favor of an interim government and fresh elections. It was too late.

Among the vultures circling for a share in the spoils of Kabul was the northern leader Abdul Rashid Dostam, one of the most astute and ruthless players of the dark, dense violent Afghan game—an amiable Machiavellian thug. He generously rewarded loyalty and brutally punished failure. When a reporter noticed some blood and flesh on the ground outside Dostam's headquarters and asked if an animal had been killed, he was told that these were the remains of a soldier who had been tied to the tracks of a tank and crushed to death that morning.

Dostam's Turkic features marked him as a descendant of the nomads from the high steppes that roll from the Black Sea across central Asia all the way down to the Hindu Kush. In Afghan tribal terms he was an Uzbek, sharing a cultural history with the newly independent Uzbekistan, across the Oxus River from the northern Afghan region he controlled. Like many other successful mujahidin commanders, he had come up through the ranks of Soviet-backed Afghan forces and owed nothing to the traditional clan structure of the country. But uniquely among those warlords who emerged as leaders from the wreckage of Soviet control, he remained part of the Soviet-backed Kabul government until almost the end. He was not a mujahid but a supreme pragmatist.

Dostam had first been recruited into a militia formed to defend the oil fields in Shebargan in northwestern Afghanistan in the late 1970s. He trained as a paratrooper, and quickly rose through the ranks of the militias that became increasingly important to the survival of the Kabul regime, particularly after Najibullah took over in 1985. Dostam's Jowzjani militia fought alongside Afghan army forces and were the only irregular force in the country to be routinely deployed out of their own area, holding ground against the mujahidin in Kandahar and Helmand as Soviet forces withdrew from the South in 1988. They developed a reputation for fighting, and for looting. Their nickname, *kilim jam*—the carpet is gathered up—referred to their habit of leaving nothing behind if they came to call.

As Soviet control drained away, Dostam maneuvered himself into a position where he was more than just the Afghan military commander in the North:

he was the undisputed leader of a region where he knew how to work the traditional levers of power. The first British envoy, Mountstuart Elphinstone, 200 years previously, had noticed the particular strength of elders among the Uzbeks: "They are assembled in tribes under powerful chiefs. This peculiarity is probably occasioned by their being separated by mountains from the kingdom of Caubul, to which they belong…which circumstances have prevented any encroachment by their own sovereign on the rights of the local chiefs."

Dostam did not encroach on the rights of the local chiefs, and secured their support by keeping the war away from the North as much as possible, arranging private peace deals where he could with mujahidin leaders, including Massud, while at the same time staying on the right side of Kabul by making his Jowzjani militia available until the end of the Soviet-backed regime. And when Soviet arms supplies stopped at the end of 1991, he was ready to play a different game, with his eye on securing a major arms dump south of the Hindu Kush.

Dostam's defection ended any hopes that Najibullah may have had. By the spring of 1992, the mujahidin already held Bagram Air Field, always vulnerable as it lay in a valley just too far from Kabul to be protected by troops in the city. Now Najibullah's deputy defense minister defected and sent planes north to ferry back 600 of Dostam's troops to take Kabul airport in the capital itself. This proved decisive and the city fell without a fight. Ex-President Najibullah was prevented from boarding a UN plane to India, and took refuge in the UN compound in town. On April 18 a tank that had been stood outside the former royal palace for almost exactly 14 years, as a memorial to the revolution that had ousted President Daoud, was taken away and replaced by pots containing pink geraniums. But the symbolic gesture was misplaced. The fighting was not over, not by a long shot.

Massud negotiated the defection of much of the Afghan air force and the army garrisons that lay between his stronghold in the Panjshir and Kabul. For the first time he could leave the fastness of his valley safely and make the journey out along its best defense, the narrow track next to the Panjshir River as it wound like a snake along the gorge below high cliffs out to the flat dusty plain beyond. A BBC reporter, Mark Urban, watched as squadrons of ex-government helicopters landed on the wide plain flanked by the high curtain of the Hindu Kush: "a most theatrical scene developed. Columns of mechanised troops snaked down from the mountains and came down to the parade ground. Massud walked along the line of vehicles and raised huge cheers. It was very much like Caesar reviewing his troops."

The newly acquired helicopters took Massud's advance guard into the city, while dozens of trucks with other troops followed by road. The scale of this armored movement, regular soldiers alongside Massud's best mujahidin, forced Hekmatyar to abandon the presidential palace and the other central locations he had occupied in the confusion of the handover. He withdrew from Kabul to positions to the east and on the Charasiab ridge to the south.

Competing mujahidin forces, armed with Soviet, Saudi and U.S.-financed weapons, now confronted each other across Kabul, and the world stood back. Just as it had abandoned the country to its fate after Soviet forces left in 1989, in 1992 the United States lost a second opportunity to bring Afghanistan back from the brink of being a failed state and the refuge of those who would destroy the World Trade Center.

There was a kind of government: "President" Burhanuddin Rabbani was nominated to take over from "President" Sibghatullah Mujaddidi later in the year. The two men were both ex-teachers in Islamic studies at Kabul University who had become mujahidin leaders. Hekmatyar, the fundamentalist who had once been their student, was offered the post of prime minister but turned it down, and when he refused to give a guarantee that he would not shoot down the plane carrying the other leaders in from Pakistan, they had to come by road instead.

In some parts of Kabul, rival mujahidin occupied opposite sides of the same street, and when reporters asked why they were not shooting, they replied, "We have not had the order yet." The same clan and tribal loyalties were in play that had made the country ungovernable when Britain had tried in the nineteenth century, but this time the centrifugal forces ripping at the center came with vastly increased firepower.

When the fighting did start, it was of an intensity unlike anything in the war in Afghanistan thus far. There had been rocketing of the capital before, but not for as long or with so little discrimination. And there had been rape before, but not used as it was now, as a weapon of war, to dominate an ethnic opposition. Massud's forces took over Afghan army positions and their heavy weapons, including tanks, armored vehicles and artillery. Between 1992 and 1995, weapons designed for total war between armies were used against people in their homes; grand avenues and whole suburbs were reduced to sand.

News footage from those terrible years has a nightmare quality. The violence had its own momentum—men shot, looted, raped, died, because that was what they did. Rationality deserted them, as they locked horns in motiveless violence, driven as if in a nightmare summoned up from the deep sludge of the subconscious. As the rockets and bullets came without warning, some survivors lost the ability to cope. A woman said, "One of these rockets hit our house. Thank God nobody was injured, but my daughter became disabled because of the terrible sound of the rocket. Once she could speak fluently, but she cannot speak now and she cannot walk either. It is as if she is five or six years less than her real age."

In an incident that became famous, a girl called Nahid, who was 15 years old, jumped to her death from the sixth-floor window of an apartment block, fearing rape. It was February 7, 1993, the night of Eid, the festival at the end of the Ramadan month of fasting. The family had recently returned from a refugee camp in Pakistan and had chosen to live on an upper floor in the bleak, Soviet-era housing complex at Microroyan because they thought their daughters would be safer. A boy and his grandfather tried to fight off mujahidin gunmen who broke in, but both were shot and wounded. After the incident, neighbors thought that a rug had fallen out of the window in the chaos. When they looked more closely they saw it was not a rug but Nahid's red dress, spread out around her where she had hit the ground. Her sister said Nahid "was really beautiful. She also had a good character. During that time when we first came back, she was always worrying about kilim jams abducting us. During the night we were very afraid and she asked another sister to tell us stories so that we'd stay awake in case anyone came in. It seemed she was aware of her coming death."

It turned out that it was not Dostam's feared kilim jams who had broken in but Massud's fighters. The family and their friends staged a protest rally the next day, carrying Nahid's body, and tried to march to the presidential palace, although according to a neighbor, "the fighting was bad that day, with rockets and bullets flying." Fighters allied with Massud fired at the mourners, and they were forced to turn back.

Nahid was only one of about 25,000 people to die in Kabul during those years. In August 1992 a carpenter came home to find his son dead: "Mohammad Ismael, who was eight years old, was killed in a very nasty way—his body was left full of holes. Other members of my family who were in other rooms were injured so badly that it took a long, long time for them to heal." On December 30, 1992, 12-year-old Baqi was killed playing in the street, by a rocket fired indiscriminately. A mother of four children was at home when another rocket hit: "The bodies could not be recognized. Their feet and hands were thrown everywhere." Another witness, Mohammed, said: "It was about four o'clock in the afternoon when a rocket hit our house near the door of the yard. My brother and eight or nine youths were standing in the lane and these eight or nine people except two of them got killed in a very bad way that you could not recognise them. My brother was injured seriously in his stomach and a piece of the rocket is still in his body. People collected body parts with shovels."

During the first phase of the fighting, in 1992, the battle set Dostam, Massud and allied mujahidin against Hekmatyar's fundamentalists. A major new Iranian-backed force also came into play in the battle for Kabul. While there had been seven mujahidin groups under Pakistan, eight further guerrilla groups, centered around the Hazara region in the West, had competed for Iranian money. They now came together in one party, the Hezb-i-Wahadat.

Historians will never agree on whether the Hazaras, who have a distinctive Mongol look, really are the descendants of Genghis Khan's cavalry, but there is enough evidence to keep this romantic notion alive. They live amid a mass of bewitching red and green mountains that appear to have fallen off the western end of the Hindu Kush, where they hear the roar of a dragon in the echo of a river thundering down one ravine and tell a local version of the old myth about the boy who saved a maiden by slaying the dragon.

Hazara literally means "a thousand," and was historically used for a unit of horsemen; so it can also be translated as "regiment" or "battalion." And the local names for their villages and hamlets appear to correspond to the names of Mongol commanders. Whatever the truth of their origins, the Hazaras certainly need a warrior tradition. In the centuries since they were left beached in western Afghanistan, as the Mongol tide receded across Asia, they have become a put-upon minority, squeezed between the Pashtun tribes of the South and the Uzbeks and Tajiks of the North—finding themselves servants at best, and slaves at worst. In Afghanistan they are also set apart by their adherence to the Shia strand of Islam, practiced in Iran.

Hekmatyar was a Sunni extremist, and at any other time might have persecuted Hazaras, but without other support, he entered a cynical alliance with them at the end of 1992. This was the signal for Massud to sanction an all-out assault on the Hazara community in Kabul, notorious even by the standards of the time. The attack on the tightly packed streets of mud houses clinging to the side of the Afshar hill in the west of the city, involving the mass killing of civilians and systematic rape of women, left the area uninhabitable.

Massud and his allies did have a military motive to move into Afshar—to neutralize hostile artillery positions and capture the headquarters of the Hezb-i-Wahadat, now that the Hazara party had allied with Hekmatyar. But an investigation by a human rights group, the Afghanistan Justice Project, concluded that the Hezb-i-Wahadat headquarters in a former college building was not even hit. "This was not a raid or skirmish but a full-scale battle, in which the Islamic State deployed the combined military resources from the old Soviet-era army and the mujahidin against targets within the capital city, all of them located in areas that were primarily residential, with the civilian population intact."

After an intensive artillery bombardment on February 10, 1993, fighters moved in before dawn the following day. The force defending the area withdrew, leaving thousands of Hazara civilians defenseless. The mujahidin who carried out the worst abuses were from a well-financed but small group led by Abdul Rasul Sayyaf, a Wahhabi fundamentalist then allied with Massud. Sayyaf's militia had been set up specifically to channel Saudi funds into the war. His men had been involved in frequent skirmishes with Hazara forces, with both sides claiming to have suffered significant abuses, including rape and murder.

The attackers moved from house to house in Afshar, raping, killing and looting. They mutilated bodies and mounted decapitated heads in windows. There is no agreement over how many were killed, but witnesses interviewed later said they saw bodies piled in the streets. Survivors were herded into shipping containers and told to dig their own graves. Some paid huge bribes to secure their release; others escaped with harrowing accounts of what had happened: "At night I was kept in a container; during the day I and other 10 to 20 men were made to dig trenches. There were lots of containers. At night some men would be taken out and not come back. We could hear shots and we assumed the men had been killed. I think some were buried in the trenches. I finally escaped by hiding in the river under a bridge." Another witness was sure the attackers were a joint force of Massud's and Sayyaf's men. Before he was taken away, he heard a commander over the radio ordering the killers not to fight each other for the loot: "I had left the door open hoping the militias would think the house empty. They came in and beat me and took me to Qargha River where I was put into a container with about 60 to 65 men. It was very crowded."

A woman described how her husband was taken away and then later the same day another group of soldiers came. "My son was 11 years old. They held him and asked where his father was. They aimed their guns at him and I threw myself over him. I was shot in the hand and leg but he was shot five times. He died." Still bleeding, she was taken down to the basement of her house and raped, along with two other women who had fled to the house for refuge and two teenage girls. One of the girls was stabbed with a bayonet when she tried to resist. The soldiers then looted everything in the house.

The Afshar massacre cast a long shadow over Afghanistan. After securing the Hazara homeland around Bamiyan, where giant stone Buddhas had once stood, in 2001, the Hazara army immediately made its way to Kabul after hearing the Taliban had fallen, because the Hazaras remembered what had happened to their families in 1993 and feared that the same thing would happen again. Securing immunity from prosecution for the killings in Kabul during those years remains one of the key preoccupations of the old mujahidin warlords to this day.

Frustrated at the inability of the mujahidin to make peace, the Saudi government invited the leaders to Mecca, the holiest place in the Islamic world, where they agreed to work together. Hekmatyar came, signed up, and went back to rocket Kabul again. Still Pakistan's favored leader, Hekmatyar had also secured the support of a number of key ex-communist leaders from a faction of the party who remembered his support when they had tried to oust Najibullah in a coup in 1990. But even when Hekmatyar persuaded Dostam, the Uzbek leader from the North, to change sides and join him in 1994, it did not break the stalemate. Neither side could deliver the killer punch, although Dostam brought a significant number of warplanes with him; so for the first time in the civil war, both sides could carry out air attacks.

The killing dragged on into another year while the world continued to look the other way. The days of journalists packing the American Club in Peshawar, growing beards and donning *salwar kameez*, waiting to be escorted across the frontier, were long gone. The reporters who had competed for superlatives in describing the legendary guerrilla leadership qualities of Ahmed Shah Massud were nowhere to be seen as his gunmen raped and looted their way across Kabul, fueled now by opium-processing workshops in the Panjshir and the proceeds of extortion at roadside checkpoints.

It was a very dangerous war to cover. Apart from random attacks, there were targeted killings, such as the death of the BBC reporter Mirwais Jalil, murdered on Hekmatyar's orders. A few journalists continued to chronicle the vortex of violence with dedication and bravery, but despite their efforts editors lost interest. With no superpower involvement, Afghans killing each other was not a story—Bosnia was the new international preoccupation. There were no debates in the UN Security Council on Afghanistan between 1990 and the arrival of the Taliban in 1996.

Forgotten by the world, Kabul suffered far more damage in the struggle between rival mujahidin than during the previous Soviet occupation. Below the ancient remnants of the city wall, winding along the hill of the Bala Hissar, Kabul's grandest streets were reduced to ruins, flattened into the dust, building by building. The southern suburbs around the zoo and the university became uninhabitable as those houses not destroyed were surrounded by unexploded munitions. Remarkably a few moth-eaten animals survived the whole war in the zoo. Hekmatyar kept the lion alive by occasionally tossing in his enemies after maiming them with a knife.

The violent stalemate in Kabul also meant there was now no check on disorder and criminality across the rest of the country. Reconstruction was at a standstill. For mile after mile, mud-walled villages had been reduced to what looked like termite mounds. The main roads were bombed into dust tracks, making it quicker to cycle than to drive from city to city. And every few miles travelers would be confronted by a chain marking the control of another petty warlord, who would claim a toll to provide protection. Kandahar, the capital of the Pashtun heartland, slid into decadence, culminating in a tank battle on the streets between two commanders who both wanted sex with the same boy.

PART FIVE

THE TALIBAN AND THE U.S.-LED INVASION, 1994–2008

12

VIRTUE AND VICE

Women you should not step outside your residence... If women are going outside with
fashionable, ornamental, tight and charming clothes to show themselves, they will be
cursed by the Islamic Sharia, and should never expect to go to heaven.

—Taliban decree, Kabul, 1996

I t would be hard to replicate the circumstances that led to the creation of the
Taliban. They were not just another Afghan guerrilla group, fighting a civil
war. They emerged like a collapsed star, sucking the war into a black hole,
then governing with the force of antimatter—of Afghan creation, but as if seen
through a dark mirror to a soul distorted by a generation of warfare. Nothing
was as it had been in the past, nor as it seemed in the present.

The men who formed the Taliban in the mid-1990s, all from the Pashtun
South, had not been connected with the most fundamentalist parties during the
war with Russia, but they developed a creed that tried to go back to the seventh
century. They said they revered women and wanted them educated when the
war was over but in fact enslaved them with restrictions worse than anywhere
other than Saudi Arabia; they opposed the use and trading of heroin but were
financed by it; and they cultivated an insular and remote worldview, looking
inward to Afghanistan, but ended up hosting Osama bin Laden, who had quite
a different vision for Islam's place in the world.

The Taliban leader, Mullah Mohammed Omar, was a figure of dark sin-
gularity, unlike any other from his country's past. Before him, Afghan leaders
had always needed to engage with the outside world; Afghanistan's position on
the crossroads of Asia demanded no less. Omar viewed the world beyond his
borders not with hostility but indifference, engaging with it on his own terms,
which meant not at all. He did not see the need for a foreign policy. I am one
of only a handful of people from Europe or North America who has even seen

the Taliban leader, and I would hardly describe our meeting as a meaningful conversation.

It was in Kandahar in 1997, a year after the Taliban took Kabul. I was traveling with Rahimullah Yusufzai, the only journalist Omar would take a phone call from. Rahimullah was well known in Afghanistan for his broadcasts on the BBC's Pashtu service, but this would be only their second meeting, and word came from Omar that it would not be "helpful" to the movement if I came too. Waiting outside, I saw him emerge afterward, tall, with a fair complexion for an Afghan and a Grecian nose, prominent above his unkempt black beard. There was not much to mark him out among a group of similarly dressed Taliban, their heads covered with large black turbans, and wearing cheap European-style polyester jackets over their traditional black salwar kameez. Omar acknowledged me with his one good eye and a simple greeting before climbing into the back of a Toyota Land Cruiser and racing away, almost running over a man who threw himself in front of the vehicle in pursuit of some local grievance.

The man who controlled more of Afghanistan than anyone since the 1970s traveled to Kabul only once during the five years the Taliban held the capital. He ruled instead from an iron bedstead in Kandahar, in a room shut off not by a door but just a dirty torn curtain, surrounded by Taliban who came and went with an easy familiarity. Rahimullah sat on the carpet among the Taliban, watching as Omar chatted, joked, signed letters and at one point unlocked the padlock on a box to give some money to two fighters who had arrived in town with nowhere to stay.

He said the Taliban had no territorial ambitions beyond Afghanistan, denying Russian claims that it wanted to export its Islamic revolution north across the Oxus River to the central Asian republics of Uzbekistan and Tajikistan. Against the evidence, he denied that the movement had been backed by Pakistan. "It is a purely religious movement which has received no support from outside," he said. He maintained the West was wrong to believe that the Taliban oppressed women; rather they revered them. In what became a standard response on the issue of girls' schools, he said there were "priorities in war," and girls could be educated in an Islamic way once the war was won.

Despite his humble appearance, this successor to the amirs of Afghanistan had a strong sense of destiny and a taste for the theatrical gesture. He was creating the world's first pure Islamic state since the time of the Prophet Mohammed, and he did not need to go to the royal palace in Kabul to be crowned. He had already gone one better, taking the cloak believed to have belonged to the Prophet himself from its case in a mosque in Kandahar, revealing it to the crowd and declaring himself not amir of Afghanistan, but Amir al-Mu'minin, leader of all the faithful. The last man to claim the title was Dost Mohammed in the 1830s.

The decade of war against the Soviet invasion had tightened the grip of Islamic fundamentalism across Afghanistan and Pakistan. President Zia encouraged this move toward Islamicization, particularly in education and Sharia law. The ratchet moved in only one direction, closing down avenues of independent thought, while the world looked the other way.

The men who emerged as Taliban leaders took it further, developing their own system, which was quite unlike that of the Kabul-educated mujahidin. They were not political revolutionaries—and in fact had little interest in politics or government. Their revolution was focused instead on controlling morality and personal behavior.

The Taliban wanted to work with the deep social grain of rural conservatism, not interfering with the power of tribal elders or landowners, as long as people followed Taliban religious practices. They viewed as superstition some of the more colorful rural religious traditions, opposing them with the same zeal as seventeenth-century Puritans in England did the practices of the Catholic Church.

Under the Taliban, religious authority would rest not with the complex layers of *syeds*, *pirs* and *alims*, traditional guardians of the Afghan Sufi tradition, but with mullahs, who qualified through the discipline of long years of strict religious education, centered around constant repetition of the Koran in Arabic, a language many of them did not even speak. Mullahs of this kind had been present in the region for a long time but now had political power for the first time. Ten years of internationally licensed holy war, followed by seven years of criminality, left a vacuum they could fill.

At the core of the new antimatter soul being forged for Afghanistan was "anti-education," in which boys were taught not about culture or the natural world, and certainly not to think for themselves—the bedrock of education in the developed world—but to believe that this was all taken care of for them by Islam. An enthusiastic talib told me of the benefits of this soon after they took Kabul. "Islam teaches when to wake and when to sleep, how to walk, how to talk, how to relate to the people. It is everything."

Taliban theology had an unbroken thread that stretched back, through the Hindustani fanatics and ghazis who had fought the British, and the Deobandi school in India, to the deserts of Saudi Arabia where Mohammed Ibn Abd al-Wahhab had refined his view of Islam in the eighteenth century.

Thousands of madrassas had sprung up not just along the frontier but elsewhere in Pakistan during the war; several of the more important were close to the capital, Islamabad, itself. They ignored not just the standard curriculum of a non-Islamic school but also centuries of Islamic intellectual achievement in astronomy, mathematics, philosophy and design. Not all madrassas, even those in the Deobandi tradition, were this rigid, but the open tap of funding from the

Wahhabi kingdom of Saudi Arabia went to those with the most austere, exclusive and intolerant form of Islam.

The madrassas became factories turning out Taliban fighters, many of them war orphans who knew no other life. *Talib* simply means "student," although the word came to mean specifically "religious student," and the madrassa system provided a formidable old-boy network, giving a sinuous strength and flexibility to the Taliban army, which otherwise lacked a formal command structure.

During major offensives, those running the big madrassas would close them to send their teenage students off as cannon fodder, with the same callous zeal as the "Mad Mullah" who had pushed boys in front of British guns a century before, witnessed by Churchill. And the madrassas provided another important support service to the Taliban campaign: fighters went straight from the front line for rest and relaxation during the wars against the mujahidin and later the U.S.-led forces in Afghanistan.

— — —

The origins of the Taliban lie in the dust of the southern desert, perhaps the most unforgiving landscape in Afghanistan, known in the local language as Dasht-i-Mango, the Desert of Death. The war here in the 1980s was quite different to the guerrilla campaigns farther north. Soviet conventional forces had a significant advantage in the wide flat areas between low hills with no cover for the mujahidin, who were restricted to hit-and-run raids, often using motorbikes.

To those fighting in the South, it felt like a forgotten corner of a forgotten war: They received far less funding than the mujahidin elsewhere, and took higher casualties. One of the more effective commanders was a former Afghan army officer who went under the nom de guerre of Mullah Borjan. He said that of the 90 men he had started fighting with, only 8 were left alive by the late 1980s—"I cannot describe the suffering." He and a small group of other Pashtun commanders became so disillusioned with the Peshawar system of funding that they had formed their own militia, the Mullahs' Front, initially led by Mullah Abdul Razzaq, and Mullah Mohammed Rabbani (no relation to the Rabbani who became president). These three men, Borjan, Razzaq and Rabbani, were among the key founders of the Taliban.

Six years before they emerged as the Taliban, the Mullahs' Front already had some of the characteristics of the movement. The mullahs lived simple lives and needed little funding. This gave them enormous power, since they owed nothing to any patron, and were remote from Pakistani control. They also appeared honest and conscientious to the villagers they lived among, caring about civilian casualties in a way that other mujahidin conspicuously did not.

Omar had not been in the Mullahs' Front but had fought farther north, sustaining four injuries, including the loss of his eye. By the time the Soviet-backed leader Najibullah was finally pushed out of office in Kabul in the spring of 1992, Omar was living a quiet life running a small madrassa in the village near Maiwand where he had lived for all of his adult life. But as criminality and corruption flourished after the collapse of central authority, he began to meet like-minded friends, who were concerned that the victory over Soviet control had been squandered. Nowhere was Pashtun nationalist feeling stronger than here. They remember the battle of Maiwand against Britain in 1880, as if it were yesterday, and like to tell visitors that it was they who first rose up against the Soviet invasion.

In 1994, when two teenage girls from his village were seized by a local commander and repeatedly raped after having their heads shaved, Omar led a group of 30 volunteers, only half of them armed with rifles, in an assault on the place the girls were being held. They released the girls, seized the commander and hanged him from a tank barrel. What happened next has taken on the aura of a legend—the founding story of a movement. Delving through the dark mirror to the antimatter beyond *how* the tale is remembered now perhaps matters more than the narrative "truth."

The exact sequence of events, and the depth of Pakistan's involvement, is disputed. Within only a few months, once the Taliban had taken Kandahar, there was clearly considerable funding and support coming from Pakistan, to the extent that Kandahar had an internal Pakistani phone code, and Pakistani troops were openly giving the Taliban technical assistance. Saudi Arabia took a close interest too; this was, after all, a movement of ex-students from schools they had funded. The Taliban leadership insist that external support came after they had seized power for themselves, and that they were not the creation of Pakistan.

Omar's successful operation to release the girls attracted considerable attention. He cemented his reputation by freeing the boy being held in Kandahar after the tank battle. He took no money and claimed no position after these exploits, spreading his Robin Hood reputation. He would say later, "How could we remain quiet when we could see crimes being committed against women and the poor." Then, at a shura in Omar's village, a former commander nicknamed Mullah Torak—the "Black Mullah"—announced the formation of the Taliban. The Black Mullah later said that although he had been the main speaker, there was no dispute over who should lead the movement: "Omar was a very brave mujahid. He was widely respected, and people knew how he had lived his life. There was no debate or confusion." There were 24 founding shura members but no fixed constitution or jobs. "If somebody was pious then he could come into the shura."

The Black Mullah had called the meeting because of concern about checkpoints along the main road. Trade was paralyzed, as every few miles there was another checkpoint, and another mujahidin group demanding money. Shortly after their founding shura, the Taliban took two Japanese-made Hino trucks from Kandahar all the way east to the Pakistan border, with 90 fighters concealed under tarpaulins in the back. Omar was in the cab of one; Borjan, the commander from the Mullahs' Front, was in the other. They paid off 42 illegal checkpoints along the way, claiming that they had sheep in the back; no one bothered to search the trucks. Arriving at Spin Boldak, the border crossing point, they took it after a brief battle, then seized an arms dump and the district headquarters.

Leaving another commander hanging from a tank barrel—already a trademark that spread their no-nonsense reputation—they fought their way back west, opening the road checkpoint by checkpoint, until they held Kandahar itself—the most decisive military shift in Afghanistan since the withdrawal of Soviet forces five years earlier. In the Afghan way, many commanders came over to them without a fight, and Taliban control of the border meant that they now had unlimited access to their main recruiting base in the madrassas.

Whatever its role up to now, Pakistan, frustrated by the inability of its protégé Hekmatyar to take power, quickly switched to the Taliban, providing them with fuel for the warplanes they took at Kandahar airport and with other crucial support. The Taliban also received donations from trucking companies for reopening the lucrative route from Iran to Pakistan that crossed the South.

In Kandahar and elsewhere in the Pashtun heartlands of the South, Taliban victories initially came as a relief. They disarmed bandits and imposed law and order. But their move on the more cosmopolitan western town of Herat in 1995 set alarm bells ringing worldwide.

Herat's control of trade from Iran, taking tariffs on secondhand Japanese vehicles that flowed through to Pakistan, made it the richest town in the country. Toyotas were only the latest business opportunity for this marketplace on the crossroads of Asia, which had seen trade come and go in rugs, blue glass, silks, spices and precious stones for centuries.

Herat contains some of the world's oldest and finest mosques, and the remains of what the godfather of travel writers, Robert Byron, called "the most beautiful example in colour in architecture ever devised by man to the glory of his God and himself." He could write this even after much of it was destroyed by British forces preparing the defenses of Herat against a Russian attack in 1885 that never came. Tamerlane and Genghis Khan had fought for control of a town from a different world like the Silk Road towns—Balkh, Samarkand and Bokhara—farther to the north. Imprinted on the DNA of Herat were long memories of civilization and cosmopolitan cultural values.

Before the arrival of the Taliban in Herat in 1995, girls were educated alongside boys and women were able to work in a limited range of jobs. The west and north of Afghanistan, Persian-speaking and outward-looking, was like a foreign country to the Pashtu-speaking hordes of the Taliban, with their two-dimensional Islamist worldview.

The Taliban had perfected a highly mobile form of warfare, using fleets of Toyota Hilux pickups and living more lightly than other forces. The austerity of their background and education, their ruthless unity of purpose, allied with the speed of their approach in Hiluxes, brought a new kind of determination to the Afghan conflict. The long-term mujahidin leader in Herat, Ismail Khan, spread his front line too wide, was drawn out too far and was overwhelmed by the Pashtun blitzkrieg. He fled for safety across the nearby border to Iran.

The new governor of Herat was Mullah Razzaq, who had been leader of the Mullahs' Front in the late 1980s. He displayed a paranoid obsession about the distraction of women, going much further than demanding that they shroud themselves in the all-enveloping burqa, a garment that came to symbolize the Taliban more than anything else. Razzaq issued orders that women were not even to pass the window of his office, in case he heard the sound of their voices or the distinctive tap of their feet.

It was perhaps only an army of orphans who could have imposed this madness on Afghanistan with such enthusiasm. Many of the fighters were still in their teens, some as young as 14, and had grown up without the company of mothers or sisters. They accepted without question that women should be banished into darkness and whipped if they were not fully covered up, or appeared outside without a male relative. The young zealots of the Taliban had no other contact with women at all, in mosques, restaurants, shops or traveling on the road. All of their conversations were with men or boys. They dreamed of virgins in paradise, making no connection between these beings and the shapeless tents who shuffled along the gutter or were carried like animals, squatting in the open trunks of cars, while men sat in the front.

Although the Taliban seemed extreme, what they imposed were no more than normal conservative countryside Pashtun values. In some villages, women do not even have a name outside their own family. I once succeeded in asking some questions of a woman in a Pashtun village near Kabul—a bizarre four-way interview, with her husband shouting my questions through a curtain. The answers were recorded by a woman camera operator and then relayed to my translator by the husband, since he would not allow his wife to be questioned directly. As we were leaving, I asked my translator to check her name. He pointed to the recently skinned carcass of a sheep, hanging glistening from a tree. "That is how I would end up," he said, "if I tried to ask." The interview, recorded during the Taliban years, revealed the frightening isolation of women's lives. The nameless, shapeless figure mumbling answers from under her burqa, had lost three sons in the war, two fighting for the mujahidin against the Soviet occupation and one fighting for the Taliban. But she hardly appeared to know that the Soviet army had left, let alone who was now in power, or whether it mattered.

The long war and decades of poverty meant that there was no impetus for progress in the Afghan countryside. The Taliban were a consequence of

Pashtun conservatism, not the original cause of women's repression, but in the black hole that Afghanistan had become, they enforced the toughest of regimes against women with a ferocious energy. At the same time the clan and tribal structure that had sustained Pashtun life for centuries, and might have provided a brake on extremism, had broken down. In the 1980s the mujahidin who first took up arms against the Soviet invasion knew where they came from, and could recite ancient legends as well as their family lineage, but an upbringing in a madrassa was a break with that past. At the height of Taliban power, a village elder I was staying with in Helmand Province expressed fond exasperation for their excesses: to him they were "just boys." He admired their zeal and honesty while wishing they had a more rounded view of human nature.

In the cities, even in their natural power base Kandahar where they had been welcomed, Taliban restrictions quickly began to grate. They had brought law and order, but with a fanaticism that made normal life impossible. The theater, a highly popular attraction in a country in thrall to the Bollywood dream machine, was flattened, and the ground cleared to build a mosque. In the spring of 1996 a new ministry for "the promotion of virtue and the suppression of vice," based exactly on the model of administration from the paymasters of the Taliban in Saudi Arabia, began to impose rules that included no music, television or non-Islamic books. Clean-shaven men were arrested and held until their beards were the approved shaggy length, and market traders stopped from displaying women's garments—or even shampoo bottles if they showed the picture of a woman.

Squatting on the floor of what looked like a stable amid ruins, in the main office of the new ministry, the virtue and vice minister cheerily said that they had realized how corrupt and decadent Western civilization had become when Prince Charles and Princess Diana both had extramarital affairs. That kind of thing would not be allowed to happen in Afghanistan. They also clamped down hard on homosexuality, although it was commonplace, indeed routine, across Pashtun areas.

From some source, not the Koran, the Taliban learned that the appropriate punishment for homosexuals was to have a wall pushed onto them. They were preoccupied for months with a debate about on how to achieve this—whether the guilty should be buried first or actually crushed by the wall, and whether it should be made with cement or loose stones. Imposing Sharia law was not easy. A rural judge told me, in the tone of a man considering a fine legal point, that he was not sure where a hand should be cut off at the wrist joint or across the bone farther up the forearm.

—   —   —

By the summer of 1996, with half of Afghanistan under Taliban control, they had Kabul in their sights. They had dislodged Hekmatyar from his headquarters on the Charasiab ridge to the south of the capital, bringing the city within range of Taliban rockets. As Britain had discovered in the Second Anglo-Afghan War, the ridge was the key to the city. The Taliban did rocket Kabul, but they also lifted the blockade imposed by Hekmatyar, allowing trade to cross the front lines, a payoff to the trucking companies that had continued to fund the Taliban since their first operation to open the road in the South.

For the beleaguered capital, the arrival of fresh food supplies in early September 1996 led some to believe that rule by the Taliban would not be all bad. Nothing could be worse than the squalor and terror of the last four years. Only foreign aid kept people alive amid the rubble. But the war had left 30,000 women without a husband to look after them, and as the days shortened, a collective shiver seemed to paralyze a city where none knew what the Islamist student revolutionaries would do once they had taken the capital.

With unbelievable cynicism, Hekmatyar now accepted the post of prime minister offered to him four years before, proposing a grand alliance with Massud. But the days of shifting alliances between rival mujahidin were over. Hekmatyar's fundamentalist Pashtun fighters were natural Taliban recruits, and after he had attempted to impose Islamist austerity on Kabul, closing the movies and imposing restrictions on women, he fled abroad and was reputed for a while to be the third largest investor on the Italian stock exchange. His forces defected en masse to the Taliban.

The main Taliban advance on Kabul did not come along the old British invasion route from the south but from the east, after Jalalabad fell without a fight in September. The story the Taliban like to tell relates how Jalalabad was taken by a handful of their fighters in two Hilux pickups. Borjan, now the overall military commander of the movement, arrived in the third. Victory was lubricated by a payment of millions of dollars to the governor to persuade him to leave. The money almost certainly came from Saudi Arabia—now backing a Taliban takeover.

In late September, on the night before he died in the final assault on Kabul, Borjan did his only TV interview as a Taliban commander. He was a slight man with a refined and thoughtful air, who picked his way toward us through a room crammed with fighters in a house commandeered from the departing governor. Most of the Taliban leadership opposed television, but he was different—undogmatic and willing to talk on camera. Spotting a talib he had sent to command the forces at Jalalabad airport, he ordered him back to his post. There was always a chaotic informality in this protean force. He was then handed a two-way radio to be given a report on a successful attack on a convoy carrying a local leader who opposed the Taliban.

Borjan calculated the effect of this news without smiling, as he sat down on the floor, resting an arm on one knee, with the other knee bent flat to the large Mauri-pattern rug that covered the floor of the room, its light-colored lozenges woven on a deep blood-red sea. He put the palm of his hand flat down on the rug and said Hekmatyar now controlled "no more than that space." The long, rather feminine fingers of his other hand, draped over the end of his knee, played around a ring of beads as he talked of the policies of the Taliban.

Unlike some other Taliban leaders, for Borjan the movement appeared to be a means to an end. He went through the ritual answers about girls' schools—"when the time was right"—and wanting an Islamic system of government. But the important things for him were peace and law and order. He was old enough to remember another Afghanistan that he wanted to see again. If he had lived, perhaps he might have moderated some of the excesses of the movement.

Leaving Borjan to plan the attack, we picked our way out through the obstacle course of tightly packed warriors, breathing the same sweet feral air as men who thought they were on the eve of victory. One man caught my arm. He was older than most, with a white beard that seemed to merge with matching folds of elaborate white cotton clothing under a brocade jacket. When he opened his mouth to smile, there was the flash of a gold tooth. In his hands he held a gleaming British cavalry sword. "My grandfather used it to cut off the head of an Englishman," he said. "Now I will use it to kill Massud." Outside, the governor's large collection of ornamental birds made an enormous racket. No one seemed to be feeding them. Borjan left before first light.

Not all of the regional commanders had gone over to the Taliban; some were helping Massud's regular troops to defend the Silk Gorge, the gateway to Sarobi, the last town before Kabul. The Kabul River plunged down almost like a waterfall here, several hundred feet, before jinking to another pass and dropping another hundred feet. It was thought impossible to break through the gorge, as the road was narrow and covered from above by hundreds of firing points, with tanks in elevated fixed positions built by Soviet forces.

Unlike at Herat, where the Taliban success depended on speed across a wide front, here victory would involve a far larger sacrifice. The Taliban advanced after dawn prayers on September 25, but faltered under a withering rain of fire and fell back. Borjan had been inside his Hilux, but now climbed out and shouted, "What's the worst thing that can happen? If you die you will become martyrs." The Taliban advanced again but then halted as the fire intensified, asking for their own tanks to go ahead first. Borjan grabbed a Kalashnikov and ran forward shouting "I am in front. Why are you behind me?" This was the defining moment of the battle that would decide the future of Afghanistan. Following the example of their commander, the Taliban force advanced at a run, and cries of *Allah hu Akbar* (God is great) were heard amid the deafening sound of gunfire and the clatter of bullets impacting on the rocks of the gorge. Borjan was hit. His driver, a streetwise 18-year-old called Naqeeb, grabbed the dying commander and pulled him into his Hilux, where his identity was concealed by smoked glass. Other fighters crowded around and asked who was inside, but Naqeeb told them it was just a wounded talib; Borjan was up ahead.

"If we had mentioned to the other Taliban that Mullah Borjan had been killed, they would have lost their courage to fight. And if we had not captured Sarobi, we would not have captured Kabul," Naqeeb later said. And he quoted with pleasure the taunting words of the commander defending the gorge, who had bragged, on the two-way radio listened to by both armies, that the Taliban would never get through, since "only men who could fight" would be able to do it.

The pace of the advance, and the ability of the Taliban to take enormous losses, broke the will of the enemy, who retreated in disarray from positions they had believed impregnable. As so often happened some local command-ers switched sides quickly to guarantee their own survival, turning a surprise defeat into a rout. Driving just behind the Taliban advance, we saw the remains of swiftly abandoned campsites, catering vehicles and ambulances—rear eche-lon kit that was not moved back in time. Only then did the Taliban launch an assault from the Charasiab ridge to the south and, in a further pincer attack, from the southeast. Massud had not expected this because that area was heavily mined, but the Taliban pushed prisoners ahead of them at gunpoint to clear the mines.

As at Herat, speed and ruthlessness ensured victory. One seasoned observer of the Afghan scene wrote, "No Afghan force, either government or opposition, had ever carried out such a swift and complex series of operations over such a wide operation area. This was mobile warfare at its most effective." Amid the chaos of retreating forces pouring into the capital, Massud withdrew to the north toward his Panjshir fastness, along the same road he had come down in such hope four years previously. The road was clogged with heavy traffic made up of those who feared that life under Taliban rule might be even worse than they had suffered during the mujahidin civil war.

As the city fell, we drove into Kabul on September 27, the only camera crew to witness the Taliban takeover, past abandoned trucks and tanks—a new accre-tion, adding another layer to the military archaeology of the road to Kabul, alongside rusting Russian hulks and, not far beneath the surface, the bones of the British, pushed into the mud above the remains of the soldiers of the Mogul emperors, Genghis Khan, Tamerlane and Alexander the Great, who had all marched this way and fought over Afghanistan.

At the presidential palace a tank had broken down the gates, and now stood guard, festooned in tinsel decorations. Inside we found a white-tiled room, drenched in blood from floor to ceiling, a scene from a horror film. This was where the former communist president Najibullah and his brother had been tortured, after being dragged from their sanctuary at the UN headquarters in

Kabul. From the amount of blood it seemed that they were already dead when they were hanged unceremoniously from a traffic police post, both bodies mutilated and mocked with cigarettes and banknotes pushed between their fingers. They were left to swing for several days; a new kind of regime had taken power.

A statement by Mullah Omar was read on Kabul Radio. He said they had no quarrel with the outside world; they wanted good relations with other countries and recognition. "We represent Afghanistan. After 14 years of jihad against the communists, the victors betrayed the nation and took up arms. Now there is order, there will be *kassas*, which means murderers will be executed. Twelve *kassas* punishments have already been carried out, and eight amputations. All stolen property must be returned, and thieves will be severely punished. Adulterers will be stoned to death or lashed. All government employees should come to work as normal, except for women and teachers, who should stay at home."

The darkness began. The Taliban were stricter in the capital than they had been in Kandahar, where they were among their own. Religious police carried short lengths of rubber hose to whip people into the mosques during the compulsory five prayer times a day. Fighters slapped people with the sides of bayonets fixed to their AK-47s to make the point. Women did not just have to cover up but told they had to have a reason to go out. Bilquis, a teacher in what had been a mixed school, said she had never worn a burqa before. "In the worst days of the war we went out. Now there's peace and we can't." Many bakeries had been staffed by women in a food-for-work scheme before the Taliban came. International donors were now told to deliver the flour and let the Taliban deal with it. Even a woman's aid program making dolls' clothing for a Western mail-order firm was banned.

Zohra, an 11-year old girl, who had an artificial foot to replace one lost in a rocket attack, complained about the "artificial mullahs" who had taken over. She knew at once that her ambition to become a doctor would have to be put on hold. We interviewed her in silhouette, disguising her identity, and also did a number of Taliban interviews anonymously, because of their prohibition against the display of faces. Within days the image of Afghanistan had slipped into the shadows—the realm of antimatter.

Letters were sent to hospitals specifying which organs could be worked on in women, while male obstetricians were banned from working with women patients at all. A group of women health workers called me over to talk, whispering their complaints through a mosquito screen. The number of women patients had gone down to a quarter of those they had seen before the Taliban takeover. They worried about what was happening to the others. A midwife said it was worse than being rocketed.

In a public display the Taliban did want filmed, 1,400 cases of beer and 400 bottles of Afghan brandy were crushed under the tracks of a tank, then covered

with earth, in case anyone licked the ground. This was a routine Islamic prohibition, but the Taliban went further. They ripped reels of film out of their cases and
burned them on a bonfire in front of the city's movie theater, while edicts from
the new rulers straying into more bizarre areas now came thick and fast. As well
as the expected bans on movies, music and TV, people were ordered to paint their
windows white, in case women were seen from outside. Normal Kabul pastimes,
pigeon racing and kite flying, were now banned. The minister for virtue and vice
said this was about orderliness, in order to keep boys off roofs where they might
look into the women's quarters of another house. But it was really about control.

In a police station responsible for a large section of the city, 30-year-old
Mohammed Ayub, who had been a witness of the founding shura of the Taliban
near Maiwand, was now the police chief. He said he had been in a madrassa for 10
years but was still not a mullah. He sat cross-legged on a couch, in flowing white
salwar kameez, his eyes beautifully lined with kohl, alongside another young man
similarly turned out, both giggling about their powers. The former police chief,
now appointed their deputy, sat rather self-consciously on a chair, in his Soviet-
era uniform, a few days' growth of beard on his face, waiting for orders.

The Taliban pursued Massud's forces north to the mouth of the Panjshir
Valley, but neither side was strong enough for a decisive breakthrough. The
Taliban had no more luck than Soviet forces taking the twisting natural defenses
at the entrance to Massud's lair, although they lost thousands of men trying. A
damaged tank with Taliban insignia marked the northernmost point of their
advance, not far up the narrow gorge.

But Massud would never threaten Kabul again, although he broke out of the
Panjshir. For the next five years the front line was fluid, with both sides carrying
out brutal reprisals against the villagers caught between them on the Shomali
plain. This had been the most fertile part of Afghanistan, until the Taliban
destroyed the complex irrigation system that brought melting snow down from
the Hindu Kush into an intricate tracery of channels crossing vineyards and
fruit orchards. It had also been one of the main battlegrounds in the war against
the Soviet Union, as mujahidin used the cover of mud walls and dykes to disrupt
the Soviet supply route to the north. Many farmers had remained throughout. The ground could not support them now though, as the remnants of vines
crumbled into decay, and their fields dried to a fine talcum-powder dust.

The Taliban were now operating openly with Pakistani artillery support,
but the information minister, Mullah Amir Mutaqqi, denied reports of this as a
"baseless allegation" although he did then explain, with no sense of irony, "It is
true to say that a large number of Taliban have come from Pakistan to congratulate their classmates on their victory."

The Taliban were difficult clients. Pakistan had tried to play the old game
and draw them into a new anti-Massud alliance, including all the other main

players, Hekmatyar, Dostam and the Hazara alliance. But despite significant pressure from the Pakistani interior minister, as well as their backers on the frontier, the Taliban did not even turn up to the meeting in Pakistan, preferring to continue the war and take power on their own. This meant that when they did take Kabul, they had few friends, and never secured the international recognition they craved. Only Pakistan, Saudi Arabia and the United Arab Emirates would recognize the Taliban as a government.

The UN made an effort to engage with the new administration, taking a copy of the UN Charter translated into Pashtu to Kandahar to show the Taliban what it meant to be a country. An envoy went through it page by page, sitting cross-legged on the ground, taking questions about what it meant when it talked of "human rights and fundamental freedoms for all, without distinction as to race, sex, language or religion." But Mullah Omar refused to meet the UN envoy then or at any other time. And the Taliban had a particular problem with Britain, where Massud's brother continued as ambassador in London, even though Massud's control was now limited to a narrow wedge of land in the Northeast.

U.S. policy was thrown into confusion by the emergence of the Taliban, whose success had not been predicted. Afghanistan had fallen off the radar since Charlie Wilson's final huge arms procurement in 1991. The head of the south Asia desk at the State Department, Robin Raphel, was a lone voice trying to raise the issue, and as late as April 1996, only five months before the fall of Kabul, she said the Taliban appeared to "have reached the limit of its expansion."

When the Taliban became stronger, Raphel backed calls for an arms embargo, but argued that relations should not be completely cut off: "The real source of their success has been the willingness of many Afghans, particularly Pashtuns, to tacitly trade unending fighting and chaos for a measure of peace and security, even with severe social restrictions...It is not in the interest of Afghanistan or any of us here that the Taliban be isolated." This analysis, appearing to leave the door open to a policy of constructive engagement, explains an odd incident in the first hours after Kabul was taken, when U.S. officials came close to recognizing of the new regime—a State Department spokesman finding "nothing objectionable" in the way the Taliban imposed Islamic law. The statement was subsequently buried, but U.S. enthusiasm for stability in Afghanistan, no matter who was in government, was more than just the pragmatism of a superpower. It derived from Afghanistan's strategic importance in a new Great Game—not this time over empire but energy.

Wanting to contain Russian ambitions and secure new energy supplies, the United States sought new friendships in the "stans," the central Asian republics that had all become independent since the collapse of the Soviet Union. One of these desperately poor and dysfunctional countries, Turkmenistan, sits on a huge natural gas field. In an effort to cut out Iran, the United States was backing a plan for gas and oil pipelines from Turkmenistan to cross Afghanistan toward markets in Pakistan and beyond.

The Turkmen leader Saparmurat Niyazov was an unreconstructed Stalinist, with a personality cult of North Korean proportions. His slowly revolving golden statue dominated the capital, Ashgabat. He banned dogs from the capital, beards, makeup on television news broadcasters, and public libraries, since "Turkmen people do not read books." He renamed the days of the week and the months of the year—using his mother's name for what had been April. If the United States was prepared to work with the megalomaniac with the revolving statue, then friendship with the Taliban should not present major obstacles. The Taliban professed a similar faith to Saudi Arabia, the United States' largest oil supplier and largest arms buyer. Perhaps Afghanistan might develop along the same lines as Saudi Arabia had, with "pipelines, an Amir, no parliament, and lots of sharia law" in the cynical but frank admission of one U.S. diplomat, who added, "We can live with that."

Even before the Taliban took Kabul, officials from the favored U.S. bidder for the pipeline, Unocal, were offering humanitarian aid as "bonuses" to Afghan groups who could unite behind the project—effectively bribes for warlords. And when the capital did fall to the Taliban, a Unocal official said it would make the pipeline project "easier to implement." The impact of the Taliban takeover on human rights seemed of secondary interest to the pipeline deal, according to one concerned UN official, who said the outside world appeared to be "just renting the Taliban for their own purposes."

Mullah Omar was no fool. He allowed Unocal to set up an office in Kandahar and sent Taliban officials to the United States to negotiate, but without control of more of the country, the deal was a nonstarter. North of the Hindu Kush, General Dostam was still in power. The battle for the North as it changed hands twice in 1997 and 1998 would turn out to be the most violent of the Taliban years, with savage consequences for civilians caught in the middle.

At the last buzkashi game played in the North before it fell to the Taliban, Dostam was unwilling to talk about their threat. He was off duty, enjoying this traditional Afghan game played on horseback, a mad fight without rules for possession of the carcass of a calf, and he even mounted up and rode for a time, although his rather solid barrel-like horse was not ideal for the fierce scrums and fast chases that characterized the game. He said the Taliban could never take the North, because "they do not play *buzkashi*."

At his overlarge house in his stronghold, Shebargan, west of Mazar-i-Sharif, he was happier talking about horses than conflict. He had never heard before of the British adventurer and horse breeder William Moorcroft, whose obsession with new bloodstock had brought him to the North, where he had died and been buried in 1825 somewhere near where we were sitting. Dostam immediately offered to arrange a search party to search for the grave.

He said he hated being called a warlord, although it is hard to think of anyone better suited to the description, and gave us the ridiculously expensive "Blue Label" Johnnie Walker, affordable only by dictators, oil sheikhs and footballers, as evening fell and fairy lights lit up plaster deer nestling in the plastic undergrowth surrounding his pool. The stewardesses he used to import from England to sit around the pool when he briefly ran his own airline had gone now, but a few days spent with Dostam in the North were a glimpse of another Afghanistan—outward-looking and central Asian; Islamic but not enclosed. He took us on a tour of a medical school, walking purposefully through the girls' dormitory to shrieks of consternation, and arranged a meeting of the Shebargan "women's committee."

One morning he called out his praetorian guard for our inspection, a couple of hundred men with well-maintained armored fighting vehicles. He told the stories of men he had recruited as children when they came to wipe the mud from his windshield, who were now his senior sergeants. These were the feared kilim jams, who left nothing behind when they came to call. They had remained loyal to him as communist militiamen, an independent northern army, allies of Massud and enemies of Massud.

Dostam's authority was strengthened by his ability to play his war games on away ground. His men may have been brutal in fighting south of the Hindu Kush, but hardly a shell had fallen on the capital of the North, Mazar-i-Sharif, as he took money at different times from Turkey, Russia, Iran and the United States. But it was all coming to an end. Soon after we met, Dostam became caught up in a local feud and was implicated in the death of a popular commander, who was shot at a funeral, his body falling, by macabre chance, into an open grave. The brother of the dead commander did a deal with the Taliban to let them into the North.

This sudden reversal of fortunes led to Dostam fleeing north across the Oxus River to Uzbekistan rather than attempting to rally his forces. He had seen what had happened to the former communist president Najibullah and his brother. The city fell with hardly a shot fired, but Taliban rule in the North was as alien as it had been in the western town of Herat. There was a significant Pashtun minority, mostly descendants of those forcibly resettled there 100 years before as a piece of social engineering to try to unite the country by the Iron Amir, Abdur Rahman. But the majority were Uzbeks, Hazaras or Tajiks. Women did not routinely cover their heads in the streets, and they expected to be able to work. External influences had affected Mazar more than anywhere else in Afghanistan, guaranteeing more rights for women, while movie theaters and video shops did a roaring trade in the latest Bollywood offerings of gory violence and stylized love.

Alongside the liberal Sunni majority, Shia customs were strong. The town was dominated by the beautiful shimmering dome of the Blue Mosque, built where Afghan legend says that Hazrat Ali, the son-in-law of the Prophet Mohammed, and revered by Shias, is buried. It is surrounded by swerving clouds of white doves, and if a black bird enters, they tell you it will turn white.

With their customary lack of nuance, the Taliban imposed their baleful rules on Mazar as they had everywhere else. It was not their restrictions on women but their attempt to disarm the local population that led to their downfall. Three days after the Taliban takeover, Hazaras in the northwest of the city began an insurrection, and when the shooting started, every man in the city with a rifle joined in—a lethal cacophony. As we scurried to safety along mud-walled alleys that offered no protection, we saw the real power in the town, a man they called *pahlawan*—strong man—the father of the commander whose fallout with Dostam had let the Taliban in. He was controlling events, unconcerned about the bullets whipping through the air, sitting incongruously in a striped deck chair, wearing soft bright-blue slippers. After two days of vicious hand-to-hand fighting, thousands of Taliban were killed and thousands more taken prisoner and killed later, some sealed in shipping containers and left to suffocate.

When the Taliban returned to power in the North some months later, again after a deal with disaffected leaders, they carried out indiscriminate revenge killings of men, women and children across Mazar. A witness said, "I could see smoke coming from the west...It was chaos. People were running and being hit by cars trying to leave, market stalls were overturned. I heard one man say, 'It's hailing,' because of the bullets." After the initial frenzy, the Taliban specifically targeted Hazaras, going into schools, business, shops and hospitals, and killing thousands. The new Taliban governor made speeches urging them to convert to Sunni Islam and said that Hazara Shias were not Muslims at all. And in an act of symmetrical revenge, once again shipping containers were used for the wholesale murder of prisoners—this time by the other side.

13

SONS OF DOST

Do you want to be remembered as a son of Dost Mohammed or a son of Shah Shuja?
—Taliban recruiting slogan, 2005

Sajjad, nicknamed "the Afghan," sat warily in the middle of a room in a prison in Kashmir surrounded by Indian soldiers. His captors were pleased with themselves. He was their prime exhibit in a display of prisoners that included a Lebanese bomb maker, another unidentified Arab and half a dozen young Kashmiris. The Afghan had fair skin, green eyes and a wispy beard. He was from the eastern mountains of Afghanistan, not the deserts of the Pashtun South.

It was February 1994, toward the end of winter in the foothills of the Himalayas, and he was dressed in a single-piece long woolen cape that pulled on over the head, a ferung, standard wear for Kashmiris. The Afghan would not say much, and did not need to, for the Indian security forces had made their point that there were increasing numbers of foreigners coming across the mountains to fight against Indian control of the Kashmir Valley. This was a very significant catch indeed. The Afghan was the military commander of a new force, backed by Pakistan to defeat India in Kashmir, using weapons and cash supplied to the Afghan mujahidin, principally by the United States and Saudi Arabia. India did not know then, could not know, that it was at the receiving end of something more than a fight for control of Kashmir. This was the first front line in a new kind of conflict—a global jihad—war without borders, progressing toward the attacks on 9/11.

The roots of the Kashmir conflict go back 200 years. When that first British envoy, Mountstuart Elphinstone, met the "unlucky Amir," Shah Shuja, in 1809, the whole of the region, arching north from Kabul to the Kashmir Valley, including the world's second highest mountain, K2, was controlled by

Afghanistan. But as Britain extended its reach through the nineteenth century, "the roof of the world" came under its influence, governed from Kashmir.

During partition between Pakistan and India in 1947, to force the issue of Kashmir's future status, Pakistan launched an invasion force of frontier tribesmen, descendants of the ghazis who had fought British forces for so long in the same region. They came close to taking the valley itself, a magical honeymooners' paradise of lakes with houseboats, woods of willow and giant plane trees, fringed by peaks topped with white snow like cake icing. That savage little war left Pakistan with one-third of the territory of the original princely state but not the valley, when the United Nations intervened to stop the fighting. The two sides had been kept apart since by a "line of control" that neither recognized as a border, locking them into what one governor of the Indian-controlled region graphically called "frozen turbulence."

Pakistan inspired a new armed struggle against Indian control of the Kashmir Valley in the late 1980s. With the United States blessing Islamic holy warriors heading into Afghanistan, this seemed the best chance yet to unfreeze the turbulence. Pakistan set up training camps on its side of the line of control, concealed in the forests and hills of the Black Mountain region that had once been the stronghold of the Hindustani fanatics, the nineteenth-century forerunners of al-Qaeda.

But by 1993, the pro-Indian lobby in Congress had persuaded the new Clinton administration to put Pakistan on its watch list as a "state sponsor of international terrorism." The reluctance of Pakistani intelligence, the ISI, to secure the safe return of hundreds of Stinger missiles missing since being issued to the mujahidin was the crucial concern for the U.S. administration, but the issue of the worsening insurgency in Kashmir was also raised. Pakistan came off the terrorist list after dismissing several leading intelligence officials and agreeing to close the training camps for Kashmiri guerrillas on its territory. Conveniently since the fall of the communist-backed government in Kabul in 1992, the perfect place was now available to hide the training camps—eastern Afghanistan.

Not for the first time, Afghanistan was a pawn in someone else's game. The military leadership in Pakistan had as great an obsession with Afghanistan as the most Forward of British analysts in the nineteenth century, wanting to control the land beyond the Suleiman Mountains, to give them "strategic depth," so they would not be left with their backs against the wall if India were to invade. Pakistan's funding of training camps in Afghanistan for Kashmiri guerrillas killed two birds with one stone—taking the camps off Pakistani soil to satisfy the United States, and giving them a stake in eastern Afghanistan.

Pakistanis and Kashmiris trained alongside Arab-Afghans, among them veterans of the Soviet war in Afghanistan. Those who answered the call had a much wider agenda than a new border for Kashmir; their horizon extended beyond all borders to a misty distant dream of a reformed caliphate in a pan-Islamic world. Sajjad, the Afghan, was the first military commander of the new force that emerged from the Afghan camps, the Harkat ul-Ansar. Before 1993 most Kashmiri guerrillas reflected a more innocent age: wearing berets and face scarves, they modeled themselves on Che Guevara and wanted no more than independence for their valley. But by the mid-1990s, the locals were finding themselves demoted to porters and guides by the foreign fighters, whose aim was not just control of the valley but control of hearts, minds and souls everywhere.

The name of new militia spoke volumes about the new mood. The main local insurgency had used an English name, the Jammu and Kashmir Liberation Front, and the long Afghan war had not introduced more imaginative names: Factions could, for example, be translated as Party of Holy Warriors or Grouping of Islam. Harkat ul-Ansar was different, reaching back to the earliest days of the faith—the Prophet Mohammed's flight from Mecca to exile in Medina. The Ansar were those who had welcomed the Prophet and his followers into their homes, and the word came to be used to describe well-armed and highly mobile horsemen, a class of warriors that more than any other were responsible for the spread of the Islamic faith in its first two centuries.

Along with the new name came a new ferocity. Several kidnappings of Western tourists in Kashmir were attributed to the Harkat ul-Ansar; some were released, others were killed. It also became harder for reporters to travel in the North-West Frontier region, to secure permission to film in the madrassas or at political rallies. There was something in the air—a new seriousness of intent, and hostility to the West.

— — —

On May 18, 1996, four months before the Taliban took Kabul, Osama bin Laden arrived back in Afghanistan after a break of six years, his fortunes at their lowest ebb. After his days as the bank manager to the mujahidin in the war against the Soviet Union, in 1990 he had briefly returned home, to Saudi Arabia, as a hero, and made what appears to have been a serious offer to mobilize his Arab-Afghan fighters against Saddam Hussein's invasion of Kuwait. He could not understand the Saudi government's decision to accept the U.S. offer of 6 aircraft carrier battle groups, 23 army brigades and 9 Marine regiments, at the head of a million-strong multinational invasion force instead.

The idea of foreign forces coming onto the sacred soil of Saudi Arabia drove bin Laden to make a decisive break with the ruling family, and in 1992 he took refuge in Sudan, where his followers said he lost hundreds of millions of dollars in useless investments, although the State Department believed he was now "one of the most significant financial sponsors of Islamic extremist activities in the world." He survived an assassination attempt and fell out with the government in Sudan, which even offered to hand him over to the United States—an offer that was declined. By early 1996, bin Laden was running out of places to go.

It was not the Taliban who had invited bin Laden to Afghanistan. He had no links with them, and did not fly into the area in the South they then held, but to Jalalabad, not yet under Taliban control, where he was remembered by mujahidin contacts from the Soviet war. When he arrived he was given a house, and Pakistan put some of the training camps it had set up for Kashmiri guerrillas under his control. Whatever the state of his own finances, bin Laden still had some backers to call on, and was developing a bigger project than the struggle for Kashmir. For this he needed publicity. He did several TV interviews and also a press conference for Pakistani journalists at a training camp, where jihadi fighters raced around in trucks, shooting in the air. A British cameraman who met bin Laden said he had almost no charisma; shaking his hand was like holding a "wet, cold fish."

Bin Laden talked in elliptical rhetoric, but buried within the looping swirls of his speeches and interviews evoking the past of Islam came his first significant statement since his return, in August 1996, issued from the Tora Bora cave complex that his construction company had extended a decade before, burrowing into the Suleiman Mountains. The "Declaration of War Against the Americans Occupying the Land of the Two Holy Sites" broke with his former paymasters, in both Saudi Arabia and the United States. But his detailed threats, including a demand for Arab women to boycott American goods (since presumably they do the shopping), were not taken seriously at levels that matter in Washington.

A month after this statement, the Taliban swept in to take the east of Afghanistan and then moved on to take Kabul. They took over the training camps, ordered bin Laden to stop threatening attacks abroad and sent him south to Kandahar, where they thought he would have a lower profile. His international agenda was a distraction from the Taliban campaign to bring law and order to Afghanistan. He moved to the South but ignored their other orders, settling into an abandoned farmhouse with his three wives and children, there to plot the downfall of the United States.

Before any attack, bin Laden always chose a deliberate symbol. In an interview in early 1998 there was a map of Africa behind him. Not long afterward, on a Friday morning, a time when all good Muslims should have been at prayer, two trucks loaded with bombs headed for U.S. Embassy buildings in Africa, one in Kenya, the other Tanzania. The bomb in Tanzania was designed to have more impact, as gas canisters had been placed around a central core of 2,000 pounds of TNT, but a water tanker in front of the embassy took most of the blast. Eleven died there, none of them Americans. In Kenya, though, the bomb took off the front of the embassy, killing 213 people and injuring many more.

The United States at the time was in thrall to the Monica Lewinsky affair. Military judgments about the scale and pace of retaliation demanded after the African attacks were weighed up in Washington while, across town, "that woman" was giving evidence to a grand jury about oral sex in the White House. Those in the Arab world believed that military action would be taken to save Bill Clinton, and in street demonstrations they held up placards: "No war for Monica."

More than 60 cruise missiles were launched, mostly from ships stationed in the gulf, with their GPS navigation systems set for the training camps around Khost in the east of Afghanistan, where there was little physical infrastructure to destroy. Fewer than 30 people were killed, none of them an al-Qaeda leader, most of them Afghans training to fight in Kashmir.

The incident defined the world's new battlefield with precision. A defense budget that would soon top $500 billion a year, designed to fight a continental war, was useless against an enemy with little to blow up. As British forces had found in the region in the nineteenth century, destroying a fanatic camp did not destroy the movement. The offensive weapons of a superpower were worse than useless against al-Qaeda. This was the reverse side of asymmetric warfare—a phenomenon usually seen from the point of view of attempts by insurgents to develop their own weapons, such as suicide bombing, in the face of overwhelming tactical superiority by conventional forces. The Khost attacks may have satisfied an understandable U.S. desire for revenge but were a public relations disaster; in fact, they were an Islamist propaganda coup.

TV pictures from Khost showed the pages of a partly burned Koran flapping in the wind, damage to a mosque and unexploded cruise missiles (subsequently sold abroad by bin Laden). Another dozen or so cruise missiles killed a night watchman and destroyed a factory in Sudan. U.S. evidence that the plant was developing chemical weapons has never been proven. Later investigations suggested it was a pharmaceutical factory, as Sudan said it was.

That was the year Osama first became a popular name for boys born in the North-West Frontier; printers could not turn out T-shirts and posters showing his face quickly enough to meet the demand, and disaffected young Muslim men worldwide had a cause. The U.S. administration played its part in creating the bin Laden brand, blaming him for involvement in a long list of attacks going back to the deaths of 18 servicemen in Mogadishu in 1993, although some officials would admit that there was little evidence to connect him with some of the attacks. The United States had defined its enemy, drawing battle lines that would develop into the Global War on Terror.

Bin Laden retreated into his cave, physically, spiritually and mentally detached from the normal world. Among the dreams of his followers was an Islamic Stealth bomber, which could fly anywhere without being detected. They drew up the plans, reasoning that their labor was free, so they would not need the billions of dollars it cost the United States to build such a plane. But amid this childish madness, a plan was developing that involved undetected planes of quite a different sort, and had asymmetric military brilliance—bringing down skyscrapers for the price of just a few pilots' licenses.

—— —— ——

The 1998 attacks in Africa, and the U.S. response, had one clear result for Afghanistan: The fate of al-Qaeda was linked with the Taliban forever. Only a few weeks earlier, the head of the secret service of Saudi Arabia Prince Turki, a frequent traveler to Afghanistan at that time, believed he had succeeded in persuading the Taliban to hand bin Laden over to him. He had offered in return 400 of the Hilux pickups that were their preferred war chariot. The vehicles had been delivered, but when he arrived to collect bin Laden, Turki found that the U.S. missile attack had changed the situation. The Taliban leader Mullah Omar insulted the Saudi royal family by saying "We may be very poor, we Afghans, and you are very rich and powerful. But we are not someone like you. You have no honour." It was the kind of answer that would win Omar respect from Muslims worldwide, especially after the prince insulted his hosts by leaving without eating the meal prepared for him. The United States did no better: Officials sent a secure satellite telephone to Omar and had several long but fruitless conversations to try to persuade him to hand bin Laden over.

The one thing the Taliban craved was recognition as the legitimate government of Afghanistan, but that the United States was not prepared to offer. Thus the third opportunity to bring Afghanistan back from the brink was squandered. Each time the country had been ignored before—when the Soviet army pulled out in 1989, and when the mujahidin took over in 1992— the suffering had been terrible inside Afghanistan. This time the world's failure to engage constructively in Afghanistan would have more far-reaching consequences.

By now, even if recognition of the Taliban had been on the table, it might not have broken through the Pashtun honor code that gave bin Laden protection as a guest. After the Saudi attempt to arrest him, the Taliban held a shura that went on for several days to decide what to do. The decision was taken that bin Laden should be asked to try to find somewhere else to live, but as Mullah Omar made the phone call to his troublesome guest, he knew there was nowhere else. This stubborn adherence to the ancient Pashtun hospitality code looks incomprehensible from outside, but those who knew the Taliban high command well deny that Mullah Omar and bin Laden were ever close friends, despite rumors enthusiastically retold by U.S. officials, that they went fishing together. Omar's family has also rejected the most persistent rumor—that they were related by marriage. The Taliban did not share bin Laden's desire to change the world— they did not look beyond their own Afghan horizon. He was going to cause the movement trouble and ultimately bring the sky crashing down on their heads, but he was a fellow Wahhabi and a guest, and that was that.

Afghan hospitality for bin Laden ended any further attempts by the U.S. State Department to take a pragmatic line on the Taliban in order to secure the pipeline deal. And the Clinton administration's room for maneuver in Afghanistan became more limited because of the Lewinsky affair. When Hillary Clinton stood by her man, female voters gave him the benefit of the doubt, and anyone wanting a more nuanced approach on the Taliban was silenced. The United States moved in a few months from a position of having no policy about Afghanistan to one that focused only on one aspect of the Taliban: their treatment of women. The cause became fashionable in Hollywood. As the Washington Post excitedly reported, "Tibet is out. Afghanistan is in."

In Kabul, a Taliban minister asked me around this time, "Why are you so interested in our women?" He was perplexed by what appeared to him to be an obsession. The Taliban thought they were being respectful by sticking to the letter of the Islamic injunction that the women's world was a private space, purdah. The view of much of the outside world that this amounted to harsh treatment and an abuse of human rights made their cause hopeless.

Western opinion was informed by stunts that the Taliban could not combat even if they had known how to try. A major U.S. network anchorwoman threw off her head covering in the middle of an interview with a Taliban minister, daring him to be shocked by the sight of her hair, while the EU humanitarian affairs commissioner, Emma Bonino, never shy of publicity, managed to engineer a situation where she and 19 Western journalists and aid officials were arrested and held for a few hours for taking photos of women patients in a hospital. Bonino absurdly described her treatment as "an example of how people live here in a state of terror."

In this atmosphere there was nothing the Taliban could do that was right. It was only after some years in power that they successfully banned the growing of opium poppies. The move was greeted with some cynicism internationally, and the view was expressed that the move had been taken to push up prices. Financial compensation to the Taliban was minimal. This grudging and small-minded response directly caused the destruction of the giant Buddhas, which had stood like sentinels in the wall of the Hindu Kush for more than 1,000 years. When Western donors appeared to care more about the Buddhas than a looming humanitarian crisis threatened by drought, the extremist wing of the Taliban that had been arguing for their destruction for years had their way and blew them up.

— — —

In 2001, among all of the consequences of 9/11, U.S. retaliation against Afghanistan was the one that was most predictable, and indeed understandable, after such trauma. The Taliban's hold on Afghanistan already looked vulnerable. Isolated internationally, and coping with the worst drought seen for many years, they were facing far more determined opposition than for some years. The former northern commander, General Dostam, had dropped by helicopter into the country at the western end of the Hindu Kush several months before the attacks of 9/11 and was rallying his forces for a cavalry assault riding buzkashi horses against the Taliban in Mazar-i-Sharif. Iran too, outraged by a Taliban massacre of Hazaras in the spring of 2001, was stepping up aid to enemies of the Taliban.

There had been no movement though on the crucial Kabul front, where Massud's forces had failed to break through Taliban lines. Just days before 9/11, an Arab "TV crew" who had been waiting for some time to secure an interview with Massud killed him with a bomb planted in their camera. The United States quickly assembled a coalition of nations for war, working on the ground with what was now called the Northern Alliance, uniting those forces whose disunity since the fall of the Soviet government had made space for the rise of the Taliban in the first place.

The Taliban were defenseless against the relentless aerial bombardment that went on day and night, degrading their ability to fight and disrupting their supply lines, so that the ground offensive was short and the Taliban were ousted from power. A separate U.S. force mounted an assault on the Tora Bora caves in a search for bin Laden. Despite an intensive bombing campaign, he escaped, probably across the frontier to Pakistan. But a quick war was not followed by the expected quick peace, as another foreign force tripped up on the other side of the Suleiman Mountains.

The simple narrative of heroes and demons—"mujahidin good," "Taliban bad"—imposed on Afghanistan was another externally drawn picture: an Afghanistan of the Western mind just as much as the one drawn by Lieutenant Macartney, when he imagined the land beyond the mountains two centuries before. The mismatch between the simplistic analysis imposed from outside and the complex reality on the ground would have a profound impact on political and military planning.

The common TV image of Afghanistan during the Taliban years—a woman in a powder-blue burqa, trudging past ruins—told only part of the story, and did not prepare Western public opinion for the reaction to the U.S.-led takeover of Afghanistan after 9/11. The first surprise was that women did not come out on the streets and "throw off their burqas" as required in the script: Afghan society did not suddenly become Western.

The explanation for this, according to a teacher in Herat, filmed making up her face before covering herself with a burqa to go out, was that the towns were full of peasants. Her face could appear on international television but not in her own high street. The former mujahidin, who became the so-called Northern Alliance forces that drove out the Taliban with the assistance of an international force led by the United States, had brought their simple rural ways with them, and that meant women still needed to cover up. Afghan society had been fundamentally transformed during a quarter of a century of conflict, more by the Western-funded mujahidin than by the Taliban. The complex and subtle tapestry of civil society had been overwhelmed by the needs of a holy war, and it was hard to stitch it back together again.

The Taliban were harsh and repressive, but only an extreme version of what was now the Afghan norm. Women's clothing did not disappear from public display in shops outside the main cities on Taliban orders. The cover-up began, even in Massud's kingdom, the Panjshir Valley, much earlier, as the ratchet of Islamicization moved in only one direction. The cheap, Russian-made, waxy-yellow plastic dummies, with their molded blond hair and a slightly unsettling stare, were removed from dress-shop windows when the communists fell from power, long before the Taliban emerged.

And the more extreme punishments demanded by Sharia law, including amputation for theft, were imposed a long time before the Taliban emerged, in some areas under the control of the forces that became U.S. allies in the Northern Alliance. The communists had destroyed the old courts and left nothing behind, so the mujahidin empowered Muslim clerics to administer justice. In 1985, a full 10 years before the Taliban, the French Afghan expert Olivier Roy wrote, "The resistance movement has brought with it a strengthening of Islam's role in shaping the social order." Sharia made sense of chaos.

An Islamic cleric in Kabul claimed that the mujahidin government in power before the Taliban had themselves wanted a Saudi-style "virtue and vice" ministry and religious police, and held back only because they were concerned about the international reaction.

Brutal, conservative and repressive the Taliban may have been, but the West ignored their significant popularity in parts of Afghanistan; the fact that they kept honest accounts, and raised more customs revenues in their last year than in the first year of U.S.-sponsored democracy in 2002; that under their rule it was possible for the first time in a generation to travel safely by day or night across most of the country (as it has not been since they fell); or that once they had taken full control of the South, they successfully stopped the growing of opium poppies—a tough challenge given the scale of the profits involved, particularly in Helmand, and something the international community has failed to do since.

The United States did not see how their Northern Alliance allies were perceived, or how they would behave, until it was too late, because they had been portrayed as heroes of the mujahidin. The Taliban regime did collapse like sand, but just as the Soviet Union had had to reconfigure its "limited contingent" within months, when it realized the kind of war it was fighting, so the U.S.-led invasion force found itself in a security situation that became worse rather than better. This deterioration was not inevitable. The simple-minded repression of the Taliban in power made it hard for them to win new recruits in the early years after they were forced out. But a unique window of opportunity, when there was goodwill for the international community to succeed, closed quickly.

Afghanistan was a unique crucible where all three recent Big Ideas about political organization were tried out. Communism and Islamism had clearly failed, now Democracy had its turn, bringing the benefits of the free market. But what came next confounded the hopes of those whose thinking had been infused by ideas about democracy's inevitable victory in a "clash of civilizations."

The countries backing the U.S.-led intervention in 2001 exhibited a lack of curiosity about Afghanistan, believing in the power of a one-size-fits-all democratic model to deliver stability. In a remarkable admission later, the European Union representative in Kabul, Francesc Vendrell, said they did not bother to find out what was really happening. "People knew that there were various tribes within the Pashtun. But because there was a feeling that things were still going to become normal, it was not thought necessary for us to understand the tribal system."

If the West forgot history, the Afghans certainly did not. It was not long before the Taliban were asking young men, "Do you want to be remembered as a son of Dost Mohammed or a son of Shah Shuja?" reminding recruits that Mullah Omar was the first leader since Dost who had displayed the holy cloak and declared himself Amir al-Mu'minin against the invaders. To them, the modern Shah Shuja, the puppet of the foreign invader, was of course President Hamid Karzai.

Karzai emerged as the only credible presidential candidate in the early heady months after the fall of the Taliban: a fastidious man, who had learned his English in the kind of boarding school in India left over from the empire, where boys are still taught to play up and play the game. Karzai's obvious good nature and his dress sense brought international attention of quite a new kind to Afghanistan. For a season, fashion magazines were full of pieces on lambskin hats and how to wear those sleeveless robes. But even in the early days big questions were being asked about whether he was the right man for a tough job.

Karzai was not Washington's first choice; they turned to him after disaster followed the return of the highly competent and popular mujahidin leader Abdul Haq, dropped by U.S. forces into the south of Afghanistan before the Taliban fell. The Taliban discovered where he was and killed him as he tried to make his escape on horseback.

When the Taliban fell, Karzai was appointed by the United States and then anointed by the loya jirga, a meeting of elders, that approved Afghanistan's first democratic constitution. To guarantee that the loya jirga would not trail on for months in the Afghan way, a deadline was imposed on the availability of a temporary purpose-built air-conditioned meeting space. Afghanistan was being kicked into a new century. Perhaps it would have been better if the elders had been allowed to sit and talk for a while longer.

Tens of thousands of refugees flooded home now that their homeland was under new rulers. Most came from refugee camps in the North-West Frontier and in Iran, but others returned from the United States, Canada and Europe, with goodwill to rebuild their country, many with degrees and foreign bank accounts. Abandoned shops in Kabul were taken over and filled with kitchen and bathroom equipment as a building boom began. In a yard behind the national bank, brick kilns 20 feet high burned night and day, fueled by bales of old banknotes, as a new currency was quickly imposed. Karzai was duly elected in the country's first presidential election in 2004. But the United States discovered, as Britain and Russia had before, that taking Afghanistan was the easy part. This time, efforts to build a nation were defeated from within, by the very tools sent for reconstruction. The billions of dollars that flowed from abroad for development might have been better used as fuel for the kilns behind the central bank as corruption set in; the new Afghanistan was rotten to the core.

During the early years after the fall of the Taliban, returning refugees set a new more progressive tone in Afghan life; the purist austerity of recent years had little appeal. Ironically, in a U.S. military assessment in 2003, it was Hekmatyar, the United States' old ally against the communists, who seemed more of a threat: "The Taliban and al-Qaeda are no longer capable of acting in a military sense, but Hekmatyar obviously has the money, influence, political will, and power to reorganize the elements under his leadership."

But in 2006, a generation after he was first trained as a guerrilla by Pakistan, Hekmatyar announced that he would now fight under the al-Qaeda banner. Both groups, al-Qaeda and the Taliban, had reemerged as serious forces in Afghanistan. The Taliban fight back started in their traditional heartland in the South, and spread north, until they controlled as much as 54 percent of Afghanistan, according to one estimate. Even a more cautious analysis by the World Bank gave them 30 percent of Afghanistan in 2007. The reemergence of the Taliban five years after their fall from power owed much to the failure of foreign forces to tackle corruption.

A drive around Kabul with the head of the capital's serious crimes squad in 2006 was an instructive experience. General Paktiawal was a large engaging man who wore a wide-lapelled pinstripe suit and carried a revolver. He led always from the front, in a locally armored Land Cruiser with a metal cover built into the bulletproof windshield for him to lift up and shoot through. As he drove he pointed out the vast tracts of land seized by various warlords since 2001, now held by force and covered in bulbous concrete mansions painted in bright colors and built, with no thought of planning controls, in that unlovely vulgar style that infects the whole region from the Mediterranean to Delhi: Dubai Kitsch.

Northeast of the capital in Sherpur, where the British army had been besieged in 1879, most of the cantonment had been built over some years previously to create the upmarket district of Wazir Akbar Khan—named after Dost Mohammed's son, who led the revolt against British rule in 1841. But the last remaining corner of the former garrison area, still government-owned when the Northern Alliance swept into Kabul in 2001, had been seized by some of those appointed to the first post-Taliban administration and parceled out between them.

The tracks across the land were not paved, so our four-wheel-drive vehicles made slow progress as they wallowed through the fine dust, past the overlarge villas some of which went on to change hands for $2 million each. With no public services, the area rumbled with the permanent thunder of giant generators, each the size of a ship's engine, with the carbon footprint of an African town; conflict is bad for climate change.

General Paktiawal then took us north on the trail of an illegal arms sale. The road went across the Shomali Plain, beneath the tall curtain of the Hindu Kush. Several years after the fall of the Taliban the fields were still not productive. Plenty of consultants had been to visit the giant Chinese-built irrigation pumping system to the north, damaged in the war, but it was still not operational. A pure white Land Cruiser with a bunch of plastic flowers on the dashboard passed at high speed, at the head of a convoy coming in the other direction. Paktiawal recognized it as belonging to the warlord in control of the area, and, sure enough, a few seconds later, the warlord was on the phone, demanding to know what the police chief was doing on his turf. Paktiawal reassured him with a story that he was just on his way to visit a friend at Charikar police station.

Paktiawal had not told anyone at police headquarters where he was going; he trusted no one except his own men. We were on our own, as the trail led up a mountain track. The pursuit ended with the arrest of two men, who carried a book containing names and dates of arms deals and some counterfeit banknotes. Only a few weeks after this incident, Paktiawal was held and beaten up in the same area.

Corruption infused all levels of the police. One appointee for police chief of a northern province was told that the price was "150,000." He turned up at the ministry of interior with his bribe and was at first received well, but then realized his mistake: the price was to be paid in dollars, not the far smaller amount in the local currency. He was thrown out with contempt.

The failure of the Karzai government and its international supporters to deliver justice or fair policing was the most significant factor in the return of the Taliban. Much of rural Afghanistan reverted to the Taliban and Sharia law, for the same reason it had turned to the mujahidin after the Soviet invasion—to provide order and justice in the face of foreign failure. In Wardak Province—not in the Pashtun South but easily accessible from Kabul, on a good road only an hour's drive west—a farmer, Nur Rahman, said, "There is no government to deal with cases. The judges, even the lowest civil servants, are corrupt and they want bribes. People go to the Taliban and tribal elders instead to sort out their problems." The Taliban government was remembered for success in basic projects such as the delivery of fertilizer and seeds and in providing electricity. The hydroelectric scheme there broke down after the Taliban fell from power. "We cannot even get an engineer from the ministry to come and look at it," he complained.

By 2007 villagers in Wardak spoke as if the Karzai government had already fallen: "During the time they had control here until this year, there were road-blocks, and lots of thieves around. There was oppression and abuse of power," grumbled a farmer, Mohammed Nazir. "Since the Taliban came back, the robbers and thieves have all vanished. Security is good. And now the Taliban are solving disputes that the Karzai government did not solve."

After taking effective control of much of Wardak, the Taliban intervened in an armed conflict between two villages, and even took a French woman journalist to see a school operating in the area under their control. Their chief spokesman admitted, in perhaps the understatement of the century, that they had got their "public relations image wrong" when they had been in power before. Increasingly the Taliban called themselves mujahidin to extend their appeal, operating an underground network of provincial administrators, parallel to the state. The Taliban military commander in Wardak, Mullah Rashid Akhond, said, "The Afghan people are helping the mujahidin a lot. All of the weapons stores from the jihad time have been given to the Taliban, who are now hand in hand with the former mujahidin. The nation, the Taliban and the mujahidin are united in fighting a jihad against the forces of the invaders."

When things did not go according to plan in Afghanistan, it became fashionable for foreign analysts to say that the problem was about "high expectations"—if only Afghan people realized that rebuilding the country would take a long time, they would be more patient and turn away from the Taliban. But this analysis ignored the negative impact of corruption in the delivery of justice and the wholesale theft of property by warlords. The perception grew in many corners of Afghanistan that the Karzai government allowed this to happen.

One minister who fell out with President Karzai in the early years over the issue of corruption, Ramazan Bashardost, had spent his refugee years as a philosophy professor in France. After he left the government, he held a weekly public "surgery" in a tent in a public park in Kabul in protest. One afternoon, a group of men arrived from the far North bearing a long list of grievances, mostly about property that had been taken from them during the years of the Karzai government.

By the light of a paraffin lamp in the gathering gloom of a Kabul winter evening, they came forward one by one, pulling ancient title deeds from beneath elaborate robes and telling their stories. One had been in charge of collecting customs revenues in his town, and although a Pashtun he was not a Taliban sympathizer, so when they took over there in 1997, he offered his resignation, since he imagined they would want their own appointee. But they told him they needed trustworthy officials and kept him in post. Following the defeat of the Taliban, when the official refused to hand over the 20 percent of revenues demanded by President Karzai's new appointee, he was thrown out of his job and lost his house and car as well. After he had made his complaint in the tent, I asked him if he would now support the Taliban. It was a dangerous question. There were police present, craning their heads forward in the group around us to listen. He nodded a quick assent.

The main engine of corruption is the world's most lucrative illegal narcotics trade, worth more than $2 billion annually, and fueling both the insurgency and officials at all levels in the government, in effect blurring the distinction between the two. In this amoral world, violence against civilians was not the monopoly of the insurgency. The Taliban, ruthless and destructive though they were, denied responsibility for some of the attacks on schools. As one international development worker in Helmand said: "To slip through the water unseen, the fish must first muddy the pool." Disorder suited a number of different elements; 60 percent of the police in Helmand Province were heroin addicts, and the governor of the province, Sher Mohammad Akhundzada, was removed from office by President Karzai at British insistence, after allegations that he too was implicated in the narcotics trade. Amid worsening tension between Karzai and the West, the president regretted agreeing to move the governor, and nominated him to the upper house of the Afghan parliament.

International efforts to tackle the drugs trade were largely ineffective. The provinces where they successfully stopped the growing of opium poppies have mostly turned to marijuana instead. Officials at the counternarcotics ministry complained that international donors spent millions of dollars abroad on a public relations contract, and on planes that they did not need, while bureaucratic obstacles made it impossible to spend any of the funds earmarked for farmers to find alternatives to poppy growing.

Meanwhile middle-ranking officials trying to stop the drug trade were picked off. Some lost their lives, others only their jobs. General Aminullah Amerkhel was removed from his post in charge of customs at Kabul airport as he was on the brink of exposing what he believed to be a major international smuggling operation. Before he was forced out, there was a remarkable insight into the power that could be exerted by the drug trade, when a woman was arrested with several kilograms of heroin strapped to her body.

She was filmed openly threatening customs officials and asking why she had been arrested; she clearly believed she had an arrangement to walk through freely. She claimed she had formerly worked in intelligence, and made specific threats against the customs officials: "I am warning you. I will come to your house and you will disappear. Use your brain. Don't you understand? I can make six men like you disappear in a day."

Later that night she was released, and rearrested only after Amerkhel went to the minister's office to complain. A few months later he was forced out of his post and went into hiding after receiving death threats. Amerkhel had also complained about the standard of work on a renovation project for the building used by customs officials at the airport. He believed that perhaps 10 percent of $1 million allocated was spent on the project, the rest going to pay off officials.

The biggest international failure, leading to worsening insecurity after 2001, was in the delivery of aid. Despite President Bush's talk of a "new Marshall Plan," matching the rebuilding of Europe after World War II, aid flows to Afghanistan were far lower than implied by that promise—just $75 a head in the first year, compared to an average of $250 a head for other recent post-conflict countries. There were some successes: Provision for women's health became possible, and infant mortality rates improved a little—from the catastrophic to the merely dreadful. But continuing problems affect not only the poor: President Karzai's helicopter pilot died in childbirth, a modern woman in a terrible medieval world.

Some schools were built, although not as many as were claimed, and to a very low standard. One of Kabul's oldest and most famous girls' schools put a plaque on its wall, proudly announcing that it was reopened with U.S. support, but there was nothing there to boast about. When I visited it, not long after the money had been spent, it reminded me of a temporary camp erected after a major disaster, such as an earthquake. Most of the girls were still being taught in tents, hot and dusty in summer, cold and muddy in the winter, and where there were classrooms, paint was peeling and the roof was leaking. The head teacher was reluctant to complain, since she told me she knew this was one of the best schools in Kabul; most were far worse.

Several years after the fall of the Taliban, health clinics, even those within easy reach of the capital, had only the most basic treatments available, and no

contraceptives, at a time when foreign consultants working for Afghan government ministries could earn $25,000 a month. The failures in development
went back to 2001. A unique opportunity was lost at the beginning when civil
servants shaved off the beards that had been compulsory in the Taliban years,
brought out their Western-style suits from under the mattress and reported
to their old ministries, only to be told to go home while an internationally
approved plan was put in place.

It would be another three years before USAID, one of the biggest donors,
finalized its strategy for Afghanistan, time during which vital momentum was
lost and a vacuum was filled by the Taliban. Along with corruption, the failure
to rebuild the country was the other powerful driver of the worsening insurgency. The finance minister in the early years under Karzai, Ashraf Ghani, was
bitter about the delay. "We had a strategy in three months. Why is it that one
has to go to parallel strategies?" He calculated that a school built by Afghans
would cost only one-fifth of the amount needed by an international agency
working in Afghanistan. Most of the aid was spent outside the state, not building its capacity, so a weak state could not even spend the funds it was given. The
effect was another kind of corruption as a parallel international system, living
like a cuckoo on top of Kabul, sucked some of the best resources out of the state
for itself.

Several years after the Taliban fell, I started a conversation with the security officer patting down my pockets at the entrance to one of the UN offices
that had taken over large parts of the center of the city. He was in his mid-30s,
and had returned home, with his wife and two children and a degree in his
pocket gained in a refugee camp—just the kind of man any new nation needed
on its side. Once the consultants had agreed the initial plan for the country, he
had worked for a while in the higher education ministry, planning the future for
Afghan universities, but the job as a doorman for an international agency paid
him twice the salary.

As insecurity increased when the Taliban reemerged, redevelopment was
further hampered: Security requirements absorbed more money, and aid workers could travel less. The International Committee of the Red Cross, which had
long experience in Afghanistan, said the security situation was worse than at
any time during nearly three decades of conflict. The head of their delegation
in Kabul, Reto Stocker, stated, "The conflict has not only intensified but it has
also spread over the last few years. Prolonged human suffering is causing real
concern in ever larger areas. There is little capacity to address it. We've never
had so little access." Across the country once again there were thousands of
displaced people fleeing fighting, and complex development initiatives had to
be shelved while direct humanitarian assistance—basic food and shelter—took
up far more of aid budgets.

I visited a literacy project in Kandahar, where women were given a sack of grain and a liter of cooking oil a month in return for attending lessons. They discarded their burqas like muddy boots in a pile by the entrance and left their children in separate classrooms in the basement while they learned how to read and count and sew. Invariably most were refugees and widows from the North. But a few were local Pashtun women who had persuaded their husbands to let them go to this subversive place in return for food. It would be hard to think of any better way of spending money in Afghanistan than on women's literacy in Kandahar, the heartland of the Taliban. But at the time I was there in 2006, the World Food Program had been forced to stop the supplies to the school because there were so many hungry mouths descending on Kandahar, displaced by the war—clever aid pushed aside for the needs of an emergency.

As they went home without the food that had been promised by the world, the women asked me what they should tell their husbands.

14

THE CHEAPER MAN

A scrimmage in a Border Station
A canter down some dark defile
Two thousand pounds of education
Drops to a ten-rupee jezail
...
Strike hard who cares, shoot straight who can
The odds are on the cheaper man.

—Rudyard Kipling, *Arithmetic on the Frontier*

Exactly two hundred years on from Elphinstone's journey to Peshawar, the Taliban rocketed the airport there to greet the arrival in the region of general David Petraeus, the new commanding officer of the latest military force to try to bring peace. His promotion in November 2008 from heading U.S. forces in Iraq to Centcom (Central Command), taking over control of the region that includes Afghanistan, signaled a shift in emphasis for the United States.

The war in Afghanistan was not going well. The United States had taken no combat casualties in the initial swiftly planned and brilliantly executed war against the Taliban immediately after 9/11; regime change without tears, at least on the U.S. side. But that had changed, and by the summer of 2008 monthly U.S. casualties on the ground in Afghanistan were higher than in Iraq. Petraeus was credited with success in turning Iraq around. Who better to send to Afghanistan? He was highly intelligent, with a reputation for surrounding himself with similarly thoughtful analysts—generals with PhDs.

Before going to head the Iraq operation, Petraeus had written a new U.S. military field manual on counterinsurgency, the first since Vietnam, in an attempt to record the lessons learned from the changed military landscape in which America found itself fighting not big conventional battles against uniformed armies, but long bruising engagements against enemies motivated to die as martyrs, whose tactics included suicide bombing. An influential book by a British general called the new environment "war amongst the people," where victory depended not on superior weapons systems and the exercise of raw force, but on a far more complex set of factors. Winning "hearts and minds" was not a soft option or an add-on to the use of force; rather it was the centerpiece of the strategic jigsaw. Petraeus refused to use the word "victory" at all, knowing that stabilizing these troubled nations needed a new approach and new language.

The most pressing military challenge in 2009 was the same as ever: how to deal with the formidable barrier of the Suleiman mountains. When it was drawn in 1893, the Durand Line had protected insurgents fleeing to Afghanistan; after 2001, the military geography of the region was turned inside out, the border now giving a safe haven to guerrillas on the Pakistani side. U.S. forces had become increasingly bullish in pursuing Taliban fighters across the frontier—and incurred Pakistani wrath for their actions as civilians were killed.

The Pakistani government did make some attempts to tackle militancy in the mountains, and some foreign fighters were arrested in operations that also led to the deaths of around 1000 Pakistani soldiers. But the crackdown was no more successful in delivering stability than the frontier campaigns of the British empire had been. Around a quarter of the Pakistani army is of Pashtun origin, and on several occasions large groups of soldiers were "captured" by insurgents in the frontier region and relieved of their weapons before being released. In two deals, in 2004 and 2006, the Pakistani government withdrew its forces from northern Waziristan altogether, agreeing to allow local villages to police themselves. The deals incensed international forces in Afghanistan. In public in October 2006 the NATO commander, U.S. General James Jones, restricted himself to a dry remark: "Preliminary indications are that the movements across the border have increased since the signing of agreements on the other side of the border."

Once again Waziristan, the place a weary British official had called "the plague spot of the frontier" a century before, played its part as the focal point of the new militancy and a place of refuge for al-Qaeda fighters. And when the United States did begin to fire across the border, a newly formed "Pakistani Taliban" allied with al-Qaeda began to gain support among tribal elders as defenders against U.S. attacks.

The radicalization of significant elements of Pakistani society that gathered pace in the 1990s had become even more pronounced since the U.S.-led invasion of Iraq in 2003. President Bush's rhetoric—"if you are not with us you are against us"—left little room for maneuver, drawing battle lines here as elsewhere in the Islamic world.

An Italian reporter, Tiziano Terzani, witnessed a rally in Pakistan of more than a million *tablighi*, men who had each agreed to give four months a year to the cause of traveling from village to village spreading a purer form of Islam. One told him, "We don't want to be like you. We don't want to watch your television or your films. We don't want your freedom. We want our society to be governed by the *sharia*." These men were not all political allies of the Taliban and al-Qaeda, but underground they were watering the soil in which the roots of the violence were growing.

"War is not a profession for bin Laden and his people" Terzani wrote. "It's a mission. Its roots lie in the faith they acquired in the closed-minded Koranic schools, and above all in their deep feelings of defeat and impotence, in the humiliation of a civilisation, Islam, which was once great and feared but which now increasingly finds itself marginalised and offended by the overwhelming power and arrogance of the West."

The barefoot missionaries, whose vision of jihad had up to now been a spiritual quest following an internal personal path, were left with no option but to back the outward jihad, the insurgency in Afghanistan against the United States and their allies; even if theirs was only silent acquiescence and not open support, it was enough. And given the failure of the Pakistani state to provide even basic services in the tribal areas, support for militancy was not surprising. Public spending per head in these tribal areas was one third of the Pakistani average; electricity, water supplies and health services hardly existed; male literacy was 17 percent, female literacy a pitiable 3 percent. An opinion poll showed there was still considerable support for *swara*, the practice of handing over girls to be forcibly married in order to resolve clan disputes.

Amid this poverty and ignorance, the inaccessible mountain terrain and deep clan loyalties in the tribal areas made a perfect base for the Islamist ideological struggle, which had been carefully nurtured by Pakistan for 30 years, initially with U.S. financing for the war against the Soviet Union in Afghanistan. By the time Pakistan realized the dangers, at U.S. insistence after 9/11, it was too late. One former official from Pakistani Intelligence, the ISI, said, "We indoctrinated them and told them, 'You will go to heaven.' You cannot turn it around so quickly." Some agents continued to fund and train fighters that others in the same service were trying to kill.

Pakistan's leader, General Pervez Musharraf, who had taken power in 1999 in a military coup, was one of the first to sign up for President Bush's "War on Terror" after 9/11 and had received $10 billion in aid in return, although little of that money found its way to develop the frontier. He assured the United States that Pakistan had stopped its support for insurgents. But he did nothing to oppose the influence of the most extremist Wahhabi-financed madrassas. Meanwhile elements in Pakistan's security forces and intelligence services never broke their links with the Taliban, who were able to regroup in 2005 to launch an upsurge of fighting in Afghanistan with a new leadership structure based in Pakistan, coordinated from Quetta—the gateway to Kandahar and the Pashtun south.

The fact was that the ISI had lost control of the monster it had created, suffering an "Islamic blowback" of the most extreme kind as the fundamentalists targeted their own society. The turning point in the history of Pakistan, defining the new battle lines, came when the government stormed the Red Mosque in the heart of Islamabad in 2007, killing around one hundred people and riddling the site with bullets and shells.

The assault on the Red Mosque was a decisive moment, since until that point the fundamentalist mullah who ran it, Abdul Rashid Ghazi, had preached his virulent message with government support and funding. Mullah Ghazi had attracted significant support from students, including a brigade of young women activists, who campaigned for a more restrictive dress code and took direct action against video shops, beauticians and massage parlors, kidnapping women working there. They had the same ardor for paradise as their male counterparts. Hameeda Sarfraz, the 19-year-old daughter of a bus driver, said, "In heaven, if a martyr feels hungry, food appears, the best quality food, and you won't even know where it came from." There were many women and some hostages among the dead at the Red Mosque, killed after President Musharraf could no longer ignore the arsenal of weapons being gathered in the heart of the capital.

Before the Red Mosque was stormed, there had been several attempts on the life of Musharraf, seen by many as too pro-American. After it was left a smoking ruin, the number of suicide attacks increased dramatically, including against the very Pakistani intelligence establishment that had such a long history of support for violent fundamentalist groups. The most ominous sign of change was the first suicide attack against buses carrying ISI employees. The insurgency went underground, with messages passed in secret meetings and on the Internet. Previously the ISI had always been able to look into the kaleidoscope and interpret the changing patterns. After the destruction of the Red Mosque, the glass was broken; they could not have controlled the militancy even if they had wanted to. Islamism had slipped its leash.

The Pakistani political establishment took heart from the defeat of fundamentalists in elections in early 2008, but missed the most significant feature of the elections—the low voter turnout in the North-West Frontier, a repudiation by many of democracy itself. Meanwhile, support grew for the new Pakistani Taliban amid a general realignment of politics after the Red Mosque incident.

The elections did seem also to offer a glimpse of another Pakistan: a significant part of society that had high hopes for democracy and opposed militancy, in the North-West Frontier as everywhere else. A new middle class was plugged into a vision of a globalized world different from the pan-Islamic caliphate of the jihadis. Private TV channels were a window into another life, where the young looked outwards to the world wearing jeans and not traditional *salwar kameez*, and women did not cover their heads with scarves.

Western policymakers liked the look of this, and backed leaders they could understand—"people like us"—who spoke the same language (and might even have been to the same university as themselves) rather than searching out other power-brokers with different clothes, customs and speech.

The high hopes for Pakistan placed on Benazir Bhutto in late 2007 in London and Washington had a similar feel to British dispatches about Shah Shuja in the 1830s. Shuja persuaded his British hosts, during his years in exile living on a British salary, that he was the answer for Afghanistan, and was disastrously imposed by force on the country.

Bhutto's assassination during the Pakistan election campaign on December 27, 2007 deprived the world of seeing whether she would fulfill her promise. She knew what the West wanted to hear, writing a book that warned of the perils of Islamic fundamentalism—although in her earlier time in office her government had backed first the mujahidin and then armed and financed the Taliban when they first emerged in Afghanistan.

And while the United States may have hoped for better democratic leadership to stabilize Pakistan, real power still lay with the army and the ISI, a state within a state, controlling much of the national economy. In the six decades after Pakistani independence, U.S. presidents *only* visited the country at times of military dictatorship, never when there was democracy. President Bush continued this dismal record when he visited Pakistan while it was still under military rule after the fall of the Taliban in Afghanistan. To the Bush White House, democracy was something to be imposed on countries that were defeated—Afghanistan and Iraq—but it was not essential for allies such as Pakistan.

There are uncanny parallels between the time after 9/11 and the early 1980s, after the Soviet invasion of Afghanistan, when President Reagan befriended the Pakistani military dictator General Zia, who had not only ousted a democratic government but also hanged the former president. Both times the United States wanted to make war in Afghanistan, a military government in power in Pakistan faced the threat of sanctions for trying to build nuclear weapons. In President Musharraf's case, the United States had to ignore even the fact of a nuclear test.

Pakistan's nuclear test in 1998 was performed under conditions of elaborate secrecy—duplicity might be a better word. The test site was camouflaged to look like shepherds' huts while U.S. spy satellites passed overhead. Any movement above ground happened only when the satellites were on the other side of the world. When it came, the explosion deep underground shook the dust from the mountains of Baluchistan, turning them white in an instant. But in the same way as there had been no U.S. criticism of Israel for its nuclear weapons program, so there would be only the mildest of sanctions against Pakistan, and even those were lifted when Pakistan promised help after 9/11.

Afghanistan's western neighbor, Iran, was treated in quite a different way. U.S. hostility to Iran had been set in stone since the 1979 Islamic revolution that brought the ayatollahs to power. In 2001 there was an opportunity for a fresh start in relations after the Taliban fell, but it was not taken by Washington. Kabul and Tehran had mutual regional interests, including Afghanistan's most important trade route, the repatriation of hundreds of thousands of Afghan refugees who had fled to Iran during the conflict, and a desire to stop illegal drugs smuggling. Iran cannot fail to be involved in the future of Afghanistan, given the length of their shared border—a line on a map of the desert. As foreign invaders come and go from Afghanistan, Iran will still be on the other side of that border.

With the Taliban gone, Iran quickly moved to exert its influence in Herat, the town nearest the border, building mosques, schools and a road, and arming Afghan police, while Iranian secret police could be seen driving about, not very secretly. But Iran's inclusion as part of the "axis of evil" in President Bush's first State of the Union speech after 9/11 complicated the potential for the new Afghanistan as it tried to form its own relationship with Iran. Local Afghan politicians were at a loss as to how to respond, given their deep links with Iran and their desire to form good contacts with the United States, the new power in the land.

The "axis of evil" speech in 2002 marked a time between 9/11 and the 2003 invasion of Iraq when international diplomacy appeared to be adrift of its moorings. Classic statecraft, employing the principle that "my enemy's enemy is my friend," should have ensured at least some U.S. contact with Iran—an appeal for neutrality if not an alliance—before embarking on an invasion of Afghanistan. But instead the United States took an evangelical stand, a realignment of the world between good and evil. It led to an invasion of not one but *both* of Iran's neighbors, as if Iran were not there, with the somewhat inevitable consequences of a multifaceted conflict developing across the region. Feeling encircled, Iran unsurprisingly turned up the rhetoric and did what it could to undermine U.S. attempts to stabilize Afghanistan and Iraq.

This factor was not taken into account by U.S. political leaders at the time, confident above all of the capacity of superior military technology to deliver results. The awesome scale of U.S. military spending and the competence and professionalism of its forces led to a suspension of normal critical faculties in that strange time after 9/11. The idea that Iran, or any other complicating factor, might affect the restoration of stability in Afghanistan counted as nothing.

But Afghanistan's ancient ability to confound invaders reemerged in a twenty-first century disguise. When the United States built the first decent road network since the Soviet invasion, Taliban attacks made it too dangerous to use. They switched to classic guerrilla warfare—inflicting damage without seeking to hold ground. Their military commander, Mullah Dadullah, explained, "Taking cities is not our present tactic…We have attacked and occupied certain locations for a short period of time, to achieve the objectives of the operation. But we will always retreat to our safe bases." Dadullah was known among his troops as *the lame Englishman*—"lame" because of a war wound, and "Englishman" because of his devious ways. With some fanfare, British forces successfully moved a giant turbine at slow speed across Taliban-held ground, fighting all the way, to try to repair power generating capacity at the Kajaki dam, which had formerly generated power for all of the south of the country. But once power was restored the Taliban could still disrupt supplies any time by taking down pylons at night.

As British forces had discovered in the nineteenth century, victory was an illusion. Gradually the realization dawned that the Karzai government did not really exist across much of the country; top-down democracy had not worked. Even where aid programs had been attempted, most were stalled by the worsening conflict, and military and civilian casualties were rising.

As a full recognition of the complexity of the task of providing security and development in Afghanistan came to be understood, there was increasing public concern in the West: political tensions over the cost in lives and cash in Canada and the Netherlands led to demands for their forces to be withdrawn. By 2007 there was little political will for the long haul except in the United States and Britain, where the mood in public statements changed, warning that securing Afghanistan would be a marathon, not a sprint.

The new somber tone matched the Soviet reappraisal with the arrival of the Gorbachev government, and in the same time frame—six years into their war in Afghanistan. The last Soviet soldier to leave Afghanistan, General Gromov, said that before Gorbachev, they had suffered from the "disease of the stagnation period: to inform the central offices only of what would be well received, rather than what was actually taking place."

Gorbachev signaled new honesty and a new direction in a politburo meeting where he read out letters from the mothers of soldiers serving in Afghanistan, demanding they should be brought home, a remarkable example of grassroots direct action having an effect at the highest level. He set a new Soviet course: "You'll have to revive Islam, respect traditions, and show the people some tangible benefits from the revolution."

Substitute "democracy" for "revolution" and Gorbachev's policy could have been written in London in 2007, as a push began to seek Afghan solutions to

Afghan problems. In Britain, a new realism became possible only with a change of leadership, once Tony Blair was replaced by Gordon Brown. For the first time officials on the ground could be honest to London about the shallow roots of democracy, the depth of corruption, the weakness of the aid effort and the growing violence. An awareness emerged that something different needed to be tried. The social advances boasted about with the arrival of democracy after the fall of the Taliban, such as a higher proportion of women MPs than in many Western countries, were hollow if it was too dangerous for the MPs to walk the streets of their own constituencies. In late 2008 one of those women members of Parliament, Malalai Joya, even said that for women in Afghanistan seven years after the U.S.-led invasion the "situation was as catastrophic as it had been under the Taliban."

Western policymakers, particularly in Europe, began to listen for the first time to those officials who had been patiently proposing that they needed to work with the grain of tribal and religious life, the real Afghanistan behind the illusion. They found a tribal structure degraded by war—working with the grain could be an ugly and complex business. But without a dramatic shift in policy of this sort, American, British, Canadian, Dutch, and other soldiers may prove to have fought and died in vain, and the US-led invasion might end up as another foreign failure during the two centuries since the modern world tried to engage with Afghanistan.

The policy change at the top was consistent with one of the most important messages in the Petraeus counterinsurgency doctrine—each word headed with a capital letter so the impact could not be missed—"The Host Nation Doing Something Tolerably Is Normally Better Than Us Doing It Well." The problem was that the host nation was becoming increasingly difficult to deal with.

On Christmas Day 2007, representatives of two of the big new international players in Kabul, the EU and the UN, were called to the presidential palace to hear unwelcome news: two of their most senior people were ordered to leave on the next available flight. It was an extraordinary diplomatic request, the kind of demand made by a pariah regime—for example the Soviet Union at the height of the cold war—not by a country liberated at no little cost.

Afghanistan was asserting itself, exactly 170 years after the first Russian and British envoys to Kabul, Alexander Burnes and Ivan Vitkevich, had sat down to a civilized Christmas dinner during their attempts to carve up the country.

President Karzai knew that the international life support system would not be turned off. Although just 5 percent of government needs could be raised from locally-raised revenue, a figure comparable with the poorest country in Africa, he was confident that the international community would not use the significant leverage that might have given them. He was flexing his muscles after successfully blocking the appointment of the ex-high representative to Bosnia, the British politician Paddy Ashdown, as coordinator of the international program in Afghanistan. As relations with Western countries, in particular Britain, became increasingly strained, Karzai grew impatient with the West's obsession with women's rights. He told a visiting minister, "The last king of Afghanistan who tried to give rights to women ended up dead."

The offence of the two men expelled, Michael Semple and Mervyn Patterson, who were working closely with British intelligence, was to attempt to talk to the Taliban in Helmand. According to Assadullah Khalid, the governor of neighboring Kandahar Province, the reason the two had to leave was because they were offering money, "It was like a business deal." He said that talking to the Taliban was the right of Afghanistan alone; Britain should not interfere.

The problem was that the Karzai government had no strategy for talking to the Taliban. The victors in 2001 had deliberately kept the Taliban out, and although Karzai talked vaguely at press conferences about ex-Taliban figures coming over, he had no interest in bringing the movement into the political mainstream—quite the opposite. His was not an inclusive process. Instead he was playing the game of a nineteenth century Durrani nobleman, refined by the warlord ethics of the late twentieth century: power was about all or nothing. When a former Taliban minister, living openly in Kabul, tried to hold a meeting of sympathetic mullahs in Jalalabad to open channels to the Taliban, Karzai put him under house arrest to prevent him from going.

That was when the first initiative to try to engage the Taliban was pursued, leading to friction with the Karzai government and the Christmas Day expulsion of the two agents. But by 2008 policy had changed, as Afghan government officials themselves began to open channels with the Taliban in a meeting in Saudi Arabia and western ministers began to say openly that there would be no settlement for Afghanistan that did not include them in some way.

The appointment of Richard Holbrooke to head U.S. policy in the region, one of the first acts of the Obama administration in January 2009, signaled that the United States would be willing to participate in this process. Holbrooke had been a key player in bringing peace to Bosnia in 1995, and had not been afraid of getting his hands dirty. In 1998, as fighting broke out in Kosovo, he had sought out the leaders of the nationalist guerrillas of the Kosovo Liberation Army, dodging Serbian checkpoints to sit rather incongruously on the floor of an abandoned farmhouse for a meeting.

Driving the new realism about the Taliban after 2008 was the worsening conflict in Helmand Province in the south-west, a region with a reputation as the most lawless in the country. Nowhere was there a bigger failure by the forces that took Afghanistan to restore security or bring development after 2001 than in Helmand. It was never going to be easy: even the Taliban took several years before they controlled it fully during their rule of Afghanistan, although

Helmand is close to their Kandahar heartland. That's why they succeeded in banning the growing of opium poppies only during the last two years of their rule, despite principled opposition from the beginning.

The spread of opium poppy fields across Helmand had increased hugely in the power vacuum that followed the fall of the Taliban in 2001. In a meeting in October 2008 in Budapest, NATO ministers made a decision that their forces would now pursue opium traders as military targets. Until then, dealing with narcotics had been seen as an Afghan police problem and the change of strategy was an admission that this policy had failed, as well as a recognition that narcotics fuelled the insurgency. Whatever the principles of the Taliban may have been, they were sacrificed to the needs of an insurgency now clearly financed by the narcotics trade.

The change in strategy was opposed by a number of European countries, led by Germany, who had been persuaded to put forces into the less-dangerous provinces of Afghanistan and now feared that they might be drawn into a new war against drugs. Political restrictions imposed on the deployment of some to these NATO forces, including rules against flying at night, being deployed for riot control, or fighting in the snow, weakened the ability of the international military response to the Taliban. There were more than fifty main "caveats" and dozens of smaller ones—a rule book that had to be consulted before any operation. NATO planners came to refer to forces from the less flexible nations as "pot-plants," useful for ornamental purposes only.

Even before the major increase in troops in 2009, the United States had already shouldered the biggest burden of the war. Apart from Britain, Canada and the Netherlands, none would commit combat troops in any numbers after the tempo of the conflict changed with a resurgent Taliban in 2005. And Britain's defense secretary, John Reid, underestimated the task, saying "We would be perfectly happy to leave in three years and without firing one shot." Even before the end of the first year British forces had fired more than a million bullets in Helmand in fierce fighting, and had had to withdraw from four towns where they had originally set up—so-called ink spots. The aim had been to spread security in widening areas, like ink seeping through blotting paper, until they all joined up, but the troops came under fierce attack from the day they arrived. They were able to withdraw with their vehicles intact from one of the towns, Musa Qala, only after a controversial deal with tribal elders who brokered a Taliban ceasefire during the withdrawal. The deal was publicly criticized by U.S. officers in Afghanistan, who saw it as a sign of weakness, and Musa Qala was not retaken for another year.

Privately, some senior British officers expressed surprise at the conditions they found in Helmand. They had come to provide support for an aid program but there did not seem to be much to support, as strict health and safety rules prevented aid workers from going out on the ground.

The army had read the new counterinsurgency manual, repeating as it did an old lesson warning against trying to fight guerrillas with the single club of military force. They knew that without effective development and a capable noncorrupt local administration, fighting would never achieve a positive result—especially as the insurgency was fuelled by drug money in an area with an open back door to a ready supply of fresh fighters across the frontier. The politicians may have taken a while to catch up, but British soldiers could see quickly that they would not be leaving "without firing one shot," as they deployed onto ground where their ancestors had once fought.

Sangin, one of the four towns taken and then surrendered in Helmand, was the place where British forces had first faced the determined opposition of those forerunners of the Taliban, *ghazis*, in the south in 1878. And it had been a fierce uprising across Helmand in the winter of 1840–41 that was the initial spark igniting the fire that engulfed British forces during that war.

A Guards officer who served in Sangin in the first deployment in the summer of 2006, Captain Leo Docherty, said that much of the military effort appeared to be just for show. There was no coherent plan for the operation in Helmand, but instead just a series of "disjointed ill-considered directives from headquarters. Everything else, all the well-meaning reconstruction stuff, is an illusion…the time spent there now seems to have been an egotistical folly." Military adventurism for no good end—it sounded like the campaigns waged on the frontier at the beginning of the twentieth century, mocked then as "General Willcocks's weekend wars."

Beyond the obvious deficiencies in development, what led to Docherty and others speaking out was the weakness and duplicity of Britain's allies, including the police, who they saw beating people and keeping confiscated drugs for their own use. "Violence will surely breed more violence, until the whole thing is beyond our control." Docherty thought the campaign was lost before it began—a "tragic replay of Soviet clumsiness." Their allies were worse than useless: the culture of corruption was deeply entrenched.

— — —

In October 2006, after several months of negotiations, I spent a few days with the Taliban opposing British forces near Musa Qala in northern Helmand. The failure of the international community to improve the lives of Afghans since the fall of the Taliban was the first issue raised by a local commander, Mahmud Khan, to explain why the Taliban were making a comeback. "We gained our freedom from Britain 160 years ago, and should remain free. We don't accept the claim that they are here to rebuild our country. They have done nothing for us."

Driving around the region with the commander was a little like visiting villages in Britain with a popular local politician. He knew everybody, and stopped often to chat. He made a virtue of the fact that he could walk around unarmed, although he carried a discreet 9mm pistol in a belt slung over the driving seat of the car. He had gathered together a display of captured weapons to show off, including two U.S. heavy machine guns—one mounted on a wheelbarrow— that the Taliban were using against British forces in Helmand.

My security was the Pashtun honor code; I was an invited guest and would be protected. I had a dramatic opportunity to see this in practice when a group of fighters heard I was there and came to kill me. My host, Mullah Abdul Manan, the overall military commander of the Taliban, told them if they wanted to kill me they would have to kill him first, and after a fierce argument he persuaded them to let me live.

He was a thoughtful man with a neat beard and soft, city hands, quite unlike the stereotype of a Taliban fighter. "You destroyed our government for just one guest—Osama," he said. He admitted that mistakes had been made during Taliban rule, and if they returned to power they would not want to impose themselves so harshly on people. But hosting Osama bin Laden was not a mistake, in his eyes. We talked until late into the night, in what must have been the women's side of a house commandeered for just that night, as he had to stay on the move all the time. The family were not there, of course, but their presence was everywhere. A Chinese-made sewing machine had been pushed aside and small scraps of cloth littered the floor, soon mingling with the rinds and pith of pomegranates thrown down by the Taliban fighters who filled the room, eating as we talked.

We sat cross-legged on thin felt mattresses lining the wall, with the commander propped up on a cushion in the corner. He spat his pips into a small bowl as we talked, breaking off frequently to listen to a two-way radio, receiving news at one point that a British military vehicle had detonated a landmine.

He denied that the Taliban supported the growing of opium poppies, claiming that they were trying to persuade people to give it up because it is against Islam. Since their attempt to return to power, the Taliban have been funded by the opium trade, but the commander said it was the British presence that allowed warlords and bandits to flourish.

The following day I was taken on a hair-raising patrol at high speed for several hours across the desert of northern Helmand, wedged between ten men sitting on the open back of a new Toyota Hilux, their legs over the side. On the way we passed the burnt-out remains of a Spartan armored personnel carrier, destroyed in August 2006 with the loss of three British lives.

I did not see a single woman while I was with the Taliban, and when we stopped in a village one evening to break the Ramadan fast, kept zealously by the Taliban fighters through the daylight hours, I was ordered to finish eating quickly so we would not lay eyes on the women who would sit where we had sat,

left with the scraps from half-eaten communal bowls of food. These remote villages, scattered across the huge expanse of the northern Helmand desert, were
very poor, and made poorer by several years of drought. The Taliban arrived
and insisted on being fed, although all the villagers had to offer was a little rice,
a stew made only of okra, and flat, roughly ground country bread.

Poppy growing has not brought prosperity to many of the people of
Helmand caught among the Taliban, drug barons and the increased pace of
the war since 2006. The Taliban did not develop Helmand when they were in
power either, but it is now easy for them to promote themselves as protectors of
the people, especially as civilian casualties increase. The Taliban took me to a
village attacked by troops from the British Special Air Service who had come at
night to arrest a suspect a few days earlier.

Two bombs fell in the raid on the village of Regan. One hit a house, killing
six members of a family, including three young girls. Two boys from the family,
Sher Ahmad and Nur Ahmed, survived the attack, although both were injured.
The other bomb partially demolished a mosque. Then villagers saw four helicopters land. Haji Mullah Sadeq ran out of his house. "I was carrying two children, one on my shoulders, and one in my arms, when the helicopters landed
and they started shooting at me. God saved me and I escaped." Some of the
villagers were too angry to talk to me because I was British. One merely pointed
to the torn and bloody women's clothing left in the ruins of the house and said
bitterly, "Are these the kind of houses they have come to build—the kind where
clothing is cut to pieces?" NATO sources said the village was strongly defended
by the Taliban, who fired on the British soldiers throughout the operation.

While the United States and its allies were being drawn into this quagmire, the political context could not have been worse. Men at illegal checkpoints
demanded money at gunpoint from every driver on the main road that crossed
the south. The checkpoints were manned mostly by Afghan police, and some by
soldiers in the newly trained and armed Afghan National Army. It was to stop
just this kind of casual theft on this very road that the Taliban was formed in
1994, and the checkpoints were a public relations gift to the resurgent Taliban
after 2006. They even began to receive payments from their former donors in the
trucking companies to sort out the problem again. The Taliban could portray
themselves as protectors of the local people and British soldiers as predators.

My trip caused a minor stir at the time, leading to questions in Parliament
and attacks by opposition politicians on TV talk shows. There were even
demands that I be tried for treason. A defense minister said, "We don't need
David Loyn to tell us what the Taliban think, we know what they think"—a
questionable assertion given that the entire political and military plan had
needed to be radically rewritten during 2006 to take account of the situation in
Helmand which was far from what had been at first expected.

A more substantial response to my report came in a letter from the British military commander in the south, pointing out that the Taliban were "tactically defeated" every time they encountered British forces. It would be remarkable if they were not, given the overwhelming superiority of British technology, training, and firepower. But at what cost? A rough back-of-an-envelope guess by an officer who knew about this kind of thing revealed that to attack a target—for example a Taliban sniper in a tree—might cost about two million dollars, taking air cover and bombs into account.

It was a new version of Kipling's poem "Arithmetic on the Frontier," in which an officer with "Two thousand pounds of education/Drops to a Ten Rupee jezail." Kipling believed the "cheaper man" would prevail. A more modern caution against the deceptive lure of tactical superiority came in Petraeus's new counterinsurgency manual that includes this warning: "As important as they are in achieving security, military actions by themselves cannot achieve success in counterinsurgency. Insurgents that never defeat counterinsurgents in combat still may achieve their strategic objectives." In other words, the Taliban have time on their side. Facing forces that could always beat them in a head-to-head confrontation, the Taliban adapted their tactics using hit-and-run raids, roadside bombs and suicide bombers. They saw that suicide bombers had had a significant impact on morale in Iraq, and although the tactic had not been part of recent Afghan conflicts, it was not unknown in the past, as seen in the assassins who faced inevitable death for an attack on a British officer in the nineteenth century. The senior Taliban commander I spent a few days with in 2006, Abdul Manan, said the tactic of suicide bombing would be employed far more extensively in the future. He was trying to keep control of it. "There are thousands waiting at the border. We are trying to stop them because they would cause chaos if they all came at once." He was killed in a targeted air attack a few months after our interview.

NATO spokesmen have characterized suicide attacks as evidence of weakness or desperation from a force with no better options against vastly superior NATO weapons, training and tactics. This is a dangerous misreading of the tactical thinking behind suicide bombing, a weapon with an impact far more widespread than the immediate casualties—damaging morale and threatening every contact the international force has with the local population. Far from being a weapon of indiscriminate terror, suicide bombers began to be deployed by the Taliban with tactical precision. Using a new strategy on June 13, 2008, an assault on a jail to release more than 400 Taliban prisoners in Kandahar deployed suicide bombers like artillery. After the suicide bombers blew open the gate, Taliban fighters on motorbikes assaulted the prison and took their comrades away with them.

The attack was another reminder that superior military technology is not crucial for success in war in Afghanistan. After watching the south go from bad to worse, the United States sent many more troops into the south, including a major surge in 2009. But there were still far fewer forces in the U.S.-led coalition in 2009 than Russian troops, defeated in the 1980s.

There were 100,000 Soviet troops in Afghanistan, double the size of the NATO force; they could be deployed anywhere, and absorb huge casualties, while NATO planners found themselves restricted by the conditions that kept the soldiers of most countries out of the front line. Soviet forces were backed up by more than half a million Afghan soldiers and uniformed militias, strong enough to hold off the mujahidin for three years after the Soviet withdrawal. In contrast, in 2009 even the most optimistic supporters of the new Afghan National Army would not expect them to hold off the Taliban and al-Qaeda for long on their own.

Soviet forces had other advantages too during their long war: they had no scruples about causing civilian casualties; they had a ruthless secret police; they used anti-personnel mines, reducing the number of troops required to defend their bases; they deployed hundreds more planes and tanks than NATO; and had access across a land border they could reinforce easily, and bring in fuel through fixed pipelines. And still they lost.

A *Pravda* correspondent was asked to report to the Soviet government on his experiences in the field. Comrade Shchedorov's letter, from 1981, contains lessons for those fighting in Afghanistan more recently, particularly in Helmand. "Upon completing an operation, the Afghan-Soviet troops as a rule return to their bases and the regions fall back under the control of the rebels...In the course of those operations, housing and the agricultural fields are often destroyed, the civilian population is killed, and in the end everything remains the same." Soviet forces found, as the United States and its allies would later, that they were fighting over the same ground again and again.

A Soviet military analysis after their war said they should have remembered the more distant past: "Alexander the Great took five years to break the resistance of the Pashtun tribes. Ten centuries later, Arab conquerors met the desperate resistance of the Afghan tribes. Six times they launched an offensive against Kabul and the area of the central plateau. Each time, they were forced to withdraw, having suffered heavy casualties."

The U.S. forces with the hardest task were those based in the harsh and remote regions on the frontier. They learned quickly and adapted to a new way of fighting that delivered some results: living among the people, spending far longer in the field than other foreign forces—more than a year at a time—and returning after a break to the same villages they had patrolled previously. It gave them a significant advantage in intelligence gathering. One of the main commanders who developed this strategy is related to John Nicholson, still remembered as "Nikal Seyn," the most effective of the British frontier political officers who began the effort to tame the frontier in the 1850s.

But once again the appearance of Afghanistan as seen by the outside world was an illusion, concealing a darker reality. Temporary successes in mountain villages were of no long-term value while there was an open door to Waziristan and an Afghan political system that did not punish corruption.

The soldiers and aid workers engaged in reconstruction worked hard, but too much of the money allocated for reconstruction went straight back to the West in the pockets of security firms and contractors. The aid was a sideshow, given the scale of theft and corruption in the country. The real invasion was the return of warlords, who carved up the country in a "victor's peace," in the graphic words of a report by the International Crisis Group: "In many ways the conflict today is a continuation of almost three decades of war involving nearly all the same players...Commanders raced to establish their own authority, creating a patchwork of predatory, competing fiefdoms. A culture of impunity was allowed to take root in the name of 'stability,' with abusers free to return to their old ways as long as they mouthed allegiance to the central government."

The jails filled with people who had had their land seized and could not afford to bribe the courts. Afghanistan did not need aid workers, it needed property surveyors and clean justice. But there was no appetite for that in the kleptocracy that emerged as drug barons, warlords and former mujahidin competed for influence in a classic Afghan power struggle.

Neither development spending nor democracy delivered results, putting even more pressure on military forces as they fought a worsening insurgency. Three of the seven parties set up by Pakistan and the United States to fight the Soviet Union in the 1980s were back in the field by 2007, fighting alongside the Taliban against the Karzai government and its foreign backers on ground that favors guerrilla warfare.

The post-9/11 move into Afghanistan by foreign forces came in a different age, when the desire to avoid civilian casualties was an important part of military planning. The tactics may have moved on from the frontier raids derided as "butcher and bolt," but as the military activity intensified, the effect on an Afghan farmer must have felt exactly the same as the war ebbed and flowed across his fields with no sign of an end.

Too many Afghans have experienced a deterioration in the basics of life—food, shelter, access to electricity, employment opportunities and security. Polio, an unknown disease in most of the world and easily preventable, increased in southern Afghanistan after 2001: a litmus test of neglect—the mark of failure. Older people remember a time before the Soviet invasion in 1979 when there was wealth not generated by poppies—a thriving agricultural economy, roads, electricity and schools, at least in the cities. Afghanistan considered itself civilized in those far-off pre-war days.

But the thirty-year nightmare that began in the late 1970s meant there was no golden age to look back to for younger Afghans, easily persuaded by preachers of the value of looking forward to martyrdom. The Taliban promoted themselves as the defenders of Afghanistan against another wave of foreign invaders, with a permanent supply of new recruits in the madrassas on the Pakistani side of the frontier.

There are 1.5 million students in these Taliban factories, where the descendants of the political mullahs who stirred up the frontier tribes against Britain, and were backed by the United States to defeat the Soviet Union in the 1980s, now preach an uncompromising Wahhabi faith, with a new line in Millennialist thinking that means some recruits for the front line believe they are fighting the battles that will bring on the end of the world. Like the emergence of the Taliban out of the dusts of the Desert of Death in the mid-90s, something else was stirring now on the frontier, fulfilling an ancient prophecy, that would sweep all before it and end the humiliation of Islam.

A saying of the Prophet Mohammed in the Hadith speaks of a new army and a new leader rising from Khorassan, an old name for Afghanistan. As the prophecy is interpreted by those telling and retelling it now on the frontier, the army will carry black flags, and be led by the Imam Mahdi, whose coming will signal the battles before the end of the world. At this point, believers say, normal technology will cease to work, so armories of swords are being assembled in Afghanistan and on the frontier, and youths are learning traditional martial arts for the war that is to come when planes and guns will not function. Osama bin Laden was still somewhere in a cave in the region, but those who believed the events on the frontier were leading to the end of the world did not think it would necessarily be him who would lead the revolt.

The prophecy of the warrior-priest Sheikh Abdullah Azzam, which brought bin Laden into the war against the Soviet Union in the 1980s, had been proved right—the Islamists had defeated one superpower. For that conflict they had funding and support from Muslim governments all the way from Saudi Arabia to Pakistan. Now, as they were taking on the last superpower those same governments were seen as enemies as much as the United States itself. In the new conflicts of the twenty-first century, al-Qaeda and the Taliban did not need to rely on governments; they collected money from individuals across the world, especially in the Islamic countries of the Gulf, where the resurgence of the Taliban was seen as fulfilling the prophecy—could this at last be the emergence of the army of the Mahdi, the black-flagged fighters from Khorassan, after many false sightings during the centuries?

The Taliban's move into the use of suicide bombers fitted the prophecy, as it said there would be killing in "ways that have not been seen before." In this fevered atmosphere, the North-West Frontier became a wartime society no less than it had been in the days of the mujahidin campaign against the Soviet Union. Every Friday in mosques, and not just those in the Wahhabi tradition, preachers ranted against the United States, before raising money for those fighting in Afghanistan. And spreading person to person through the bazaars, on DVDs and through the Internet, were speeches demanding total sacrifice. In one made at a wedding, a mullah condemns the use of music for weddings, and tells the groom that he should not paint the traditional henna on his hands.

"Allah loves blood not henna now. Blood is a beautiful color and Allah wants this blood. You should encourage each other to get married without henna, at a young age. If you don't get married then the Americans will take your young girls from you. The reason for Americans to come here is not to make us prosperous, they are lying, I swear by Allah. They are your enemies. Do not sit with them. They are here to dishonor you and enter your houses. They look at your women with dishonor."

It was an appealing message to some Islamic youth, and did not even need to be backed by a majority to fuel worsening violence in Pakistan as well as in Afghanistan. "In order for a guerrilla war to succeed, a *portion* of the local populace must support or acquiesce to the presence of the indigenous guerrillas in their midst," wrote U.S. General Theodore Mataxis, whose credentials as a counter-insurgency expert went back to Vietnam. "There must be a willingness to accept significant casualties—combatant and non-combatant. Guerrillas must have a safe haven and a source of supplies." The Taliban and al-Qaeda could tick every box—significant local support, a safe haven and source of supplies. As Mataxis remembered: "The guerrillas remained when the French left Algeria and Indochina, the United States left South Vietnam, and the Soviets left Afghanistan. The side with the greater moral commitment, be it patriotic, religious, or ideological, eventually won because of higher morale, greater obstinacy, stronger national will, and the determination to survive."

That was the challenge that made the battle for hearts and minds not a soft add-on but an essential part of any strategy. General Petraeus liked to say that there was no fixed plan for counterinsurgency—each situation was unique. By 2009 he was supported by a new administration that was willing to listen. One of the few foreign policy commitments made by Barack Obama in his campaign for the presidency was to take a more active interest in Kashmir—a glimpse of a more coherent strategy emerging for the region. After all, it was in Kashmir that the radicalization had begun in the early 1990s that had now spread worldwide.

But it was very late in the day to be building a coherent policy. The mistakes went back before 9/11. U.S. involvement in Afghanistan did not begin with the war in 2001 but in 1979. Responses to the Russian invasion of Afghanistan and the seizure of embassy officials in Iran—pursued then with the best of motives—had unintended consequences, and then worsened with the corrupt-ing effect of Charlie Wilson's funding, particularly in the two years after the Russians left Afghanistan in 1989. And since the warlord economy had been allowed to reestablish itself in Afghanistan under the nose of U.S. forces after 2001, it became easier for the Taliban to regroup in reaction to it.

Events outside the country made their job easier. The war in Iraq helped them recruit in Afghanistan and on the frontier in the name of jihad, Saudi Arabian funding continued for education that provided the seed-bed of mil-itancy, while Pakistan played its double game—saying it backed the United States and still supporting Islamist fighters on the frontier and in Kashmir.

By 2009 stabilizing Afghanistan was a far harder task than it had been in 2001. An opportunity had been lost. Two hundred years after Elphinstone was the first envoy to encounter the country, his caution about war there still held true. He concluded that even if a western power succeeded in taking the coun-try and putting its choice of leader in power, "maintaining him in a poor, cold, strong and remote country, among a turbulent people like the Afghans, I own it seems to me to be hopeless."

After all, the terrain had not changed. The frontier was just as it had been when it was visited by that earlier British traveler George Forster in the 1780s—"a chain of rocky mountains, whose scanty slips of valley afford but the coarsest provision for human wants," inhabited still by people who "have made so slow a progress in civilization."

Notes and Sources

One constant theme across two centuries of foreign intervention in Afghanistan has been short-termism. The aspirations of invaders and nation builders alike have never matched the challenges of this magnificent, sometimes harsh country and its complex and courteous, warlike but always gracious people. I owe a particular debt to the insights of a number of journalists and historians in telling the story: Charles Allen, who has done the hard work researching the connections shared by Wahhabi warriors on the frontier of the past and present; Christina Lamb, for her account of motorbike journeys with the young warriors who later led the Taliban; the late George Crile, for chasing down that larger than life character Charlie Wilson; and Ahmed Rashid, who understood better than anyone the importance of oil and the bigger strategic questions around the Taliban, working more as a detective than a journalist. The politics around the First Anglo-Afghan War have been researched by J. A. Norris, and no one told the military story of that war better than Patrick Macrory. I have drawn most of the narrative for Chapter 3 from Lady Sale's extraordinary diary.

I am grateful for the assistance of retired Brigadier Bill Woodburn, who was generous and hospitable while sharing his impressions of how Kabul felt in the nineteenth century. As well as understanding the importance of the Bala Hissar itself, Bill has brought his military engineer's mind on to the layout of the cantonments set apart from the rest of the city that were to play such a key role for British forces. The house the BBC has rented for many years, where I usually stay in Kabul, is inside what were the walls of the large cantonment at Sherpur built by Shir Ali for his army and held by the British force led by General Roberts during the desperate days of the siege of December 1879. It is so big that Bill believes it must have been originally conceived as a new fortified town.

I commend the work of the archivists of the nineteenth century who collected diaries, notes and reports from the frontier and the battlefield for what was called the "Political and secret department" of British administration in India and for Parliament, and to their successors in the India Office section of the British Library who preserve this collection with such dedication.

I am grateful to Alex Maxwell, for her skill in drawing maps that show what the country feels like, and illustrating them with such beauty. And I pay tribute to my agent Annabel Merullo, for constant support.

Other than those already named in the introduction, during the years I have been reporting on Afghanistan I have variously shared large plates of rice, nights in goat sheds and/or perceptions and useful conversation with, among others, Fisnik Abrashi, Robert Adams, Ashraf Ghani, Amir Shah, Nicholas Barrington, Baqer Moin, Roderic Braithwaite,

John Burns, Kate Clark, Tom Coghlan, Daud Qarizadah, Tony Davis, Lyse Doucet, Farah Durrani, James Fergusson, Dick Fyjis-Walker, Phil Goodwin, Adam Holloway, Ismael Saadat, John Jennings, Clare Lockhart, Anthony Loyd, Dominic Medley, Mostapha Zahir, David Page, Colin Peck, the late Juliet Peck, William Reeve, John Simpson, Rory Stewart, Mark Tully, Mark Urban and Elizabeth Winter. Vaughan Smith was brave and resourceful during several long trips when we traveled light in the months after 9/11, dropping by helicopter behind Taliban lines. He made TV history by transmitting the first news pictures to be sent to the BBC from a laptop through a lightweight satellite telephone link—technology that is now commonplace. And I want to make special mention of some other crews I have traveled with, in particular Fred Scott, Andrew "Sarge" Herbert and Vladimir Lozinski, who shared the risks, shooting and editing pictures during the turbulent years between 1995 and 1997 on both sides of Taliban lines as the country fell to this strange new force. Vlad carried the first pictures of the seizure of the Afghan capital by the Taliban on an epic drive from Kabul to Islamabad, bribing guards to let him through the Khyber Pass, in time for the evening news on the day the city fell.

There is no right or wrong way to spell many of the terms used in this book that are transliterations from other scripts. I have tried to steer a course between clarity and authenticity, wanting to retain archaic usage where appropriate—Caubul, Affghanistan, Mahometan—but not where it would obscure meaning. For consistency I have used the term "British" when writing about armed forces from the Raj, although the term was hardly used in the earlier period, when the word "English" was far more widespread, and forces were distinguished between those who were native or Queen's army. Similarly I have used "U.S.-led" for the fluctuating coalitions of foreign forces that have been in Afghanistan since 2001, since the U.S. military contribution has been by far the largest, although under varying leadership as the needs of the intervention have evolved.

I have used "Pashtun" as the term for Afghanistan's largest tribe, although "Pakhtun" tends to be used on the Pakistani side of the frontier. The old term "Pathan," which long predates the British presence in the region, is now considered derogatory.

CHAPTER 1

11 It was the first meeting between......
Mountstuart Elphinstone, *An Account of the Kingdom of Caubul.*
12 John Crokatt, an analyst with...
John Crokatt, *Thoughts on the External Defence of India,* January 28, 1808.
An early British traveler...
George Forster, *A Journal from Bengal to England.*
13 Personally charismatic, as a teenager...
Sir Edward Colebrooke, *Memoir of the Honourable Mountstuart Elphinstone.*
18 The risk of the French winning...
This extraordinary tale of diplomatic incompetence was put together by Sir John Kaye, *History of the War in Afghanistan.*
22 One of the early travelers...
Alexander Burnes, *Cabool.*

24 When the British horse-breeder...
William Moorcroft and George Trebeck, *Travels in the Himalayan Provinces.*
25 A few months later Burnes set out...
Mohan Lal, *Travels in the Punjab Afghanistan &c*
26 "These accounts only confirm...
Ellenborough, *Diary.*

CHAPTER 2

28 The ambassador who had sent the note...
John McNeill, *Progress and Present Position of Russia in the East.*
"In lieu of distributing...
All Kamran Khan quotes are from Mohan Lal, *Travels in the Punjab.*
29 "the best rampart India could have."
J. A. Norris, *The First Anglo-Afghan War 1838–1842.*
"females, both of high and low family...
Mohan Lal, *Travels in the Punjab.*
31 "tall stature and haughty...
Mohan Lal, *Life of Dost Mohammed.* (This account was written from memory; his first interviews were seized by in 1842 in the chaos in Kabul by Akbar Khan, who refused to return them.)
"Of later years, by all accounts he had been ambitious...
Arthur Conolly, *Overland Journey to the North of India.*
33 "Vitkevitch had a colorful past...
Russian Expedition to Khiva under General Perofski in 1839.
34 "The English, who are not soldiers...
All of this colorful detail comes from Lal, *Life of Dost.*
"ex-king at Loodiana...
Norris, *The First Anglo-Afghan War.*
36 "a riddle, wrapped in a mystery, inside an enigma."
Coined by Winston Churchill in a broadcast in October 1939.
37 "The Russian fiend...
Peter Hopkirk, *The Great Game.*
38 "The magnitude of the measures...
Norris, *The First Anglo-Afghan War.*
"a picture of military splendor...
J. H. Stocqueler, *Memorials of Afghanistan.*
"an unseemly display of dancing girls"...
This was Henry Havelock, later the hero of the siege of Lucknow, quoted in Norris, *The First Anglo-Afghan War.* His statue stands in Trafalgar Square, London.
39 "You have brought an army into...
Lal, *Life of Dost.*
41 "The only objection is that of expense...
Norris, *The First Anglo-Afghan War.*

"forlorn hope...
Term used since the sixteenth century for raiding parties sent out ahead of a main force in face of overwhelming odds.
"If Shah Shuja is really a king...
Norris, *The First Anglo-Afghan War*.

42 A chief who had come across...
The story of how Outram was foiled in pursuit of Dost is in Stocqueler, *Memorials*.
"not more than three hundred effective men...
Outram quoted by Stocqueler *Memorials*.

43 "respectful, decorous, even cold reception...
Norris, *The First Anglo-Afghan War*.
"I cannot but congratulate you on quitting this country...
Patrick Macrory, *Signal Catastrophe*.

44 "The cession by the Sikhs of all the countries west of the Indus...
Macnaghten letters.
"most firm friends and most steadfast allies...
Letter, September 1837 British Library D 1165/5.

45 "the most unhappy step taken during the campaign...
Lal, *Life of Dost*.
"I am far from able to decide...
Lal, *Life of Dost*.
"drive these Ferengee Kafirs out of the country...
Stocqueler, *Memorials*.

46 "Why is it that Englishmen everywhere are rough....
Macrory, *Signal Catastrophe*.
"The Iron is hot...
Norris, *The First Anglo-Afghan War*.

47 Shuja's agents went ahead to spread the word...
Lal, *Life of Dost*.
they heard the unearthly clang...
Thomas Seaton, *From Cadet to Colonel*. Seaton has a wonderful and warm eye for detail.

CHAPTER 3

49 "a rampart and ditch an Afghan could run over...
Lady Florentia Sale, *Journal of the Disasters in Afghanistan*.
"as great a scoundrel as ever lived...
Norris, *The First Anglo-Afghan War*.
"a season of such profound tranquillity...
Norris, *The First Anglo-Afghan War*.

50 The drama that played out on the night...
Lal, *Life of Dost*.

52 "death to dishonour...
Lady Sale, *Journal*.

53 **"Dangerous it is, but if it succeeds, it is worth all risks...**
Lal, *Life of Dost.*

54 **"All was confusion from before daylight...**
Lady Sale, *Journal.*

55 **"An immense number of poor wounded wretches...**
Vincent Eyre, *The Military Operations at Cabul.*
a persistent Afghan legend...
Louis Dupree walked through the route in 1963 at the same time of year as the retreat, and uncovered strong folk memories of the events. *Journal of the Folklore Institute [Indiana] Vol 4 1967*

56 **"The confusion became terrible, all discipline was at an end...**
Quoted in Dupree, *Afghanistan.*

57 **Captain Arthur Connolly, without fear of retribution...**
It was a bad time for the Connolly family: Arthur's brother John died in captivity in Kabul, and another brother had been killed two years before by a sniper.

58 **When he had set out to "thrash" the rebel tribes...**
Seaton, *From Cadet to Colonel.*

59 **"most conspicuous from the city...**
Stocqueler, *Memorials.*

60 **Returning to Istalif the morning after its sack...**
Charles Allen, *Soldier Sahibs.*
"I'm sorry; it's the fashion in earthquakes"...
When Shelton died in Dublin after falling from his horse in 1845, his regiment went out onto the parade ground to raise three cheers.
The retreat from Kabul, with Lady Sale waving a sword...
Macrory, *Signal Catastrophe.*

61 **But the Select Committee of the East India Company...**
Dupree, *Afghanistan.*
As the blame game began...
Norris, *The First Anglo-Afghan War.*

62 **"We could prevail upon our dear Friend...**
Norris, *The First Anglo-Afghan War.*

CHAPTER 4

65 **In 1836 an old man arrived in the Russian...**
Russian Expedition to Khiva under General Perofski in 1839.

66 **"The position of Russia in central Asia is that...**
Sir William Fraser-Tytler, *Afghanistan.*

67 **"I never heard a word uttered of doubt as to our success...**
Parliamentary Papers L/Parl/2/182.

68 **"Yours is an army of tents and camels...**
John Lawrence, *Lawrence of Lucknow.*
"a good, honest, useful piece of rascality"
Fraser-Tytler, *Afghanistan.*

69 "(1) you will never be able to get the Afghans to make a treaty…
Fraser-Tytler, *Afghanistan.*

70 Fifteen years previously, in his first campaign…
Allen, *Soldier Sahibs.*

71 "There is an air of masculine independence about him…
Paget and Mason, *Record of the Expeditions against the North-West Frontier Tribes.*
"between the eyes, and there they found—a man…
Olav Caroe, *The Pathans.*

72 Hardly a year passed between 1849…
Parliamentary Papers L/Parl/2/284.

73 And now something else was stirring on the frontier…
Much of this narrative is drawn from Charles Allen, *God's Terrorists.*

74 Mohammed Jafar believed…
Allen, *God's Terrorists*
"the inhabitants, a semi-civilised race, are fanatical Mahometans."
Edward Thornton, *A Gazetteer of the Countries Adjacent to India.*

75 mobilized by the *akhund* of Swat, a revered figure…
Remembered in the Edward Lear poem of 1862:
　　"Who or Why, or Which or What, is the Akhund of Swat?
　　Is he tall or short, or dark, or fair,
　　Does he sit on a stool or sofa, or chair or squat
　　The Akhund of Swat?"

76 "the only danger to British rule in India…
Abdur Rahman, *The Life of Abdur Rahman.*
Tolstoy may be best remembered…
Tolstoy's image of the tough daisy is echoed in the description of the mountain tribes
by Badshah Khan, known as the Frontier Gandhi for his efforts to unite and liberate
the Pashtun people in the 1930s. "The courage of our tribal brothers is described as
wildness, passion for freedom as lawlessness, their proverbial hospitality as an irrepressible urge [for] begging, borrowing and pillaging…Like untended, wild daisies
they bloom and fade away in mountain ridges." Quoted in Rajmohan Gandhi, *Ghaffar
Khan.* The Frontier Gandhi's grandson was elected chief minister of the North-West
Frontier Province in 2007 with a mandate to change its colonial name.

78 "savage with a touch of insanity…
Fraser-Tytler, *Afghanistan.*

CHAPTER 5

79 "A non-recognition of their failures…
General Soboleff was the former chief of the Asiatic Department of the Russian
General Staff and wrote this highly critical account of British military prowess in
Afghanistan in order to make the case for an invasion of India. It was translated in
Calcutta and widely distributed by Forward policy advocates.
"Afghanistan as a whole could no longer exist"…
Fraser-Tytler, *Afghanistan.*

81 "the immense importance to us of the triangle...
    Parliamentary Papers L/Parl/2/284
    "affectation to apply the nice distinctions...
    Political and Secret Department papers, L/PS/20/memo3.
    offered the same as before, 87,000 rupees...
    Official Account of the Second Afghan War.
    The first shots in the Second Anglo-Afghan War...
    Official account of the Second Afghan War.
85 "Some of the cavalry I have dismissed...
    Parliamentary papers L/Parl/2/182.
86 "only by those who know the coldness of the nights...
    Official account of the Second Afghan War..
    "act of retributive justice...
    Lord Roberts, *Forty-One Years in India.*
    "Towards the afternoons the main bazaars...
    Nancy Hatch Dupree, *An Historical Guide to Kabul.*
87 "The prolonged occupation by foreign troops...
    Official Account of the Second Afghan War.
    This was an enormous site with low walls...
    I owe this and much other intelligence about the forts of Kabul to retired Brigadier
    Bill Woodburn.
90 "rights of the savage...
    Roland Quinault, "Afghanistan and Gladstone's Moral Foreign Policy."
94 "Total defeat and dispersion of General Burrows's force...
    Leigh Maxwell, *My God—Maiwand!*
    "Everything which belonged to the state...
    Political and Secret Department papers L/PS/20/memo3.
    In the words of an anonymous diary...
    Political and Secret Department papers L/PS/20/memo3.

CHAPTER 6

This chapter is drawn almost wholly from three sources—the beautifully observed narrative by Sir T. J. Holdich, *The Indian Borderland,* and the accounts left by the two negotiators who locked horns over the frontier, the amir Abdur Rahman and Sir Henry Mortimer Durand.

101 did not know a "Pathan from a Poobah."
     The reference is in Gilbert and Sullivan's opera *The Mikado.*

CHAPTER 7

111 On November 3, 1895, before first light...
     Parliamentary papers L/Parl/2/284..

"liberate Afghanistan for Islam from the English"...
Abdur Rahman, *Life*.
His book on jihad, passed from hand to hand on the frontier...
Abdur Rahman, *Jihad*.

112 "The priesthood, knowing that their authority...
Winston Churchill, *The Story of the Malakand Field Force*.

116 Lieutenant Harry Rattray, the commander of the detachment...
Son of the founder of his regiment; "Ratrray's Sikhs."
"a boy aged thirteen or fourteen on whose head he bound a turban...
Parliamentary papers L/Parl/2/284.
"Bands of *ghazis*, worked up by their religious enthusiasm...
Quoted in Allen, *Soldier Sahibs*.

118 "most open and audacious violation...
Parliamentary papers. House of Commons. Session 1898. vol. 63. C. 8713, 8714.

119 "the unprovoked aggression on Khyber pass gravely affects...
Parliamentary papers L/Parl/2/284.
the gateway to the Khyber Pass, was under Subedar...
Colonel H. C. Wylly, *From the Black Mountain to Waziristan*.

120 "Burning houses and destroying crops unless followed up...
In 1900, when he was made commander in chief in South Africa during the Boer War, Lord Roberts did not sanction the burning of villages. It was only after he returned to Britain that Boer settlements were systematically burned and the controversial policy was begun of bringing families into camps, where many died from disease.

121 "The Commander-in-Chief dissents...
Parliamentary papers L/Parl/2/284.
"deal with the hearts and minds of the people"...
Commons debate in 1898, the year after the conflict, L/Parl/2/284.. One Liberal MP said in the debate that Britain was now facing "patriotism inflamed by fanaticism, and this was a very much more formidable force than patriotism independent of fanaticism."
The Marquess of Salisbury, prime minister...
Parliamentary papers L/Parl/2/284.

CHAPTER 8

123 "His Highness asked me about his marital duties"...
Bird's diary is in Dane family papers in the British Library. D659 1–11.

125 had long been opposed to the "infatuated nonsense...
David Gilmour, *Curzon*. Curzon had traveled in the region as a young man, meeting Abdur Rahman, and had won the Gold Medal of the Royal Geographical Society, credited as the first European to reach the source of the Oxus River.
"The sudden alarm, the long dust-choked ride...
Fraser-Tytler, *Afghanistan*. Fraser-Tytler later served on the frontier in several leading roles and never forgot the pointless excursions he had undertaken as a young officer.

126 **"None had any substantial experience of the frontier."**
Parliamentary papers L/Parl/2/284..
"young British officers have gone in and out among the tribes...
Parliamentary papers L/Parl/2/284..
"I do not advocate the crushing and disarming of the tribes...
George Roos-Keppel, *Papers.*
Germany has the distinction of being the first country to exploit jihad...
Britain was doing it at the same time in Arabia, of course.
129 **Since 1911 a highly influential fortnightly...**
L. B. Poullada, *Reform and Rebellion in Afghanistan 1919–1929*
130 **"a French municipal office....**
Robert Byron, *The Road to Oxiana.*

CHAPTER 9

135 **Congressman Charlie Wilson from Texas....**
George Crile, *Charlie Wilson's War.*
one of the richest, and certainly the most influential...
Ishtiaq Ahmad, *Gulbuddin Hekmatyar.*
As a student leader in Kabul in the late 1960s...
Olivier Roy, *Islam and Resistance in Afghanistan.*
136 **Development meant that in the 1970s...**
Louis Dupree, *Afghanistan.*
The travel writer Bruce Chatwin...
Introduction to Byron, *The Road to Oxiana.*
137 **In Kabul student elections in 1970...**
Roy, *Islam and Resistance in Afghanistan.*
Daoud rejected offers from the Saudi government...
Author interview with ex-student.
Pakistan quickly recognized the potential...
Ahmad, *Gulbuddin Hekmatyar.*
The Afghan Islamist exiles were open to...
Roy, *Islam and Resistance in Afghanistan.*
138 **Massud was released.....**
Michael Griffin *Reaping the Whirlwind,* quoting Jane's Defence Weekly.
The Panjshir uprising gave...
Roy, *Islam and Resistance in Afghanistan.*
Daoud told the Soviet leader...
Henry Bradsher, *Afghan Communism and Soviet Intervention.*
"We will never allow you to dictate...
Bradsher, *Afghan Communism and Soviet Intervention.*
The communists changed the national flag...
Edward Girardet, *Afghanistan—The Soviet War.*

139 **Hekmatyar led the first successful raid....**
Ahmad, *Gulbuddin Hekmatyar.*
As events spiraled toward the Soviet invasion...
The scale of the bloodshed in the initial uprising in Herat is usually overstated. Antonio Giustozzi has researched it at www.crisisstates.com/download/wp/wpSeries2/WP4.2.pdf.
Nur Mohammed Taraki made the first...
Details of Soviet moves toward war are translated and available on U.S. open access Web sites. Most were drawn from the online archive at George Washington University, www.gwu.edu/~nsarchiv/NSAEBB/NSAEBB227/index.htm.

143 **"What unnerved everyone was the suspicion...**
Crile, *Charlie Wilson's War.*
"make Soviet involvement as costly as possible...
Bradsher, *Afghan Communism and Soviet Intervention.*

144 **"lawlessness, disobedience, embezzlement, bureaucracy...**
Bradsher, *Afghan Communism and Soviet Intervention.*

145 **"Begin active operations for destruction...**
Alexander Lyakhovsky, "The Tragedy and Valor," documents translated on George Washington University website.

CHAPTER 10

148 **"If America challenges the Soviets at every turn...**
Crile, *Charlie Wilson's War.*

150 **Britain's answer to the hard-drinking...**
Author interview with the Marquess of Salisbury.

151 **Soviet equipment was unsuited to the terrain...**
Lester W. Grau, *The Bear Went over the Mountain.*
An Estonian conscript remembered...
Mohammad Yousaf and Mark Adkin, *Afghanistan: The Bear Trap.*
A Russian ex-soldier told of an incident...
Artyom Borovik, *The Hidden War—A Russian Journalist's Account of the Soviet War in Afghanistan.*

152 **Some were signed up by deception...**
Girardet, *Afghanistan—The Soviet War*

153 **"typical tribal fighting for immediate tangible gains...**
Yousaf and Adkin, *Afghanistan: The Bear Trap.*

154 **"The Feds spent a million bucks trying to figure out...**
Crile, *Charlie Wilson's War.*

155 **"traitors and filthy vultures...**
Bradsher, *Afghan Communism and Soviet Intervention.*
"a circulatory system without blood"...
Letter by Colonel K. Tsagolov translated for NSA archive.

156 **"more the kind that women liked"...**
Borovik, *The Hidden War.*

157 **Between them, the mujahidin and Soviet forces...**
Document on George Washington University website.
About 1.5 million people died....
Estimate by Human Rights Watch: hrw.org.

CHAPTER 11

159 **The way the freelance cameraman Rory Peck...**
With thanks to Colin Peck for making the diary of his late brother available.
160 **"All the dominating heights belonged to Pakistan...**
Yousaf and Adkin, *Afghanistan: The Bear Trap.*
161 **A Russian journalist who spent a few days...**
Author interview with Vladimir Snegirev, then with *Pravda.*
dangerous traveling companions as they invited martyrdom...
Author interview with Rahimullah Yusufzai.
A woman in Kabul said...
John Fullerton, *The Soviet Occupation of Afghanistan.*
162 **Among them was a bank clerk called Ramia...**
Christopher Walker, *The Times,* February 28, 1989.
walk down the middle of the road...
Afghanistan Justice project, *War Crimes and Crimes against Humanity 1978–2001.*
Tajwar Kakar, a schoolteacher who had been tortured...
Mark Fineman, *Los Angeles Times,* February 12, 1989
163 **Cranborne survived because he had been...**
Author interview.
Hekmatyar turned his attentions to the south...
Ahmad, *Gulbuddin Hekmatyar.*
"a true monster and enemy of Afghanistan...
Ahmad, *Gulbuddin Hekmatyar.*
"Supplying military aid to the Afghan rebels...
Crile, *Charlie Wilson's War.*
164 **"a policy that began to be characterized...**
Washington Post, March 31 1990.
"I am confident of a military victory...
Christina Lamb, *Financial Times,* July 28, 1989.
165 **"the smell of political expediency and compromise...**
Yousaf and Adkin, *Afghanistan: The Bear Trap.*
"We've been denying our activities there...
Bradsher, *Afghan Communism and Soviet Intervention.*
166 **"shovelled into the ideological pockets...**
Author interview with the Marquess of Salisbury.
167 **When a reporter noticed some blood and flesh...**
This was Ahmed Rashid, who told the story in *Taliban—The Story of the Afghan Warlords.*

168 **"a most theatrical scene developed…**
Author interview with Mark Urban.

169 **"One of these rockets hit our house…**
The personal accounts of horrors during these years, including the uncovering of the Afshar massacre, are taken from Afghanistan Justice project: *War Crimes and Crimes against Humanity.*

CHAPTER 12

180 **The origins of the Taliban lie in the dust…**
Christina Lamb, *The Sewing Circles of Herat.* Among her companions on her travels in the South then was a young Hamid Karzai.
"I cannot describe the suffering…
Lamb interview with Borjan.

181 **In 1994, when two teenage girls from his village…**
Author interviews in Kandahar.
"How could we remain quiet…
Rahimullah Yusufzai interview with Omar.
"Omar was a very brave mujahid…
Rahimullah Yusufzai interview with the Black Mullah.

182 **"the most beautiful example in colour…**
Byron, *The Road to Oxiana.*

185 **reputed for a while to be the third largest investor…**
Ahmad, *Gulbuddin Hekmatyar.*
It almost certainly came from Saudi Arabia…
Rashid, *Taliban.* The Saudi ex–spy chief, Prince Turki, has denied that he personally handed over this money.

186 **"What's the worst thing that can happen…**
Author interview with driver Naqeeb.

187 **One seasoned observer of the Afghan scene…**
Tony Davis, "How the Taliban Became a Military Force," in William Maley, *Fundamentalism Reborn?*

188 **"In the worst days of the war we went out…**
Author interview.

189 **"It is true to say that a large number of Taliban…**
Author interview.

190 **The head of the south Asia desk at the State Department…**
Raphel had a curious personal connection with the region. Her former husband, Arnold, from whom she was divorced at the time of his death, was the U.S. ambassador to Pakistan killed in the plane crash that killed General Zia in 1988. All Raphel quotes here are from Rashid, *Taliban.*

191 **"pipelines, an Amir, no parliament, and lots of sharia law…**
Rashid, *Taliban.*

At the last buzkashi game...
Author interviews.

193 **"I could see smoke coming from the west...**
Afghanistan Justice project, *War Crimes and Crimes against Humanity.*

CHAPTER 13

195 **Sajjad, nicknamed "the Afghan"...**
Witnessed by the author.

196 **"frozen turbulence"...**
Title of book by Jagmohan, governor of Jammu and Kashmir, 1983 to 1987.
Pakistan inspired a new armed struggle...
Sati Sahni, *Kashmir Underground*
Pakistan's funding of training camps in Afghanistan...
Daniel Benjamin and Stephen Simon, *The Age of Sacred Terror*, and U.S. intelligence documents in the online archive at George Washington University.

197 **attributed to the Harkat ul-Ansar...**
Or its affiliates; the names of organizations changed often.
Osama bin Laden arrived back...
Lawrence Wright, *The Looming Tower—Al-Qaeda's Road to 9/11.*

198 **shaking his hand was like...**
This was Peter Jouvenal; the story is told in my earlier book, *Frontline.*

199 **TV pictures from Khost showed the pages...**
These exclusive pictures were taken by Rahimullah Yusufzai.
Among the dreams of his followers...
Documents found by Peter Jouvenal and Anthony Loyd in Osama bin Laden's house in Kabul after the fall of the Taliban revealed this and other farfetched plans.

200 **The vehicles had been delivered...**
Rashid, *Taliban.*
Turki found that the U.S. missile attack...
Wright, *The Looming Tower.*
"We may be very poor, we Afghans...
Author interview with Rahimullah Yusufzai, who spoke to several people at the meeting.
Officials sent a secure satellite telephone to Omar and talked...
Rashid, *Taliban.*

201 **"Tibet is out...**
Quoted in Rashid, *Taliban.*

203 **The cover-up began, even in Massud's kingdom...**
Witnessed by Rory Peck in 1989.
An Islamic cleric in Kabul...
Author interview.

raised more customs revenues in their last...
Author interview with Clare Lockhart, adviser to the Afghan finance ministry.

204 **"People knew that there were various tribes...**
Interview with Alastair Leithead for BBC *Newsnight*, December 2007.

205 **"The Taliban and al-Qaeda are no longer capable...**
Spokesman for the International Security Assistance Force, March 31, 2003; quoted on Agence France Presse.

Hekmatyar announced that he would now fight...
Interview with al Jazeera quoted in International Crisis Group (ICG) report, 2006.

controlled as much as 54 percent...
Estimate by Senlis Council, 2007.

206 **seized by some of those appointed...**
ICG report, "Countering Afghanistan's Insurgency."

One appointee for police chief...
Anthony Loyd, *The Times*, November 24, 2007.

207 **"There is no government to deal with cases...**
BBC interview, December 2007.

Their chief spokesman admitted...
Author interview.

it became fashionable for foreign analysts...
For example, the deputy head of the UN mission Ameerah Haq, interviewed for the ICG report, "Countering Afghanistan's Insurgency."

208 **The provinces where they successfully...**
Author interview.

209 **General Aminullah Amerkhel was removed...**
Author report for BBC *Newsnight* 2006. (This report was part of a portfolio that won the first Orwell prize for TV news.)

just $75 a head in the first year...
Report by CARE: 2002.

President Karzai's helicopter pilot died in childbirth...
There is a poignant photo of her at the controls of a helicopter in Katherine Kiviat and Scott Heidler, *Women of Courage—Intimate Stories from Afghanistan*.

210 **"We had a strategy in three months...**
Author interview.

"The conflict has not only intensified...
Richard Norton-Taylor, *The Guardian*, February 13, 2008.

CHAPTER 14

213 **Petraeus had written a new U.S. military field manual...**
www.fas.org/irp/doddir/army/fm3-24.pdf

214 **An influential book by a British general...**
General Sir Rupert Smith, *The Utility of Force*.

around 1,000 Pakistani soldiers...
Figure often quoted by the former President Musharraf to answer critics who said he had not done enough.

"Preliminary indications are that the movements...
The News, (Islamabad) October 28, 2006.

the plague spot of the frontier...
This was Lieutenant Colonel Sir George Roos-Keppel, a senior British frontier-official during the first two decades of the twentieth century. He went on: "The history of the tribes of Waziristan...has been a story of raiding, outrage, murder, abduction and fanatical assassination."

215 **An Italian reporter, Tiziano Terzani...**
Tiziano Terzani *Letters against the War.*

Public spending per head in these tribal areas...
New York Times April 10 2007.

An opinion poll...
Community Appraisal and Motivation Programme *Understanding FATA* 2008.

"We indoctrinated them and told them...
Carlotta Gall and David Rohde, *New York Times*, January 15, 2008.

and had received $10 billion in aid in return...
Husain Haqqani of Boston University calculates that the overt and traceable U.S. aid to General Musharraf's Pakistan amounted to $9.8 billion, of which 1 percent went for children's survival and health and just one-half of 1 percent for democracy promotion (and even that went partly to a commission controlled by General Musharraf), *New York Times*, April 10, 2007.

216 **a new leadership structure...**
Taliban sources speaking to the author.

"In heaven, if a martyr feels hungry...
Somini Sengupta, *New York Times*, July 23, 2007.

217 **writing a book that warned of the perils...**
Benazir Bhutto, *Daughter of the East.*

but also hanged the former president...
And by a horrible ironic historic symmetry, that president was Zulfikar Ali Bhutto, Benazir Bhutto's father.

Pakistan's nuclear test in 1998...
Author report for BBC News.

218 **U.S. hostility to Iran had been set...**
There is good evidence that the crucial part of the jigsaw, tipping the Soviet Union to invade Afghanistan in 1979, was the belief that the United States would invade Iran, threatening to change "the military-strategic situation in the region to the detriment of the interests of the Soviet Union." Georgy Kornienko, "The Cold War: Testimony of a Participant," online archive at George Washington University.

Iran quickly moved to exert its influence in Herat...
Author report for BBC *Newsnight*, January 2002.

219 **"Taking cities is not our present tactic...**
Interview for Al Jazeera 2006. Dadullah was targeted and killed in May 2007.
"disease of the stagnation period...
Artyom Borovik, *The Hidden War.*
"You'll have to revive Islam...
Anatoly Chernyaev, "Notes from the Politburo," October 17, 1985, online archive at George Washington University.

220 **situation was as catastrophic...**
Malalai Joya was speaking at the Frontline Club in London October 8 2008, on receiving the Anna Politskovskaya award.
Although just 5 percent of government needs...
U.K. International Development Secretary Douglas Alexander in evidence to International Development Committee of House of Commons, January 17, 2008.

221 **"The last king of Afghanistan who tried...**
Douglas Alexander in evidence to International Development Committee.
According to Assadullah Khalid, the governor...
Author interview, February 2008.
When a former Taliban minister, living openly in Kabul...
Author interview on condition of anonymity, December 2007.
he had sought out the leaders...
Author report for BBC News June 1998.

222 **"We would be perfectly happy to leave in three years...**
BBC interview, April 24, 2006.
only after a controversial deal with tribal elders...
Author interview with the Taliban who did the deal; this aspect remained strongly disputed by British commanders on the ground.

223 **"disjointed ill-considered directives from headquarters...**
Leo Docherty, *Desert of Death.*

225 **A defense minister said...**
Adam Ingram on BBC *Newsnight*, October 26, 2006.

226 **the British military commander in the south...**
Brigadier Ed Butler letter to the *Independent* (London). October 27 2006.
deployed suicide bombers like artillery
Tom Coghlan, *Daily Telegraph*, (London) June 15, 2008.

227 **There were 100,000 Soviet troops...**
These figures are from a military analyst with long experience in Afghanistan, who was not willing to be named.
Comrade Shchedorov's letter...
Letter to the Central Committee of the Communist Party, November 12, 1981, online archive at George Washington University.
"Alexander the Great took five years...
The Russian General Staff analysis of the Soviet war in Afghanistan, translated and edited by Lester W. Grau and Michael A. Gress.

228 **"victor's peace," in the graphic words of a report...**
ICG, "Countering Afghanistan's Insurgency."

The jails filled with people who had had their land seized...
Author interview with Sibghatullah Mujaddidi, Speaker of the upper house of the
Afghan parliament 2006.

229 **There are 1.5 million students in these Taliban factories...**
Estimate by Hanif Atma, Afghan education minister, in author interview,
November 2007.

230 **"Allah loves blood not henna now...**
DVD found in Peshawar and translated by Najibullah Razaq.

"In order for a guerrilla war to succeed...
General Theodore Mataxis, quoted in introduction to the Russian General Staff
analysis, translated and edited by Grau and Gress. Mataxis was an adviser to the
mujahidin in Afghanistan during the Soviet war.

231 **"maintaining him in a poor, cold, strong and remote...**
Mounstuart Elphinstone *Kingdom of Caubul.*

"a chain of rocky mountains...
George Forster *A journal from Bengal to England.*

BIBLIOGRAPHY

BOOKS

Ahmad, Ishtiaq. *Gulbuddin Hekmatyar* (Pangraphics Pvt).

Allen, Charles. *God's Terrorists* (Little, Brown 2006).

Allen, Charles. *Soldier Sahibs* (John Murray 2000).

Benjamin, Daniel, and Stephen Simon. *The Age of Sacred Terror* (Random House 2002).

Bergen, Peter. *Holy War, Inc.—Inside the Secret World of Osama bin Laden* (Weidenfeld & Nicolson 2001).

Bhutto, Benazir. *Daughter of the East* (Simon & Schuster 2007).

Binyon, T. J. *Pushkin* (HarperCollins 2002).

Borovik, Artyom. *The Hidden War—A Russian Journalist's Account of the Soviet War in Afghanistan* (Faber and Faber 1991).

Bradsher, Henry. *Afghan Communism and Soviet Intervention* (Oxford University Press 1999).

Burnes, Lieutenant Colonel Sir Alexander. *Cabool—a Personal Narrative of a Journey to, and Residence in that City* (1841, reprint Indus Publications 1986).

Byron, Robert. *The Road to Oxiana* (reprint Pimlico 2004).

Campbell, Alastair. *The Blair Years* (Hutchinson 2007).

Caroe, Sir Olaf. *The Pathans* (Oxford University Press 1958).

Caroe, Sir Olaf. *Soviet Empire—The Turks of Central Asia and Stalinism* (Macmillan 1953).

Churchill, Winston S. *The Story of the Malakand Field Force: An Episode of Frontier War* (Longmans 1898).

Coll, Steve. *Ghost Wars* (Penguin 2004).

Conolly, Arthur. *Overland Journey to the North of India* (Richard Bentley 1834).

Crile, George. *Charlie Wilson's War* (Thorndike 2003).

Curzon, George Nathaniel. *The Pamirs and the Source of the Oxus* (1896, reprint Elibron Classics 2005).

David, Saul. *Victoria's Wars—the Rise of Empire* (Viking Penguin 2006).

Dey, Kally Prosono. *Life of Sir Louis Cavagnari* (J.N.Ghose & co 1881).

Docherty, Leo. *Desert of Death* (Faber 2007).

Dupree, Louis. *Afghanistan* (Princeton University Press 1978).

Dupree, Nancy Hatch. *Afghanistan* (Afghan Tourist Organisation 1978).

Dupree, Nancy Hatch. *An Historical Guide to Kabul* (Afghan Tourist Organisation 1972).

Eggermont, P. H. L. *Alexander's Campaigns in Sind and Baluchistan* (Leuven University Press 1975).

Elliott, Jason. *An Unexpected Light* (Picador 1999).

Ellenborough, Lord. *Diary 1828–1830* (1881).

Elphinstone, Mountstuart. *An Account of the Kingdom of Caubul* (1815, reprint Indus Publications 1992).

Eyre, Sir Vincent. *The Military Operations at Cabul, which Ended in the Retreat and Destruction of the British Army* (John Murray 1843).

Forster, George. *A Journal from Bengal to England, through the Northern Part of India, Kashmir, Afghanistan and Persia, and into Russia by the Black Sea* (1790).

Fraser-Tytler, Sir William. *Afghanistan—A Study of Political Developments in Central Asia* (Oxford University Press 1950).

Fullerton, John. *The Soviet Occupation of Afghanistan* (Methuen 1984).

Gandhi, Rajmohan. *Ghaffar Khan* (Penguin India 2004).

Gilmour, David. *Curzon* (John Murray 1994).

Girardet, Edward. *Afghanistan—The Soviet War* (Croom Helm 1985).

Giustozzi, Antonio. *Koran, Kalashnikov and Laptop—The Neo-Taliban Insurgency in Afghanistan* (Hurst 2007).

Grau, Lester W. *The Bear Went over the Mountain* (Frank Cass 1998).

Green, Colonel Sir Henry. *The Defence of the North-West Frontier of India, with Reference to the Advance of Russia in Central Asia* (1873).

Griffin, Michael. *Reaping the Whirlwind* (Pluto Press 2003).

Halliday, Fred. *Threat from the East* (Pelican 1982).

Hensman, Howard. *The Afghan War of 1879–80* (Allen 1881).

Herodotus. *The Histories* (translated by Aubrey de Selincourt Penguin 2004).

Hodson, Peregrine. *Under a Sickle Moon—A Journey through Afghanistan* (Abacus 1986).

Holdich, Sir T. J. *The Indian Borderland* (Methuen 1901).

Hopkirk, Peter. *The Great Game* (Oxford University Press 1991).

Hopkirk, Peter. *On Secret Service East of Constantinople* (Murray 1994).

Jafar, Muhammad. *In Exile–A Strange Story* (New Delhi reprint 1964).

Jalal, Ayesha. *Partisans of Allah—Jihad in South Asia* (Sang-e-Meel Publications 2008).

Kaye, Sir John. *History of the War in Afghanistan* (W.H. Allen 1851).

Kepel, Gilles. *Jihad—The trail of political Islam* (I.B Tauris 2004)

Khalil, Jehanzeb. *Mujaheddin Movement in Malakand and Mohmand Agencies 1900–1940* (Hanns Seidel Foundation 2000).

Kipling, Rudyard. *Kim* (Macmillan 1901).

Kiviat, Katherine and Heidler, Scott. *Women of Courage—Intimate Stories from Afghanistan.* (Gibbs Smith 2007).

Lal, Mohan. *Life of Dost Mohammed Khan of Kabul* (Longmans 1846; reprint 2004 Asian Educational Services).

Lal, Mohan. *Travels in the Punjab Afghanistan &c* (W.H. Allen 1846).

Lamb, Christina. *The Sewing Circles of Herat: My Afghan Years* (HarperCollins 2002).

Lawrence, John. *Lawrence of Lucknow* (Hodder 1990).

Lermontov, Mikhail. *A Hero of Our Time* (translated Paul Foote, Penguin Classics 2001).

Loyn, David. *Frontline—The True Story of the British Mavericks who changed the face of war reporting* (Penguin 2006).

Macrory, Patrick. *Signal Catastrophe—The Retreat from Kabul 1842* (Hodder & Stoughton 1966).

Maley, William, ed. *Fundamentalism Reborn? Afghanistan and the Taliban* (Hurst 1998).

Maxwell, Leigh. *My God—Maiwand!* (Leo Cooper 1979).

Molesworth, G. N. *Afghanistan 1919* (Asia Publishing House 1962).

Moorcroft, William, and George Trebeck. *Travels in the Himalayan Provinces of Hindustan and the Panjab from 1819 to 1825* (reprint Oxford University Press 1979).

Mortimer, Edward. *Faith and Power—The Politics of Islam* (Faber & Faber 1982).

Norris, J. A. *The First Anglo-Afghan War 1838–1842* (Cambridge University Press 1967).

Official Account of the Second Afghan War 1878–1880 (John Murray 1908).

Paget and Mason. *Record of the Expeditions against the North-West Frontier Tribes 1873 and 1884* (Whiting and Co 1884).

Poullada L. B. *Reform and Rebellion in Afghanistan 1919–1929* (Cornell University Press 1973).

Rahman, Abdur. *Jihad* (translated by Najibullah Razaq 2008).

Rahman, Abdur. *The Life of Abdur Rahman, Amir of Afghanistan* (John Murray 1900).

Rana, Muhammad Amir. *A to Z of Jehadi organisations in Pakistan* (Mashal 2007).

Rashid, Ahmed. *Taliban—The Story of the Afghan Warlords* (I.B. Tauris 2000).

Roberts, Lord. *Forty-one Years in India* (Richard Bentley 1897).

Robertson, Charles Gray. *Kurrum, Kabul and Kandahar—Three Campaigns under General Roberts* (reprinted Sang-e-Meel Publications 2002).

Robertson, Sir George. *Chitral: The story of Minor Siege* (reprint Bhavana Books 2001).

Roy, Olivier. *Failure of Political Islam* (Harvard University Press 1994).

Roy, Olivier. *Islam and Resistance in Afghanistan* (Cambridge 1986).

Russian Expedition to Khiva under General Perofski in 1839 (translated and printed by Office of Superintendent of Government Printing, Calcutta 1867).

Russian General Staff. *The Soviet-Afghan War*, translated and edited by Lester W. Grau and Michael A. Gress (University Press of Kansas 2002).

Sahni, Sati. *Kashmir Underground* (Har-Anand Publications 1999).

Sale, Lady Florentia. *Journal of the Disasters in Afghanistan* (John Murray 1843).

Sale, General Sir Robert. *The Defence of Jellalabad* (private edition 1843).

Seaton, Major General Sir Thomas. *From Cadet to Colonel* (Hurst and Blackett 1866).

Smith, General Sir Rupert. *The Utility of Force* (Allen Lane 2005).

Smith, Vincent. *Oxford History of India* (Oxford University Press 1981).

Soboleff, Major General L. N. *The Anglo-Afghan Struggle* (translated and printed by the Office of Superintendent of Government Printing, Calcutta 1885).

Spear, Percival. *The Oxford Modern History of India 1740–1975* (Oxford University Press 1965).

Stewart, Rory. *The Places in Between* (Picador 2004).

Stocqueler, J. H. *Memorials of Afghanistan* (Calcutta 1843).

Terzani, Tiziano. *Letters against the War* (India Research Press 2002).

Thornton, Edward. *A Gazetteer of the Countries Adjacent to India* (1844, reprint Indus Publications 1996).

Tolstoy, Nikolai. *Hadji Murat*, translated Hugh Alpin (Hesperus 2003).

The Truth about Afghanistan (Novosti Press Agency Publishing House 1986).

Urban, Mark. *War in Afghanistan* (Macmillan 1988).

Vigne, Godfrey T. A. *Personal Narrative of a Visit to Ghazni, Kabul and Afghanistan and of a Residence at the Court of Dost Muhammad; with Notices of Ranjit Singh, Khiva and the Russian Expedition* (1840).

Wright, Lawrence. *The Looming Tower—Al-Qaeda's Road to 9/11* (Allen Lane 2006).

Wylly, Colonel H. C. *From the Black Mountain to Waziristan* (Macmillan 1912).

Younghusband, Captain F. E., and Captain G. J. *Relief of Chitral* (1895).

Yousaf, Mohammad, and Mark Adkin. *Afghanistan: The Bear Trap* (Pen & Sword Books 1992).

INDIA OFFICE RECORDS IN THE BRITISH LIBRARY

Crokatt, John. Thoughts on the External Defence of India from the Projected Invasion of the French and Russians 1808. Mss Eur D1070.

Dane, Sir Louis William. *Papers*. D659 1–11 (includes Dr. Bird's diary).

Durand, Sir Henry Mortimer. *Papers*. D727/17.

Keane, Baron Edward. *Papers*. 1840 Mss Eur B315.

Macnaghten Sir William Hay. *Letters* D727/17.

Masson, Charles alias James Lewis. *Private Notes of Mr Masson as Drawn Up from Memory: 1827–1829*. Mss Eur B218.

Parliamentary Papers. L/Parl/2/182; L/Parl/2/284.

Parliamentary papers. House of Commons. Session 1898. vol. 63. C. 8713, 8714.

Political and Secret Department papers L/PS/memo3.

Roos-Keppel, Lieutenant Colonel Sir George. *Papers*. Mss Eur D613.

Wade, Sir Claude, *Letter*, September 1837 British Library D1165/5.

ARTICLES

"Administration of Sir John Lawrence" (*Calcutta Review* 1869).

An "Anglo-Indian," *Our Russian Neighbours and How to Deal with Them* (*Calcutta Review* 1868).

Colebrooke, Sir Edward. "Memoir of the Honourable Mountstuart Elphinstone" (*Journal of the Royal Asiatic Society* 1861).

Dupree, Louis. "The Retreat of the British Army from Kabul" (*Journal of the Folklore Institute* [Indiana], Vol. 4, 1967).

Green, Colonel Sir Henry. "The Great Wall of India" (*The Nineteenth Century* May 1885).

Mcneill, John. "Progress and Present Position of Russia in the East" (1836).

Office of the Geographer. "Afghanistan-USSR Boundary" (U.S. State Department 1983).

Quinault, Roland. "Afghanistan and Gladstone's Moral Foreign Policy" (*History Today* December 2002)

Trench, Captain F. "The Central Asian Question," Royal United Services Institute lecture (1873).

WEB SITES

Afghanistan Justice Project, "War Crimes and Crimes against Humanity 1978–2001": www.afghanistanjusticeproject.org/warcrimesandcrimesagainsthumanity19782001. pdf.

CARE report 2002 at: www.care.org/newsroom/specialreports/afghanistan/09302002_ policybrief.pdf.

Frontier opinion poll 2008:

Community Appraisal and Motivation Programme : www.understandingfata.org.

Giustozzi, Antonio at: www.crisisstates.com/download/wp/wpSeries2/WP4.2.pdf.

International Crisis Group reports available from: www.crisisgrOxfordUniversity Press.org:

"Afghanistan: The Need for International Resolve" (Asia Report No. 145, February 6, 2008).

"Afghanistan's Endangered Compact" (Asia Briefing No. 59, January 29, 2007).

"Countering Afghanistan's Insurgency: No Quick Fixes" (Asia Report No. 123, November 2, 2006).

U.S. counterinsurgency doctrine at: www.fas.org/irp/doddir/army/fm3–24.pdf.

George Washington University online archive of U.S. and Soviet documents on Afghanistan at: www.gwu.edu/~nsarchiv/NSAEBB/NSAEBB227/index.htm.

INDEX

WITHDRAWN

7/6/09 $ 27.95